KILL OR BE KILLED

◆

THE AUTHOR AT GONDOKORO

KILL OR BE KILLED

The Rambling Reminiscences of an Amateur Hunter

Major W. Robert Foran

Peter Capstick, Series Editor

St. Martin's Press
New York

To the Reader:

The editors and publishers of the Peter Capstick Adventure Library faced significant responsibilities in the faithful reprinting of Africa's great hunting books of long ago. Essentially, they saw the need for each text to reflect to the letter the original work, nothing having been added or expunged, if it was to give the reader an authentic view of another age and another world.

In deciding that historical veracity and honesty were the first considerations, they realized that it meant retaining many distasteful racial and ethnic terms to be found in these old classics. The firm of St. Martin's Press, Inc., therefore wishes to make it very clear that it disassociates itself and its employees from the abhorrent racial-ethnic attitudes of the past which may be found in these books.

History is the often unpleasant record of the way things actually were, not the way they should have been. Despite the fact that we have no sympathy with the prejudices of decades past, we feel it better—and indeed, our collective responsibility—not to change the unfortunate facts that were.

—Peter Hathaway Capstick

KILL OR BE KILLED. Copyright © 1988 by Peter Hathaway Capstick. All rights reserved. Printed in the United States of America. No part of this book may be used or reproduced in any manner whatsoever without written permission except in the case of brief quotations embodied in critical articles or reviews. For information, address St. Martin's Press, 175 Fifth Avenue, New York, N.Y. 10010.

Library of Congress Cataloging-in-Publication Data

Foran, W. Robert (William Robert).
    Kill, or be killed : the rambling reminiscences of an amateur hunter / W. Robert Foran.
        p.   cm.
    "From Peter Capstick's library."
    ISBN 0-312-02227-1
    1. Big game hunting—Africa.   I. Title.
SK251.F67   1988
799.2'7'096—dc19   88-11496
                                                                      CIP

First Edition

10 9 8 7 6 5 4 3 2 1

EDITOR'S NOTE TO THE REPRINT EDITION

Hamisi bin Baraka lay crushed and hemorrhaging, smashed and tusked into the dark forest floor, white sprays of shattered bone poking like strange, sharp mushrooms through his black and bloody skin. A few feet away, a misshapen red tarboosh lolled on its side as bright butterflies already gathered to drink the moisture of the man's gore.

The elephant was gone, dying of its wounds as it crashed mindlessly and irresistibly through the dense bush. The birds were still. Even the wind was dead. The only motion was the jerky approach of a bleeding, tattered white man, stark and horrified. His heavy rifle made a dull sound as he dropped it to the ageless African dirt and knelt beside the semiconscious man.

As he wetted the gunbearer's lips with a damp finger, dark, frank eyes opened in the ripped face, locked with his, then closed. Forever. W. Robert Foran, adventurer, soldier, policeman, explorer, journalist, author, and ivory hunter of some four hundred elephant, swore that day he would never hunt *tembo* again.

And, as long as he lived, he never did.

Back at camp, Hamisi bin Baraka buried, Foran sat for many hours at work, the silence of the great Ugandan Akuma Forest hollow in his chest as he chipped away at the flat stone, the tombstone of his friend of six years. As he sat near the low fire, the memories of those half-dozen years came back to him as sharply as the pain of his own wounds. Perhaps through the silence of his morose porters he could hear the distant, ragged tear of rifle fire, the war cries of the Nandi and Kisii, the scream of enraged elephants, or the soft campfire chatter of his safari friends. But it was all in his mind. The only sound was the finality of steel on stone.

Major W. Robert Foran was one of the most fascinating and entertaining characters of early East Africa, an area that probably sported more of his breed that anywhere on earth at the time he arrived in Kenya Protectorate in 1904. No stranger to violence as a distinguished veteran of the Boer War, Foran came of a family steeped in military tradition. The eldest of four sons, he was born in Eastbourne, England, in 1881 and graduated from the Royal Military Academy of Sandhurst, the equivalent of America's West Point. Despite his birth, he was an Irishman and the green in his blood held sway throughout his life.

After the Boer War and a severe bout of enteric fever, Foran was sent back to England, where he served at the Coronation of Edward VII before returning to his regiment in the Transvaal. He then sailed for India in the hopes of serving in the Indian Army, which, unfortunately, did not materialize. But before a transfer back to South Africa, Foran did manage a few weeks' service in the Waziri Campaign on the North-West Frontier in 1902 and also enjoyed some excellent tiger and buffalo hunting.

Back in Johannesburg, the young officer/adventurer was dismayed to learn that he was about to be posted back to Aldershot and peacetime soldiering. As he so vividly puts it: "Africa, the mystical and inscrutable, was my first love. . . . Only those who know Africa can understand how potent is her appeal." Foran began hatching plans in the historic Rand Club in Johannesburg and was encouraged all the more by what was being said in the local newspapers about British East Africa and its prospects at the time, more specifically, the then Kenya Protectorate.

He and a friend soon left for Lourenço Marques in Portuguese East Africa, where they embarked for the sea voyage to Mombasa, arriving there in March 1904, all thoughts of an army career now shelved. The train ride up to the infant Nairobi was a revelation, the passengers being treated to an amazing spectacle of game in their thousands on the Kapiti and Athi Plains. Foran also learned of the tribulations of the early Indian station masters at places like Simba and Tsavo who would send frantic telegrams to Nairobi such as the following:

"Four lions with consorts aggressively on platform and completely in charge my official functions. . . ."

"Two lions on platform . . . I very nervously frightened and secured in office. Cannot dare give 'line clear' signal oncoming train . . . ."

Foran was on the threshold of tremendous adventure. It was in the air.

Once in Nairobi, Foran set about hiring a gunbearer—Hamisi bin Baraka—and porters, as well as seeing to the general outfitting of his first safari in British East Africa.

It was while Foran was busy preparing for his second safari, this time into the Sotik country, that he was approached to join the British East Africa Police, a paramilitary outfit composed of Indian and black troops under white officers who wrote some of the more amazing pages of early Kenyan history. The BEAP combatted anything from maneaters, murderers, and defrauders to fires, plagues, infidelity, and armed uprisings by the local tribes. Foran's complete ignorance of both the law and police work was not considered an impediment to his appointment as one of the first four white officers of the BEAP. Foran's African fate had been sealed.

Kill: Or Be Killed is a charming collection of anecdotes and adventures concerning the African bush, hunting dangerous game, tribal life, and the many zany characters of early Kenya. Published in 1933 during the Depression, when few people could afford the luxury of books and the true adventure of their pages, this particular book is now rare and is considered prize Africana. Foran wrote twenty-two books, one appearing posthumously, which ranged from children's stories to travel books, African reminiscences, history, novels, and a biography. Because of his experience in Kenya, Foran was chosen by the American Associated Press to cover the Roosevelt safari of 1909/1910 and spent thirteen months with the former President. In all, he wrote for more than half a century.

Foran was widely traveled, having also hunted in Ceylon, Burma, Mexico, Canada, and America. Many of his peers and friends were famous hunting personalities such as Selous, Stigand, Ryan, Hunter, Sutherland, Neumann, and Bell. Like some of those pioneering hunters, Foran poached with great success in the Lado Enclave, that curious piece of Africa that was home to incredible herds of elephant at the turn of the century. His only posthumous book concentrates on the Lado experience.

It is a strange story how Foran came to resign from the BEAP in January 1909. Four and a half years of the most pestilential climate, coupled with the cynical inflexibility of the British colonial bureacracy, pushed Foran into a nervous collapse. Two incidents typify what he had to endure. I'll call them "the serious emergency" and "the three cents."

Foran had already succumbed to a severe case of "tropical nerves" and was given three weeks' leave to recuperate. He set out on an elephant safari in the Mount Elgon region, hunting over two hundred miles from base when a runner came into camp with urgent orders for him to return immediately. Foran made a forced march over terrible terrain, arriving in record time. The emergency? Dire, indeed. The Inspector General was rumored to be coming and Foran was needed to form a guard of honor. Of course, the august official never showed and Foran's recuperative leave was ruined.

It didn't stop there. The Foreign Office could not get it straight that the natives, not having money, were taxed in cattle. Obviously, anybody who had ever taken a course in biology would have realized that the cattle tax could not remain static as cows had calves. The Foreign Office could never understand the surplus and suspected dark dealings by Foran and the other beleagured civil servants. Then came the seeming impossibility of reconciling the difference in exchange rates between Kenya's *two* currencies, rupees and shillings. Whenever these currencies had to be exchanged, there was always a fraction of surplus or deficit in the account books. The British Government never got it straight and were becoming downright nasty about the three cents' overage on Foran's books. Foran cracked in the face of this querulous, stupid correspondence, collapsing across his desk in hysterical tears.

Invalided back to England, Foran soon recovered and was assigned to the Roosevelt Safari as a special correspondent. At the end of that historic trip, he went to America, where he worked for four years as a journalist with major newspapers and also founded the famous Adventurers Club in Chicago, lecturing on African hunting too.

The First World War erupted and Foran saw action that resulted in part of his face being blown away, permanently affecting his speech. It was only after this that he began writing in all earnestness. He subsequently farmed near Marandellas in Mashonaland for a few years, but his ranch did not prosper and he faced ruin.

Foran lived in Singapore for a time and became the editor of the *Straits Times*, a position he held until ill health forced him back once more to England in 1933, where he remained until 1947. He served in the War Office and in the Home Guard during the last World War.

Despite his extensive writings, Foran remained a private man. He refers fleetingly to his once being married, and his 1958 book *A Breath of the Wilds* is dedicated to "Audrey." Could she have been Mrs. Foran? Were they divorced or did she die? The answer does not come cascading from Foran's pen. I suppose if he didn't want to share the details we should consider the matter his private business anyway.

Foran returned to Kenya permanently in 1947, where he continued to write. He had an excellent memory and leaves no doubt as to the accuracy of incidents he witnessed in person. He does, however, slip up here and there. By way of example, he incorrectly reported the date of Stigand's death, even though they were close friends. Such details do not in any way spoil the thrill of a great "read" such as *Kill: Or Be Killed*.

Robert Foran lived in a time when you could actually meet lions in the dusty streets of Nairobi. He did. Not once but twice, the first lion having to be shot in front of what passed as the post office and the second having to be dealt with by a Foran ". . . garbed in dinner clothes and patent leather shoes."

It was Major Foran who introduced that elite Indian Army officer sport of pigsticking, known among the anointed as "hog-hunting" in the Raj. Warthogs took the place of the Indian wild boar on the Athi Plains outside Nairobi. He also witnessed the early bow-hunting expeditions from America and the roping of lions by American cowboys on horseback. The Masai invited him as an honored guest to their traditional lion hunt in the shadow of Mount N'Gong, a spot later immortalized by Baroness von Blixen-Finecke in *Out of Africa*. These were "the palmy days of big game shooting," as that great Kenya pioneer Lord Cranworth once said.

The Sportsman's Arms Hotel in Nanyuki, north of Nairobi, was Foran's home in the last years of his life. It was a fine, bright day in August 1968 when W. Robert Foran knew death was coming. Calmly, he ordered a bottle of champagne and, raising a last toast to his eighty-eight years of life during which he had outlived all the legendary African big game hunters and pioneers, he died, like the gentleman he always was.

One wonders if part of that toast was not a greeting to Hamisi bin Baraka, waiting for him on a jungle hillside in Uganda.

—PETER HATHAWAY CAPSTICK

TO THE MEMORY OF

that fast-dwindling band of gallant sportsmen, my friends of the past, who experienced the same joys and thrills in treading the game paths of Kenya, for they knew that:

The fellow who fights the fight alone,
   With never a word of cheer,
With never a friend his help to lend,
   With never a comrade near,
'Tis he has need of a stalwart hand
   And a heart not given to moan ;
He struggles for life, and more than life—
   The fellow who fights alone !

INTRODUCTION

IN this overstocked world there are a number of people for whom a safe, routine existence is inert and boring. They actually delight in the hardships and dangers of the wild parts of the earth; they have a hungry urge to contend with rough nature in a battle where no quarter is given; they accept the challenge to kill or be killed.

They gratify this wanderlust in various ways: the traveller, explorer, naturalist, and hunter are all devotees, all actuated by the same desire for direct sensation—to sample life from the original source. The readiest outlet for this ambition is in the hunting of wild beasts: the first and most natural occupation. This pursuit takes men into strange and wonderful environments; they see solemn dawns from the summits of unknown mountains, and terrible sunsets in the midst of wildernesses of inspiring solitude; their days are bright with danger, their philosophy the most comforting because the most simple.

This book is written by one of these men—a wilderness hunter. In its pages the reader will be able to experience vicariously risks and excitements, where death stands at his elbow, watching for the unsteady hand, the failing eye, to nudge him into eternity; the customs of strange peoples will interest him; the tropic sun will warm his blood to the gay, hazardous adventure of the chase.

Major Foran is a hunter of large experience in India and Africa. He went to Kenya in the early days, before the tourist got there, and made good use of his fine opportunity to explore and hunt in that delightful country. He has reconstructed a period as rich in excitement and romance as any in the history of colonization.

His own adventures are sufficiently thrilling and entertaining, but to them he has added many of those of the famous hunters of the past who, in his young days, were still in their prime, and able to relate these stirring tales to their friend the author.

This is no tourist's wonder-book, nor movie-maker's advertisement, but real live adventure such as will always outshine the synthetic variety. Major Foran has lived the wild life at its best, and he has given us a vivid picture of it.

C. T. STONEHAM

PREFACE

IT is thirty-four years since I fired my first shot in Africa at either man or beast, and thus found myself launched in the everlasting warfare waged between all living creatures. At intervals, during the past three decades, I have hunted big game in Asia, Africa and North America ; and have fought against men in a number of savage wars.

I write chiefly of the pioneer days in Kenya, long before civilization had changed the face of the land and driven the vast herds of wild creatures to seek sanctuary further and further into the backward regions. Those were days of golden joys, of tramping through lonely lands, of the adventure of hunting wild beasts, and of the companionship of many men of sterling worth.

Alas, most of those good friends have already joined the " Great Majority " ; but few still survive. All were red-blooded he-men. I treasure the memories of the many happy hours spent with them in Eastern and Central Africa. Their friendship was always a valued reality ; their courage a thing to greatly admire ; their store of knowledge readily available ; and their lives an inspiration.

For the first six years of my hunting, I employed mostly a rifle to provide me with sport. Thereafter, I relied almost solely upon a camera. I infinitely prefer the latter.

It is well to emphasize that I have no pretensions of being a " famous " game shot or more than averagely experienced in the sport. The title of " famous big game hunter " is far too often given or claimed without any real justification. I have merely hunted and photographed wild animals in their natural surroundings, both large and small varieties, dangerous and otherwise, with the instincts of an amateur sportsman-naturalist.

Such sport as I have enjoyed has been obtained in the course

9

of my military or Government duties,.or else during occasional periods of leave in countries wherein I chanced to be serving for the time being. Having a penchant for the wild regions in preference to the more settled portions of a country, unusual opportunities for hunting and studying big game have not been lacking. In this, my lot has indeed been fortunate.

Many of those with whom I served in Africa and elsewhere seldom had an inkling that I had done more than " shoot for the pot " when on safari and in the performance of my lawful occasions. I have always felt a reluctance to share my adventures and experiences with others, for such have appealed to me as being of rather a sacred and personal character. Also, I strongly resent having my private affairs or amusements under public discussion.

Furthermore, my reticence was often a necessity. I had been playing truant and actually shooting big game when supposedly engaged on my official duties as a Government servant. All very reprehensible, no doubt, but adding to the spice of the adventure. If these little " unofficial " expeditions had come to the ears of those set in authority over me, I should have suffered a severe reprimand, if not worse than that.

Such peccadilloes, therefore, are best kept to oneself. The more particularly so in the old-time Kenya where tongues habitually wagged too freely : largely for want of something better than idle gossip to occupy the mind. To have mentioned one of these little lapses from grace in Kisumu would have been to know it was common talk in Nairobi within forty-eight hours. So I was silent.

It has often been urged upon me that the time for secrecy having long since passed, the fear of the official wigging having ceased, and the conditions in Kenya having altered so much in the past quarter of a century, I should no longer keep the memories of those glorious days to myself. Rightly or wrongly, many of my friends insist that they should be shared with others. Perhaps they are right ; but I would have preferred to have retained them in my storehouse of memories.

It was a great life, while it lasted : none better. Such adventures must make a strong appeal to all, and not just for the lust of killing. Great pleasure is to be found in the joy of living next to Nature and the excitements of taking big risks. These two factors count most of all. Those who have once tasted these delights must ever afterwards hunger to repeat the great experience. Perhaps, Robert W. Service had just this kind of life in mind when he wrote :

> Let us probe the silent spaces,
>   Let us seek what luck betides us,
> Let us journey to a lonely land I know,
>   There's a whisper on the night-wind,
>   There's a star agleam to guide us,
>   And the Wild is calling, calling—let us go.

My hunting days are over, to my lasting regret. I can look back over that long stretch of years, however, without remorse. I am not conscious of ever having done any deed in hunting big game, except by sheer accident, of which any sportsman might feel just cause for shame. And I can remember, with satisfaction, the many chances taken with dangerous animals in the wild regions ; and on equal terms.

It is impossible to put back the clock ; but, if I had those years to live all over again, I would not have them changed except in one single particular. And that would be to substitute a camera for a rifle.

My thanks are due to Mr. Fred A. Parrish, the late Captain J. H. Cumberlege and Dr. L. R. Magoon for their kind permission to reproduce photographs.

W. ROBERT FORAN

LONDON,
  February 15, 1933.

CONTENTS

LIST OF ILLUSTRATIONS

KILL: OR BE KILLED

CHAPTER I

THE LAW OF THE JUNGLES

ALL living creatures are instinctively destroyers of life. Since the dawn of Creation one beast has hunted and killed another: human beings have hunted animals, or been slain by them.

There is only one law prevailing in the wild regions of the earth—kill: or be killed. No mercy is ever given: none ever asked. Every form of life goes in constant fear of destruction. Its very existence is threatened both by day and by night; year in and year out, for one preys on another for means of sustenance. In this eternal fight for life there is only one dominating factor—the survival of the fittest.

Nature has provided each species of animal with the capacity to reduce these dangers and guard adequately against the constant risk of total extinction; but not entirely to eliminate them. Again, in some animals, she has furnished an instinct whereby they can overcome the protection given to other species. So even a balance is maintained that the extermination of any one or more species is rendered impossible.

Man has always been the most deadly foe of the wild creatures from the beginning of Time. The relentless advance of civilization into the unpeopled wastes of the earth has driven the wild fauna further and further from their age-old habitat, and done much to upset the even balance so cleverly devised by Nature.

Certain rare species of animal life have been wiped out completely; others have been brought to the brink of annihilation. Modern deadly weapons, coupled with improved means of transport and easier communications, have all played their parts in bringing about this ruthless extermination of the fauna in many parts of the world.

In South Africa the settlement of the country brought in its wake the wholesale slaughter of the wild animals. In district after district the destruction was complete and irrevocable. It can never be replaced. Some of the finest gifts which Nature bestowed so lavishly on South Africa have been lost to posterity. Six species are now extinct and may never be seen—the bloubok, the quagga, the Orange River buffalo, the red hartebeest, the Namaqualand giraffe and the black-maned Cape lion.

It may seem incredible to many, but Johan van Riebeeck, writing of Capetown in 1652, recorded that the land about the present site of the city then swarmed with kudu, eland, steen-buck and hartebeest; lions raided the cattle kraals nightly; leopards came down from Table Mountain in broad daylight and carried off sheep from under the eyes of the herdsmen ; and hippopotami wallowed in a pool where now stands Church Square, the heart of the city.

Now these animals can only be found in established game reserves or in small and scattered areas of the Union of South Africa.

How far distant is that same state of affairs removed from Kenya and other parts of the continent of Africa ? I wonder !

On my return to Kenya for a short visit, after an absence of twenty years, I noted with poignant regret the vast changes that time and closer settlement had wrought in that colony. Two decades only, but what a difference ! When I knew Kenya first, the wild animals could be found almost at your front door in Nairobi. In another quarter of a century or less, it is probable that few beasts will be found outside the game reserves.

In Kenya, where Nature had been more generous than elsewhere in the world, it was early realized what a great asset the game was to the country ; and steps were taken immediately to prevent the ruthless butchery which occurred in South Africa. The colony is still a naturalist's wonderland, thanks to this sane view-point. The increasing demands of civilization, however, have driven the game much further back ; and only in the reserves can they now be found close to the settled lands.

The interests of the colonists had to be safeguarded, though the average settler is a first-class sportsman. His outlook on the controversy that rages round the subject of the preservation of the wild fauna of the British Empire is healthy and rational.

Most governments concerned with the problems of game protection have devised laws which, in so far as is possible, maintain a happy mean between the rights of the settlers and those of the animals. The regulations provide for the continued existence of the wild beasts in sufficient numbers to allow a reasonable amount of hunting on fair terms to sportsmen and naturalists. This is a statesmanlike policy.

There are some who think that all game shooting is quite indefensible, and who believe that mankind could still continue to live and prosper even if all wild animals were permitted to increase unchecked. This is nonsense. Nature knew far better than that.

Man's efforts to develop the lands of promise and cultivate virgin soils have entailed a stern fight for the right to live; and the fauna, both dangerous and defenceless, has had to make way before the wave of human invasion. If man had not won that grim battle, civilization must have been dealt a mortal blow.

To men with both ample means and leisure, the collection of trophies in the game fields is limited only by the terms of their shooting licences; and by the amount of time and money they can devote to the sport. Yet I have known men who have lived in India or Kenya for over twenty years and never have killed even a tiger or lion. They have hunted them, and failed.

The aim of most sportsmen is to obtain the very finest specimens of each species procurable. When actuated solely by this motive, they may often work hard for days on end without even a chance to fire their rifle. The narrow limitations of their licences to hunt, kill or capture wild animals relieve them of all responsibility for the heavy reduction in the numbers of the various species. All they have done is to pick out for themselves the very best in the matter of heads and trophies; not to ruthlessly butcher animals on sight. For this reason, in the localities most frequented by sportsmen, the really good trophies have become increasingly rare. The latter all require time and, in most cases, a long period of years to grow into first-class proportions.

Sport, as distinguished from butchery, needs neither excuse nor apology. The former is the moderate and humane exercise of an inherent instinct worthy of a civilized being; and the latter is the revolting outcome of the undisciplined nature of the real savage. Game butchery is as grossly objectionable as any other form of wanton barbarity; but to protest against all hunting of wild animals, as some do, is a sign of softening of the brain, not of soundness of heart.

The genuine sportsman is never a butcher of game. Among them will be found some of the most gentle and tender-hearted of human beings. Those who do slaughter animals heedlessly, and often with wanton cruelty, can never justly be styled sportsmen; not even by the widest stretch of the imagination.

Personally, I have never killed any living creature just for the sheer lust of slaying, except the crocodile. In the first year or two of my hunting adventures, it is true, I did seek out exceptional trophies; but this object was never allowed to become of paramount importance. My joy and pride in collecting really good heads died an early and unmourned death. I soon discovered that it was a costly and futile pastime, owing to my frequent change of stations and the limited space available for display or storage. Taxidermy costs were also prohibitive to one of my very limited means. I found difficulty even in giving away really splendid trophies. All were faced with the same handicaps as myself.

Carnivores have been killed as vermin; elephants for profit from their ivory; defenceless animals for food for myself or native porters; buffalo and other dangerous beasts in actual self-defence; and some for the acquisition of a really exceptional trophy. Not one single creature, except a crocodile, was ever killed just wantonly.

I soon found a greater joy in spending hours tracking down or watching game in their natural surroundings, so that I might observe all they did and thus profit, at some future date, by that knowledge. It repaid me a thousandfold. Only thus is it possible to learn the hundred and one things of the real intimacies of jungle life.

After my first year or two of big game shooting, I often tracked down a much prized trophy for several hours or even days, sometimes under the most trying conditions, and then never fired a shot at my quarry. The reason for this abstinence was that I became absorbed in observing the habits of the beast or those of the herd to which it belonged. I found this so very fascinating that the trophy, for which I had worked so hard, was completely forgotten. I have always experienced a sense of gladness at my forbearance.

I have tried always to live up to a self-imposed rule of never shooting at any animal unless reasonably sure of killing my quarry outright or as soon as possible after wounding it. Unquestionably, it is much better to lose your prize than to fire when there can be only a hope of maiming the beast. This is much easier to say than to do ; but efficient stalking and accuracy of aim should be the primary equipment of all big game hunters. The creed of every true sportsman should be one animal, one bullet.

It is not always possible to adhere to this golden rule, for circumstances, beyond all human control, sometimes are too strong to be surmounted. I have always hated myself whenever I wounded and did not kill outright. Occasionally, my only average marksmanship was at fault ; at others, to my bitter regret, I lost my temper ; and there have been times when I was forced to act swiftly and without due regard to aim.

You have to get accustomed to many bitter disappointments in hunting big game. There is nothing in the world, to my way of thinking, which teaches a man more patience, iron self-control and self-discipline in most difficult circumstances than this royal sport. Moderation in taking life and in one's own personal habits, and cool courage, are just as much essential factors for success in the game of life in the wilds as are accurate shooting and efficient stalking. You may be guilty of a number of foolish acts which combine to rob you of your trophy, but there are always others to be had. You can profit by your past errors in the next round of the contest between man and beast. Many a hunter has lost his temper or lacked cool judgment in difficult circumstances, and paid very highly for his temporary lapse from grace. As many more again have known keen remorse for the unnecessary slaying of a wild animal.

If every hunter killed all the animals he ever stalked, then the sport indeed would be a poor one. If the game was as easy as all that, it would not have so many ardent devotees and there would not remain many beasts to serve as targets.

When in pursuit of the larger and more dangerous animals, it is never wise to take the slightest liberty. Then you are up against the cold, unrelenting law of the jungle. It is the beast's life or yours that must be forfeit. It behoves you, therefore, to kill quickly and cleanly ; and not be killed in the attempt.

Only the man who is physically fit may hope to hold his own in the wilds with the savage beasts. Animals in their own natural haunts are trained to perfection. Always they are keyed up to kill, well knowing that, if they fail, their own death is inevitable. So the sportsman who is pursuing dangerous animals must learn to keep perfectly cool in moments of acute and sudden peril. He must strive automatically to do just the correct thing and at the psychological moment, and frequently when there is no time for deliberation.

There is a great fascination about hunting big game which cannot be found in any other form of sport. Those who go out into the wild spaces with rifle or camera, and with a real sporting instinct, not only to take life but to study the habits of the denizens of the forests, plains, lakes, swamps and rivers, always find the adventure very much worth while. They open out, and are able to read, a book of Nature with many vastly interesting pages. There is not one single dull paragraph.

Always there is something new to be seen and learned. Every single thing is found to have a meaning, not only in the ways of the wild creatures themselves, but also in those of the primitive human beings who fight for existence among the savage beasts.

So often the unexpected happens. That is the chief part of the immense fascination of big game hunting. It can never, never grow stale. No two animals of any one species ever behave exactly alike in the same circumstances. No man living can state definitely that an animal of this or that species always acts in a certain manner, any more than one hunter can question the actual experiences of another with creatures in their wild state.

Only the law of life in the jungles never changes a particle. It always has been, and always will be, kill : or be killed.

CHAPTER II

AN UNREHEARSED JUNGLE DRAMA

SHORTLY after the conclusion of the South African War, my duties as a soldier took me to India. I was obsessed by one ambition : to kill a tiger. I knew no rest until I got the chance to test my nerves and skill with a rifle against the king of the jungles.

To the true sportsman, this is quite an understandable frame of mind.

I was out after my fifth tiger, and my experiences on that hunting adventure were epic. It was my last chance at a tiger in India, as it happened ; and the final curtain could not have been bettered. That great day will always stand out most vividly in my recollections.

By great good fortune, I was a silent witness of an unrehearsed comedy and then a real drama in the heart of the jungle. Both were staged and produced by a real expert at show-craft —Mother Nature.

It is the drama which stands out so clear-cut in my mind ; and always will. The comedy was merely a light-hearted curtain-raiser ; but deliciously played.

I sat literally in the " gallery," and was an enthralled spectator of a terrific duel between two mighty beasts of the jungle-lands of India. I looked down upon Nature in the raw, and saw a scene that surely must have stirred even a blasé Nero to a display of genuine enthusiasm. I am prepared to wager that he never saw a greater combat waged in the amphitheatre of ancient Rome !

That fierce battle for life brought home to me, as nothing else could, the actuality of the savagery of animals in wild regions ; and how every hour is beset with extreme perils and hedged round with constant threats to life.

One moment they know and enjoy a carefree existence, kill and eat their fill, and know happiness and contentment ; and

23

the next, they are fighting a mortal duel against an unexpected foe. It is ever the law of the jungle that they are up against : kill : or be killed ! Bluff, strength, cunning, trickery, agility, ferocity and sureness in attack—those are the only suits of armour worn by these jungle gladiators. No man, however, could ever teach them a single trick in the game of life. They know it all.

I was alone on this final tiger-hunt. I sat perched high on a machan, firmly secured in a lofty but solid tree on the very edge of the vast jungle. Before me stretched a vista of open ground and a swamp ; beyond that was a grim hedge of almost impenetrable forest and tangled undergrowth. It offered a most forbidding prospect : cruel and sinister.

I had gone early to the chosen spot, so as to complete my plans for attacking a notorious tiger of the district ; and had climbed up to my post an hour or two before sundown. I like to have some daylight in which to make sure all is prepared, to study life at sunset, and be rested and ready before the fight begins.

A tiger had killed not more than fifty yards from my tree, and was suspected to be the very animal I wanted. I felt quite sure that he would return to finish his meal. So I waited patiently for his advent, watching and enjoying this peep at Nature.

Early in my vigil, I saw a jackal come forward from the jungle and loaf round the kill. He moved in an aimless sort of way, and kept at some distance from it. To read through his pretence was simple, for plainly the intention was that the world should believe he had not even seen the kill. It was most amusing to watch his antics. The tiger had been interrupted after killing, and had devoured but a small portion of the carcass. It must have been a terrible temptation to that jackal.

After a time, however, he disappeared into the jungle. I was real sorry to see him go, for his clownish behaviour had relieved pleasantly the tedium of my wait for the lord of the jungle. He was just about due to arrive for the feast, and the jackal obviously was taking no risks of being caught red-handed by the tiger in pilfering the larder.

To my great surprise, the jackal presently stepped out once more before the footlights and gave an unsolicited encore. He must have made a complete, or almost complete, circuit of the

THE AUTHOR'S SAFARI FORDING A RIVER

spot, for he reappeared from the direction in which he had first shown himself to me.

Now he walked up to within a few paces of the carcass of the domestic buffalo, boldly and without hesitation. No sooner was he within reach of it than he jumped backwards hastily, as if alarmed. For a moment or two he stood still, listening and ready for instant flight. He repeated this performance several times, each time going just a little nearer to the coveted beef. Then he craned out his neck as far as possible, and gradually and cautiously touched the kill with his nose.

Immediately nose met beef all his fears seemed to evaporate and he dropped the mask of shyness. Evidently, he had made up his mind that the tiger was not yet in the vicinity. As his preliminary acrobatic performances had not elicited even a warning growl to intimate that this was a private, very private larder, patently the tiger had not come back to his meal. The coast being clear, fortunately, immediate action was now indicated.

The jackal set to work in a very businesslike manner, and tore open the extended stomach first of all. The stench was so dreadful that I squirmed slightly on the machan, my senses in revolt and seized by acute nausea. While struggling to get my handkerchief to clamp over nose and mouth, I must have made too much noise. The jackal heard the slight creak of the machan at once, looked up at me for a brief second, and vanished like a wisp of smoke. I saw him no more.

It had all been most interesting and amusing, and I had thoroughly enjoyed that little curtain-raiser.

I sat on my machan, absorbed in watching the jungle actors pass across my stage. Believe me, I was far from bored with this vigil. The scraggy trees surrounding the swamp were silhouetted against a setting sun that blazed in the West like a ball of incandescent copper. The day insects gradually ceased their irritating humming and biting ; and the fairy life of the night, whose dawn is the setting day, came buzzing in myriads from their hiding-places like the ballet of an elfin chorus.

A stately crane stepped daintily through the reeds ; and fat-breasted little birds of brilliant plumage settled on twigs, twittered and kissed good night, ruffled their gorgeous feathers, and then tucked tiny heads under their wings. Nature was retiring to rest : only the killers were on the prowl.

There is never an armistice in the wild spaces of the earth.
It is always war : and war to the death. No quarter is given
to any living thing, and only the very fittest and most cunning
can escape for long from their ultimate fate.

I breathed deeply, stirred and delighted with all I saw.
The swamp air, sweet to my nostrils, almost intoxicated ; a
cool night wind sprang up and soothed my sun-baked body ; and
my senses revelled in this picturesque unveiling of Nature's
own bed-chamber. Surely no human being could have remained
insensible to, or out of tune with, the charms of that perfect
picture !

All at once, I was alert. I had heard heavy feet forcing
their way through the tangled masses of the jungle. The giant
grass ahead of me now swayed and bent down ; and, a moment
later, a magnificent cow buffalo breasted her way out of that
thick mat of grass and undergrowth, and stood out in the open.
She had a massive sweep of horns ; one of the best I have ever
seen on one of her kind. Powerful bulk, terrific shoulders and
gigantic head, she made a grand picture. She offered a perfect
target ; and I had not yet bagged an Indian buffalo. For a
fleeting instant or so I hesitated, fingers clutching my rifle.
But I wanted that tiger, and so refrained from shooting. Oh,
how glad I am to-day that the tiger was uppermost in my
thoughts !

Suspiciously, she sniffed the air ; and then, throwing her
face skywards, bellowed like a thunderclap. The tree seemed to
quiver under me to the vibrations of that majestic challenge to
all in the wilds.

A moment later came an answering bellow, as if from miles
away. It sounded faint and distant after the volume of her
great voice. The cow replied joyously to her mate. She shook
her huge head, and then drove the cruel points of her horns
viciously into the soft earth. Evidently she was feeling good,
and wanted the world to know it.

Leisurely, she walked over to the tiger's kill, and sniffed at
it thoughtfully for a minute or two. Again up came her splendid
head, and the thunder of her throat burst and shattered the
silence of the dying day. It was a sound of challenging defiance :
arresting, menacing and utterly provocative.

Suddenly she showed signs of palpable uneasiness. She
turned about swiftly, facing the suspected point of danger.
Her head was lowered now, eyes peering intently at the edge of

the jungle beyond my tree. My own followed the direction of her steady gaze. Almost at once I saw what she had seen.

The tiger was there, just clear of the fringe of the dense jungle. He was skulking along silently, furtively, and with white belly sweeping the grass.

He saw the cow buffalo and halted instantly : motionless save for his twitching, writhing tail. The buffalo scattered the loose earth with a swift stroke of her forefoot, eyes never wavering from that intent watch on her ancient foe. Both animals were alert, and fully on guard. Eyes held eyes, unflinching and savage. There was deadly hate in the whole attitude of each great beast.

Shoot that tiger I would not. I desired now only to see this wonderful jungle drama played out to the final drop of the curtain.

Slowly the striped jungle-cat crept forward more into the open, never once straightening his elastic body, eyes glaring fixedly at the buffalo, and tail swishing the grass angrily. The massive jaw hung half open, low to the ground and dripping saliva. The cow buffalo moved only to keep facing him, neither advancing nor retreating. There was a deadly menace in her whole intense attitude.

Round and round, in an ever-narrowing circle, went the tiger, trying to get in behind the buffalo for a sudden spring on to her back ; but she was always too quick for him. You could not teach her much in ring tactics, and her footwork was perfect. She knew every trick of the jungle.

Abruptly the tiger paused and drew himself up into a ball, tail lashing the ground savagely. Then, without sound or warning, his body shot through the air like a rocket. At the same instant, with a thunderous bellow and the fine sweep of horns levelled, the buffalo charged. She met the tiger's body in mid-air. The shock of that impact hurled both to the ground ; but, in a flash, they were up again. With a roar and answering bellow, they charged at each other once more. The tiger missed, but his leap landed him behind the buffalo.

With almost incredible agility, he turned and sprang upon her back. Before his terrible fangs could sink deep into her neck, she threw herself over backwards and tried to roll upon him. The move was both astute and effective.

The tiger, in order to save himself from being crushed beneath that massive body, loosened his hold on her. As she regained her feet, he was ready ; and now fastened himself on her right shoulder. The cow shook him clear of her and, with a furious bellow, charged full at him. She bowled him over like a ninepin, and then rammed him against the thick trunk of a large tamarisk tree.

Blood was flowing freely from her bellowing mouth, streaming also from the great gashes in neck, shoulder and back made by those cruel talons. She retreated to gain charging distance to finish off her enemy.

The tiger, however, was still fit to fight, though badly gored and crushed. He was game, too. Again he sprang in, and this time landed fair and square between her great horns, his beautifully striped body hanging down and completely smothering her face. His teeth and claws sank deeply into her flesh, blood filled his mouth and ran down the cow's sides in great rivers of carmine. She bellowed aloud in her agony.

Lowering her head almost to the ground, she charged full speed at a big tree trunk. Her burden was still festooned over her face. There came a sickening thud as they met the solid tree. She staggered back and almost sat down on her rump, but quickly regained her poise. A feeble roar told me that the tiger's distress was very great indeed ; and that the result of that terrific impact would be his complete undoing. In a limp heap, he collapsed on the ground.

The cow buffalo had delivered a real upper-cut and knocked him out.

I saw her draw back, and carefully measure her mark. A short rush forward, a sharp twist of her cruel horns, and she had gored him again and again. He tried to crawl away into the cover of the jungle growth, and hide from that pitiless onslaught. Now he had had enough : rather more than enough. But there is no referee in the jungle to count " time." He was not to know escape from the relentless law. Only the death of one, or both, could end that fierce combat.

A triumphant bellow of victory shook the swamp-grass and made my machan shiver. The cow buffalo charged home for the final effort. She lifted that mangled, crushed body on her great horns, gave a sharp twist of her head, and threw the big jungle-cat, as if he was a wisp of straw, some distance away.

He must have died as he hit the ground. She did not even trouble to follow his body, and make certain that he was killed. She *knew.*

I could not resist a loud shout of : " Bravo ! " All through that titantic battle my sympathies had been with the buffalo, even though she had robbed me of my trophy. But no tiger skin in the world could have compensated me for having failed to witness that stupendous fight to the death. It was an opportunity that comes but once to a man in a lifetime : even if then.

The black pall of night descended and shut out that great picture. A young and tender moon shed an ethereal light over the stage, and twinkling stars began to wink at me from the darkening canopy overhead.

The buffalo bellowed again, triumphantly ; and was answered immediately from close at hand in the dense jungle. I heard the crash of her thundering departure from the stage to meet her mate in the wings of the forest. The curtain fell soundlessly then, and shut out the last act of that thrilling jungle-drama.

I was glad that she had won : glad with all my heart that the tiger had gone down to such a splendid creature. She had asked no mercy : given none.

I wanted to say something to that dumb heroine in her hour of triumph ; but I was tongue-tied. Never till that moment had I realized how narrow are the limits of human speech. There were no words in the cold English language to express adequately all I felt.

The tiger's body I left where it had fallen. It was not mine.

CHAPTER III

TIGER! TIGER!

ONLY those who have actually experienced the thrills of hearing, when in the heart of the Indian jungle, the insistent warning of the shikaris : " Tiger ! Tiger, sahib ! " can understand the real joy of those three words.

The lucky man who has killed his first tiger has just cause to feel proud of his prowess ; while he who has made a bag of a number of striped-cats of the jungle has but a poor opinion of other forms of shikar in India.

To mention this entrancing subject to an Indian forest official, or to any of those who have lived for long on the edge of the jungle in India or Malaya, is to bring forth a tale of experiences, personal and otherwise, which might well daunt the most case-hardened lion-tamer.

The man who speaks truthfully of his first tiger hunt almost invariably confesses to having experienced a feeling of genuine awe at the sight of his quarry. In many cases, he will own to a sickening, paralysing fear. The latter, I freely admit, was undoubtedly my own first reaction to a tiger seen in the wild state. In the few meetings with this ferocious beast, during my service in India, I was always conscious of a feeling of acute discomfort until I warmed up to the work in hand.

Although one's first impression of the tiger as seen in its native haunts may always be remembered with a thrill of dread, yet the fascination of the sport soon becomes over-mastering. One British officer of the Indian Army had a record of over three hundred tigers to his credit at the time of his death. Long after he had retired on pension, he remained in the wild regions of the East. He refused to return to England and shiver in sunless days or to abandon the game of the jungle for the driven birds of the English covert. His name, of course, was famous among all shikaris.

It is a fallacy to believe that tigers are common in India, Burma or Malaya ; or that a keen man has only to desire a personal interview with the lord of the jungle in order to secure an abundance of trophies. As a matter of fact, exactly the opposite is the case. Practically every sportsman has ascertained the falseness of this pleasing fiction soon after his arrival in India, or just as soon as individual circumstances have made it possible for him to hunt tiger.

The fact is that tigers are necessarily rare animals, for ordinarily they prey upon other *ferae naturae* ; and it follows from this that were they to become plentiful in any one locality, then the game on which they exist would soon be killed off and the tigers forced to emigrate. Undoubtedly the ultimate result would be that the tiger would quickly become extinct. Nature, however, rules the jungle and all life therein with an iron hand, and has guarded adequately against such a contingency. Though the final extinction of the tiger may be a probability, there are still so many vast solitudes but rarely inhabited by man in the immense spaces of India that, though it is an uncommon beast, its final extermination is still far distant.

But for the havoc wrought by men among the wild animals upon which the tiger preys, no doubt there would be food for far more of the latter within easy range of actual civilization. The growing scarcity of the food supply of the tiger has forced it to seek haunts more remote from the limits of man's invasion, and where the game still exist plentifully and without being butchered. If the tiger is rarer to-day than Nature intended this species to be, it is solely due to mankind having cut short its supply of natural food. All creatures have to eat to live, and the tiger is no exception. Deprive it of the game, and it will exact toll from the village cattle, flocks and even human beings.

Run your finger across the map from Baluchistan to Singapore —an eighth of the globe. Between these points lie the mighty States of India, Siam, Burma and Malaya ; towering mountain ranges ; broad and stately rivers—the Indus, Ganges, Jumna, Brahmaputra, Irrawaddy and Salween—all flowing to the sea from the high Himalayan gable of the earth ; and a vast area of jungles, deserts, tumbling hill country and dense forests. This is one of the world's greatest hunting grounds. The only serious rival is Equatorial Africa. Time was when the whole

continent of Africa, from the Cape to Cairo, was a teeming
mass of wild animals of infinite variety; but man robbed the
future generations of the heritage which Nature had bequeathed
to them.

It is the natural ambition of most sportsmen to test their
nerves on a tiger, for it appeals strongly to that love of sport
inherent in all Englishmen. It is not given to all, however, to
achieve the height of their desires. Many keen sportsmen,
who I know personally, have resided in India or Malaya for
many years, have expended a good deal of time and money
in trying to kill tigers, and yet have not succeeded in slaying
a single specimen. It is cruel hard luck ; but all in the game.

Shortly after my arrival in India, in 1902, I was told the
story of one such case. On the eve of returning to England
on pension, a veteran Colonel of the Indian Army decided to
make one final effort to accomplish his life's ambition. Year
after year he had failed, but craved just one single tiger before
he bade farewell to India.

One day his Indian shikari reported that a fine male tiger
had been seen in the neighbourhood. He set out, accompanied
by three of his junior officers, to hunt it down. It was agreed
that he was to have the first shot, unless the tiger rendered
it impossible to carry through this arrangement.

When his quarry emerged from the thick jungle into full view
of the four sportsmen, the Colonel took the first shot. He
severely wounded the handsome beast, but did not kill it. In
such an event, it is usual, and much wiser, to wait at least
an hour or two before going in pursuit. This enables the angry
animal to be found when growing stiff from the wound and weak
from loss of blood. But this veteran soldier was within sight
of realizing his lifelong ambition ; and grew reckless.

After an exhausting search, the beaters finally located the
wounded beast in thick cover ; but it had too much life to offer
a fair shot to kill. Suddenly springing past the rest of the
hunting party, the tiger did its enemy to death and then bounded
off into the thick jungle before the others had time to shoot.
Their Colonel was at death's door when they reached his side,
and a moment later was dead. Instead of killing, he had been
killed.

It is only the boldest and most experienced sportsmen who
venture on foot into the dense jungles after tiger. The most
common method employed is to sit up in a machan—a rough

A TSESSEBE GRAZING

A ZEBRA AT WATERHOLE

Photos by Fred A. Parrish

platform or native bed erected in a tree overlooking a kill, and shoot the beast as it comes for its meal.

I once heard a good story of a sportsman who was weak enough to grant his wife's request to accompany him to the machan and see the tiger killed. When the critical moment arrived, the lady doubted the safety of their position, and offered up loud and pious appeals for the tiger to be kept away. Once again her wish was granted. For all time to come, her husband's advice to his friends was : " If you want good sport, for God's sake don't take a praying woman with you ! "

The other method—far more picturesque, exciting but very costly—is to pursue the jungle-cat with the aid of trained shikar elephants and an army of Indian beaters. The sportsmen are in the howdahs on the backs of the elephants. Their giant steeds crash their way through the long grass, reeds, young bamboos and everything else while searching for any lurking tigers. At last one is driven from cover into the open, and bullet after bullet is poured into it. The tiger is not always killed at the first salvo ; and, in its final efforts to save its life, often turns upon its tormentors with astonishing fury.

The Bengal tiger is such an awful scourge to the Indian villagers and herdsmen near the jungle-lands that it is little short of a kindness to kill them at every possible opportunity. They are treated and classified as vermin, much in the same way as are lions and leopards in Africa.

Tigers are great travellers, and each one wanders over a very large tract of land. He may prey on twenty or more villages, visiting one to-day and another to-morrow ; and his kills frequently occur at places situated long distances apart. Sometimes, however, a big beast will make his headquarters for a time near a cluster of villages, and then will levy a regular toll upon cattle or flocks, or even upon the human inhabitants. Such a beast is often quite well known to the villagers, and is generally given a special nickname as a mark of distinction. The natives often meet him on the jungle paths, crossing their fields or else gliding noiselessly through the shadows of the dim forest depths.

Sometimes he is a confirmed man-eater. In this case, he strikes acute fear into the hearts of the simple Indian forest-dwellers ; and they become so terrified that nothing will induce them to leave their villages or work in the fields until the man-eater has been killed.

Man-eating tigers are not infrequent in India. In one single year's statistics it is recorded that tigers killed 809 people ; and the total mortality caused by wild animals, snakes included but crocodiles excluded, was no less than 18,471. That is rather staggering to contemplate. In that same year under review, it was recorded that at least 48,400 cattle became the prey of marauding beasts of the jungle.

This destruction of life is not all one-sided. During that same period it was reported that 27,000 dangerous animals were killed and 116,500 snakes destroyed. How many more could be added to either side of the ledger in this eternal war in the jungle it is quite impossible even to guess.

Could such a state of affairs exist elsewhere than in India ? I very much doubt it.

The indifference of the natives of India toward this grave situation is incredible. Life of any kind, human or animal, is of very little account in their eyes. They have paid heavy tolls in death to the wild beasts of the jungle for untold ages, yet remain as passive as their meek cattle. The timidity of the Indian peasant encourages the wild beasts to attack human life, or else we should not find a record of 18,471 human beings destroyed by animals in one single year.

One forest officer told me cynically that the life of the average Indian peasant was so miserable in any case that he made no real effort, or very little, to preserve it.

The man-eating tiger goes about his deadly work in a dreadful silence. To my mind, there is nothing that so chills the blood with horror as the mental picture of such a sinister brute venturing into an Indian forest village in the middle of the night, and passing from hut to hut, silently as a cloud's shadow over the face of the moon, in search of an easy means of entry to claim a victim.

The native householders lie awake, staring blankly and utterly terrified at the frail doorway, while listening intently for the least hint of the monster's approach. It is a night of abject terror, a ghastly period of horrible expectancy. Mentally, they review every single detail of their crude defences, and visualize the weak spots in their hut.

The sharp crackling of a twig suddenly startles one man. He strains his eyes through the darkness, clutches at the knife which is the only weapon he possesses, ears tensely listening and body trembling with mute apprehension. Then he hears the soft tread of the tiger pause at the doorway of his own hut. A moment later, the fierce beast has launched itself against the flimsy door and crashed it inwards. As if born out of the silence of the night, the man sees the man-eater standing in the shattered entrance, silhouetted against the moon's silver flood.

He knows full well that this is no apparition created by his terrified brain : but the real thing. Before he has even time to call out for help, the tiger has felled him with a blow of its paw and seized him in its mouth. It bounds off into the jungle with its human prey, carrying the body much as a terrier does a rat.

At dawn, the other frightened villagers crowd round the deserted hut. The writing is plain on the earth for all to read; and there is a wail of mourning throughout the small village.

That scene is a matter of daily occurrence in one or other parts of India. Whole tracts of country and clusters of villages have become depopulated owing to the depredations of the king of the jungles, so that the advent of a European sportsman to tackle the brute is welcomed joyously, and much as the coming of a public benefactor. He spells deliverance from this deadly scourge ; relief from their hourly terrors ; and the defender of their right to live. So the villagers will always keep Europeans well posted as to the movements of tigers in their districts, and are keen to act as beaters in the hunt—for a monetary consideration. You may not even save their miserable lives without being asked to pay for doing so !

It was at the Nerbudda River near Jubbulpore, in the northern part of the Central Provinces, that I had my first tiger shoot.

Shortly after my arrival in India, a brother officer told me that he had been invited to join a tiger hunt. At my earnest pleading, he managed to wangle an invitation for me also. By his kindness, the path to crown my ambition was rendered easy. On our arrival at Jubbulpore, we found all in readiness.

On the great day, the elephants were driven up to us. They were commanded to fall down upon their knees, ladders were placed against the howdahs, and we climbed up to the backs of the big beasts. Once all were safely there, the signal was given for a start to be made. Each elephant unhinged itself into altitudes with rather the sensation of a mountain in the throes of an earthquake ; and off we started in a long string toward the Nerbudda River. This spot had always been noted for big tiger bags.   Time may have altered this since my early days in India.

It struck me at once that the tiger would not have much of a chance against such a large battery of guns.   Our elephants had been well trained, were supposed to stand when a tiger charged, and not even to flinch when a rifle was discharged from their backs.   I say supposed, for I doubt if any elephant ever born is wholly devoid of fear of the tiger.   Besides the beasts we rode, there were others to be utilized in beating the jungle for the tiger.   We had much the appearance of an elephant-mounted army on the line of march.   So far, it all looked superlatively easy and lacked all the element of danger.

After a consultation, our head shikari turned off into a part of the jungle where a kill had been made on the previous night.   A "kill" is the carcass of an animal slain either by the tiger or some other agency.   Ordinarily, the killer will hang about its larder ; and, in the meantime, drives away the jackals, hyenas and vultures from its supper.   As the tiger is nocturnal in habit, it generally dozes during the hours of sunshine in some shady spot near the banquet prepared by its own efforts.   Naturally and instinctively, it shuns all dens ; and very rarely will a tiger hunt even game for a long period in the same district.

We hoped to bag this tiger ; and my excitement was intense. As we approached near to the kill, the head shikari drew our attention to a flock of scraggy-necked vultures perched in nearby trees.   It was an auspicious sign, for it proved that the tiger was lurking near its kill and exercising its rights over the meal.   Some of our elephants were twitching their ears, swaying their trunks from side to side, and treading uneasily. Evidently they had got a whiff of tiger-tainted wind.

The beaters now made a detour of half a mile to get behind the tiger, while we took up our position in an open space on the edge of the jungle.   We were to wait there until the tiger had been driven towards our guns, and actually broke cover.

As the elephant walks at the rate of at least six miles an hour, it was not long before the din of the drums and the shouts of the beaters reverberated through the jungle, scaring monkeys, peacocks, smaller birds and other jungle dwellers.   Sambar, barking-deer, swamp-deer and other varieties broke past us singly, in twos and in threes ; and a diminutive mouse-deer, not over twelve inches high, plunged madly between our elephant's legs. That little mite started a riot !

With a snort of fear, the large beast turned to bolt. Had it not been for the mahout's steel-goad treatment, we might have been carried off into the jungle and probably brained against a big tree-branch. This extreme nervousness on the part of our elephant rather shook my confidence in his alleged courage in the face of a tiger's vicious charge.

The din made by the beaters grew momentarily louder ; and we heard, too, the peculiar drumming sound made by some elephants as a signal that a dangerous animal is near at hand. This brought us to our feet in the howdahs, rifles ready and fingers on triggers, and eyes searching the edge of the jungle. Just at that moment, a deer in full flight swept past us ; and our shikari, pointing to our left-front, whispered : " Tiger, sahib ! Tiger ! "

And then I saw him ; my very first tiger in the jungles. It was a red-letter day for me ! Before us was a very large beast, his jaw almost touching the ground as he sneaked, half crouching and half crawling on his white belly, through the fringe of the jungle. He stood for an instant in suspense, seemingly undecided which way to turn.

This is always the moment when the hunt is gravely dangerous. With a terrifying, coughing roar, the tiger will generally hurl itself with tremendous bounds straight at its foes. Its pace is terrific. When at springing distance, it hurls its heavy body through the air upon the nearest elephant. This is the great moment for testing a sportsman's nerves and steadiness of aim. Unless the tiger is killed now, and at once, it will land with claws and teeth on the flanks of the elephant, striking and tearing with ghastly effect.

I knew this, having been carefully warned what to expect and what I must do. I got my sights on to him, but not before I saw the brute's eyes blazing at us like green emeralds, while the cruel fangs were bared and glittering like polished ivory.

Just as I was about to press the trigger, my elephant suddenly charged straight for the tiger, uttering a shrill scream of rage and hate. The movement was so totally unexpected that it caught me off my guard. I found myself shaken clear out of the howdah into some bushes before I could clutch at the side of the basket. Luckily for me, they broke my fall and I escaped injury.

As I landed on my back, my rifle exploded. Where the bullets went, I have not the least notion; but no harm was done. The kick of that double explosion, however, bruised my shoulder badly.

An instant later, my companion in the howdah fired; but only succeeded in wounding the tiger. All in all, there was plenty of excitement for some minutes. The noise of the two rifles being discharged, the trumpeting of the elephants, the tiger's howling roar, the shouts of the beaters and the beating of their drums all combined to create a nerve-racking cacophony of sound.

Hastily scrambling to my feet, I stood entranced as I watched that fearsome scene. The tiger was undaunted, and met the charge of the elephant without flinching. With a lithe spring, he landed on its head, and sank claws and fangs into the huge beast's neck and trunk. I could see the mahout beating at the tiger with his steel-goad, while the elephant was trying to throw its enemy to the ground. As I watched that amazing fight, I could not avoid a feeling of immense relief that I had been thrown out of the howdah. I did not relish my position on foot at all, but it did seem safer than being in the howdah so close to that savage brute.

Quickly reloading my rifle, I tested the mechanism and found all in order. I glanced around rapidly. The other sportsmen's elephants were circling round the combatants, trying to get a chance of a clean shot at the tiger. Then I stood ready to fire at the first available moment, and watched that Homeric battle with the keenest possible interest.

Because of their position, it was quite impossible for any of the guns to get into action. The tiger and elephant were too mixed up for a safe shot. My friend in the howdah was equally powerless to intervene, unless he risked hitting both elephant and mahout instead of the tiger.

Resenting the blows of the mahout's goad, the jungle-cat now sank its claws into the man's thigh and tried to pull him down from the elephant's neck. This attack revived me into rapid action. I took a long chance, and fired my right barrel into the tiger's spine. With a roar of pain, he fell backward to the ground; and our enraged elephant, bleeding profusely from many terrible wounds, was upon him instantly. He tusked and trampled the tiger to pulp before he could be driven off the hated foe.

The fascinating part of all big game hunting is that almost always the totally unexpected happens. I had not been prepared to have an elephant bolt from a harmless and minute mouse-deer, and then turn to charge boldly at an unwounded tiger. But this is exactly what had happened, for the big beast had started his charge before my friend had fired and wounded the tiger.

I did not forget that experience; and I give our elephant full marks.

I had seen my first tiger, and it had been killed; but the trophy was my friend's. In any case, I wasted no vain regrets over it. The skin was quite valueless, thanks to the elephant's angry onslaught on the dead body.

It was real tough luck on my friend, for it was his first kill among the tigers.

CHAPTER IV

A FEW TIGERS I HAVE MET

IN the light of personal experience, I do not consider big game hunting in India is as dangerous as in Africa. Every sportsman is entitled to his own opinion, provided always he can speak from actual knowledge of conditions in both countries. No man living can be dogmatic, reasonably, about such things. So often circumstances vary widely.

If one looks for danger in India, however, it can be found readily enough. Danger enough, indeed, to daunt even the stoutest heart. But the adventurous or foolhardy spirit can find real danger anywhere in the world, by acting like an idiot and ignoring all commonly accepted safeguards. Even in the streets of London, one may face bigger risks than in the wildest regions of untamed Africa or Tibet.

In India there is no real hardship in hunting tigers. Most of the shooting is done in real comfort, if not in the height of luxury. You are either carried to your game or else it is driven right up to the muzzle of your rifle. At times even, you just sit and wait for it to come to the bait, live or dead, prepared as a lure.

On the other hand, in Africa, generally speaking, the hunter follows and faces his dangerous quarries on foot. He has to work real hard to get to grips and take big risks; and often only gets a shot after days of strenuous tracking. There one commonly hunts alone. In India, the crowd turns out; and I hate a crowd when hunting. I would much prefer to be alone, and have generally been so.

My second tiger hunt was of a very different character from the first. It was conducted from a machan, which had been built cleverly in a convenient tree. The headman of the local village had informed a cavalry officer friend of mine that a tiger was carrying off the cattle every night. He invited me to accompany him in an effort to rid the neighbourhood of this pest and thus confer a blessing on the Indian peasants.

To entice our quarry into the vicinity of our machans, we bought two domestic buffaloes from the headman and had them tethered under our trees as bait. It sounds cruel, but two buffalo in exchange for a tiger means a big saving of life among the herds ; and these two beasts, unknown to themselves, were offered up on the altar of sacrifice. They were ancient beasts, long past their prime and real utility. But I have never quite liked the idea of using " live " bait.

We had been told that the marauder was an old offender, and well known to the villagers. Though many earnest efforts had been made to destroy this brute, all had failed. In fact, we gathered that the simple peasants regarded this beast as blessed with supernatural powers. We were both most eager to try our luck with the village scourge, and hoped earnestly that fortune would smile upon us. Both had still to bag his first tiger.

I found it far from comfortable to sit in a cramped position all night on an unsteady platform in a tree which swayed with the wind. The slightest movement of my body made the machan creak, and this would alarm our cunning quarry. To sit hour after hour, perfectly motionless, and straining one's eyes for a shot at a dark smudge that moves in the blackness of night, is no sinecure. Fireflies wave their lamps in your face, and every conceivable insect beats about your head and bites every atom of your body exposed to view ; while, for full measure, a few venturesome lizards playfully drop down the neck of your shirt and wriggle about on your chest or back. I loathe soft, clammy creatures ; so suffered the torments of the damned during that night's vigil. I still consider it was worth all that I endured.

The hours of this rank discomfort dragged by slowly. The time seemed interminable. Towards dawn, I heard the buffalo below my tree begin to tug at its tether. Straining my eyes for a glimpse of the expected tiger, I saw a large black shape slowly moving across the open space in front of my platform. A dull thud followed. Immediately there was a terrified bellow from the buffalo, and the sounds of a brief but violent struggle. A few minutes later all was still. I waited, perhaps for half an hour, and then heard the sloppy, tearing sound always made by an animal when eating unbled meat.

I could scarcely see to shoot, but levelled my rifle, which had luminous sights, at the dark mass below me. I fired plumb into the centre of it. A roar and several snarls echoed from

the target, assuring me that my mark had been hit somewhere.
The sound of my shot had scarcely died away, when two loud
reports on my right told me that something of importance was
happening to my companion at his machan.

With the eagerness and stupidity of the novice, I jumped
down from my roost in the tree and landed on all fours. Picking
myself up, I made my way slowly and cautiously to the black
mass at which I had shot. I kept it covered with my rifle, in
case the tiger should rise and charge.

I learned some sense after that night's adventure. My
action was simply shrieking aloud for trouble : frankly, it was
suicidal !

More lives have been lost by sportsmen following up a wounded
tiger on foot than in any other way. Often the tiger will lie
up in the jungle, to all outward appearances stiff and out of
action. It is, however, only shamming death. The daring
and foolish hunter approaches too close and, to his sudden
dismay, finds there is still a considerable kick left in that striped
body. Before he has time either to fire or retreat, the wounded
beast puts forth its last ounce of strength and gains a terrible
revenge on its foe.

As I neared my quarry, I heard my friend call out loudly :
" I've got him, old chap ! "

" So have I ! " I shouted back ; and really believed it.

I fired another shot at my fallen tiger, and it did not move.
To make doubly sure that it was dead, I gathered and lit a
bunch of dry reeds and saw, to my astonishment, that I had
killed a large leopard instead of the tiger.

The unexpected had happened again !

While I was examining my kill, I heard two more shots from
my companion ; and then, in rapid succession, six shots from
his revolver. Instantly I knew that he was in serious trouble.
Crying out loudly that I was coming to his aid, I ran swiftly
towards him, reloading as I stumbled across the rough ground
in the darkness.

When I reached his side, he told me breathlessly that, just
as my first shot had been fired, he saw the tiger quite distinctly.
He let drive, and the tiger went down. Immediately it rose
again, and he let it have the second barrel. As the brute lay
still, he felt certain that it was dead. As I had done, he waited
for a time and then climbed down from the machan, and walked
proudly toward his first tiger. When within twenty yards or

so, the beast again leaped up and charged full at him. He fired twice, and it rolled over with a furious growl ; but promptly rose and charged once more. Whipping out his revolver, he emptied the chamber into the beast as it came on. One well-directed bullet penetrated the tiger's brain, and it fell dead at his feet.

When we skinned his fine trophy after sunrise, we found nine bullets in the carcass. Only one of his shots had missed.

On our triumphant return to the village with our two trophies, the headman assured us that we had killed the wrong tiger. Only that very night, he insisted, the old marauder had slain a village bullock. The beast had been seen and recognized as the real raider. Tired as we were, we hurried off to the spot where the kill had been located. Still I had not got my tiger, and could not rest content until I had. Every rebuff served to make me the more determined to slay one.

We waited under cover on one bank of the shallow nullah, in which the partly eaten carcass of the kill lay. It was an asinine thing to do, as we learned afterwards ; and time wasted. Up to dusk, when we abandoned the futile vigil, the tiger had not put in an appearance near the kill. It was most disappointing. We both badly needed a night's rest and sleep, and neither fancied sitting up for two nights in succession.

On the following morning, soon after daybreak, we went off to see if the tiger had been to the kill during the night. He had, undoubtedly, for the carcass had been dragged some distance away from the spot where we had last seen it. Now he had cached his larder in a very dense and thorny thicket. This would not suit our purpose at all, so we got the villagers to act the rôle of scene-shifters.

We had two machans fixed in nearby trees, and the carcass was dragged from under the dense canopy of thorn-bush. On our instructions, it was left in the open close to our two trees. Then, the stage set to our liking, we returned to camp for tiffin. It had been arranged that we should go back to the machans and take up our posts about the middle of the afternoon.

A little before sunset, while it was still quite light, I saw the tiger advancing slowly through the thicket in which he had placed his kill ; and from which it had been dragged so as to afford a clear shot at the beast. He looked back over his shoulder only once, and then came straight up to the kill without further hesitation. I was afraid that he might see me and dash off in alarm, if I raised myself before his head was hidden by my machan. It was only with the utmost self-control that I waited for him to disappear from my view. Then I carefully elevated myself, fired downwards, and hit him.

He dragged himself away slowly, however, but with obvious pain and difficulty. I fired my second barrel at him, but missed badly. After a long wait, I climbed down from my machan. I was joined almost immediately by my companion and our beaters. I was positive that the tiger was severely wounded, but knew now that it would be the height of folly to follow up at once. While we waited, darkness descended ; and we were forced to abandon the hunt. Neither of us was quite mad enough, though both Irish, to pursue a wounded tiger in the dark and through such thick jungle. Our beaters, very rightly, stoutly refused to even consider such a project. To-morrow, yes ; to-night, most decidedly not ! We agreed with this verdict, and trailed back to camp.

Before dawn next day, we were out once more after my tiger. I was already speaking of it as " my " and not " the " ! We followed the blood trail through terribly thick stuff, in which the danger was extreme. Our advance was marked with great caution, and was slow.

Presently, I heard the tiger groaning somewhere ahead of us, but nobody could see him. The trail now took us into a very densely jungled and narrow nullah, and I went well ahead of my friend and the beaters. It was my tiger and, therefore, the point of danger was rightfully mine ; but my heart was in my mouth. The beaters were directed to go along both banks of the nullah, and throw in stones but not to enter it under any circumstances.

The beat began. Very soon the big, round head of the tiger appeared. It showed up on my side of the nullah, and only twenty to thirty yards away. The head alone was visible, but he seemed to wish to break out on that side. A fool beater made a noise, and the tiger stood up and turned broadside on to me. He saw me instantly, and charged. I fired my right barrel, and dropped him in his tracks. Then I let him have the second barrel, aiming at the small portion of his body which I could still see. I was taking no undue chances with a wounded tiger ; and my first, at that. I wanted to kill him, but not be killed.

Now I stood still and waited for what might happen, but the

SERGEANT HARNAM SINGH

LEOPARD CAUGHT IN A TRAP AT SAIGAI-SAI

beast remained where he had fallen. I could hear him making a smothered sort of groaning noise at short intervals. At last, even this weird sound ceased abruptly; and a deadly silence reigned. Thinking he was now dead, I advanced slowly to my kill. While I was walking up to his body, he suddenly struggled violently, raised his head, and tried to get up. This was too much! I had not forgotten to reload in my excitement, and now fired at the back of his neck. Again he collapsed and remained motionless. I thought he was quite dead this time, and so threw all caution to the winds. Keeping my eyes on the quarry, I went in close and pulled the tail.

I dropped that tail as if it was a red-hot coal. Immediately I touched it, he began to gasp and then open and shut his massive jaws. It looked as if he was on the point of death, so I stood over him with my rifle held ready. I did not think another shot was necessary, even for humanity's sake. Still the laboured breathing and gasping went on for several minutes; so I fired a bullet into him, and killed. We found no less than five of my bullets in the carcass, everyone having taken effect in a vital spot.

That tiger died hard!

Here was a remarkably good illustration of the care that should always be exercised in approaching a tiger which you have every reason to believe is dead. Lack of caution in such a case may lead to your own death instead of that of the tiger. Too much care cannot be taken. It was a lesson to me; and I never forgot it.

My friend was very angry with me for having gone up and pulled the beast's tail, while still alive. He said some very scathing things, all of which were deserved. I freely admit that it was a most stupid thing to have done, but every game hunter has to acquire wisdom through bitter experience. I have never since repeated such a gross piece of lunacy.

Having achieved my ambition and killed my first tiger, I was immediately conscious of a keen wish to bag another. The sport grows on you.

A notorious man-eater was the subject of my fourth tiger hunt. This particular beast preyed on human beings exclusively, and had struck terror into the heart of every villager in the entire district. The local District Officer had done his level best to destroy this pest, but had failed. Rewards offered to the villagers were equally ineffective. Having heard about this brute, I wrote offering my help in a determined effort to kill the beast. To my joy, I received a most cordial invitation to join the District Officer at a certain village and aid him in hunting down the man-killer. I accepted gladly, obtained leave from my Colonel, and hurried away to the rendezvous.

My host met me at the agreed spot, and already had everything arranged for the hunt. The man-eater had been reported as seen near this very village on the previous day. Our chances of success looked reasonably hopeful.

The stage had been set expertly before we went out to the selected site, a little before sundown. Two machans had been built in trees, close to the known drinking pool of this man-eater, and a domestic buffalo had been tethered close to our posts. We hoped that the tiger might fancy a change of diet. When we mounted to our machans, the sun had already set. It was with a feeling of exultation that I made myself comfortable on my perch, for I had murder in my heart after hearing the harrowing tales of the villagers concerning this brute's dastardly conduct in the neighbourhood.

Hour after hour passed without incident. My heart was heavy within me, for it looked as if all our most carefully laid plans must fail.

It was approaching dawn, and I was half asleep. Then the report of my companion's rifle rang out sharply twice from his machan. In a split second I was wide awake, every sense keenly alert. An instant later, I saw the tiger not thirty yards from my own tree. I fired haphazard at him, but evidently did no particular damage. He disappeared into the jungle-growth. I swore savagely.

My companion shouted to me that he was positive he had severely wounded the beast, and was going to climb down from his machan. I followed his example, and quickly joined him. With a wounded tiger, and probably the man-eater, in the unknown vicinity, I preferred company to standing alone.

The sky was now flecked with grey, and faint streaks of pink showed here and there on the eastern horizon. A new day was about to be born. We held a hurried consultation, and it was decided to follow up the tiger's trail as soon as it was light enough and our beaters had arrived from the village. We knew that they would join us quickly, for our shots must have been heard by their anxiously expectant ears.

As soon as they had joined us, we set out in hot pursuit.

The trail was quickly found by a shikari who, after following it for a few yards, stooped and picked up a large leaf. Examining it carefully for a brief moment, he turned to us and exclaimed: " *Kuhn*, sahib, *kuhn* ! And he pointed to a big smear of blood on the leaf. This was a heartening sign. The tiger had been hit, but how badly had yet to be discovered. Through not killing him cleanly, we had left ourselves dirty, very dirty work to be done ! A wounded man-eater is just about the nastiest kind of wild beast to tackle in thick country. We knew it.

We were afraid that the brute might get clear away, and set off at once after it. Our village shikaris and beaters, however, did not like the idea at all and protested sullenly at such great folly. They knew this man-eater far too well to wish to play with him. The District Officer ordered them to walk behind us, if they felt so frightened. They did not object to this new arrangement, seeing they were not called upon to take the major risks. And it was *their* beastly man-eater we were trying to deliver them from !

The trail was easy enough to follow, and passed down the centre of a dry ravine. Eventually, we reached a point where the ravine made an abrupt turn past a small thicket of tamarisk. Here we divided our forces. My companion went round one side of it, while I took the other. As I reached the far end of the thicket, a water-hole came into full view ; and there was the jolly old tiger, lying down in the water and with only his head showing above the surface. Taking careful aim, I fired at the only target offering ; but though my bullet hit true, it failed to kill. I fancied it must have been a glancing shot ; or else he had an exceptionally strong skull. With a short, sharp roar, the man-eater sprang out of the water and rushed round the other side of the thicket. I shouted at the top of my voice to warn my hunting partner ; but he later swore that he never heard me.

A second later, I heard two shots from the District Officer's rifle, followed instantly by an angry roar and a shrill cry for help. Running at top speed round the end of the thicket, my eyes beheld a scene that made my blood run cold. My companion was on the ground ; and standing over him, his mouth dripping with blood, was the wounded man-eater.

The shikaris, who carried our second rifles, had gone by another route to the water-hole ; but, on hearing the shots and our loud cries, came running toward us. They broke through the dense jungle at a point almost opposite to the tiger. Instantly the beast abandoned his victim and charged straight at the new enemy. They opened fire with our rifles, but none of the shots stopped the infuriated brute. One of the shikaris dropped his rifle and ran : the other stood his ground, firing steadily as the tiger rushed him. When the magazine was empty, he tried to reload ; but there was not time.

The great bulk of the man-eater sailed through the air and bore the unlucky shikari to the ground. All this time I had been unable to shoot, for I was afraid of hitting the man instead of the tiger.

The beast used only his claws on the man, but the weight of his body and the violence of the charge knocked the man down. The tiger fell over the body of the shikari, and then began to wipe his face with a paw just like a house-cat after lapping up a bowl of cream.

For a moment or two I stood still, too horrified by the swift developments for my brain or body to function ; and then ran forward in the hope of being able to get a safe shot at the man-eater. I was feverishly handling my rifle, eyes intent on the animal.

At last, I got within easy range. My sights came on, and I steadied my jumping nerves. A second later, I fired at the head of the man-eater. At the shot, the huge beast sank down in a limp heap on his victim. I made sure he was dead, and then called to our followers to come to the aid of their comrade.

When I returned to the District Officer, I found him sitting up and wiping the blood from his clothes and face with bundles of grass. He had not been hurt.

He told me that, as he had fired at the tiger, the beast sprang and knocked him down. The blow of the paws stunned him for a few minutes. When he recovered his senses, he found the heavy body of the man-eater lying across him, and the hot blood was flowing freely over his head and chest. To his surprise and relief, the man-eater had not attempted to maul him. At the sudden appearance of the shikaris, the man-eater had got up and charged them. My companion was pretty sore and badly shaken, but had neither been clawed nor bitten. It had been a most miraculous escape !

In the meantime, the other natives had been caring for the mauled shikari. When we reached the group, the poor fellow was scarcely breathing. We had him carried back to the village, where he died a few hours later without regaining consciousness. His skull had been severely fractured by a blow from the man-eater's paw.

On examining the tiger, I found that the first shot I had fired, and easily identified as I was using the only expanding bullets, had shattered the lower jaw after first passing through the bridge of the nose. It was for this reason that the big brute had been unable to use his wicked teeth, which fact saved the District Officer's life. Once more the unexpected had happened! To be knocked down by a wounded man-eater, and to escape without a single scratch from claw or tooth must indeed be rare.

The trophy was my companion's. He had hit it first, and there could be no argument about it. In any case, he deserved it.

We returned in triumph to the village with the carcass of the old man-eater, and found ourselves acclaimed as popular heroes. The exuberance of the simple villagers' welcome can readily be understood. At last they could sleep at night in peace, without the constant fear of being taken by a man-eating tiger.

I bet they enjoyed their first night of real freedom, and slept like logs.

CHAPTER V

THE LEOPARD'S CUNNING

IN point of pluck, cunning and ferocity, the leopard is the
peer of either lion or tiger ; but its small size renders it
probable that the beast merely will maul and not kill a
man. A leopard will charge just as readily as one of the
larger animals, and is rather more apt to get home on its objec-
tive ; but a human being, so attacked, runs less risk to life than
to limb.

A very good illustration of this is furnished by the actual
experience of Carl Akeley, the famous naturalist of the Field
Museum in Chicago, when collecting specimens in Kenya some
twenty or so years ago. I saw a good deal of him then, and
spent a couple of days in his camp at Londiani. This was a few
months after he had engaged in a hand-to-hand fight with a
wounded leopard. He actually killed the beast with his bare
hands when it sprang upon him. He showed the scars, and told
me the grim details of that nasty adventure.

He had already wounded the brute twice, crippling it in one
front and one hind paw. Thereupon it charged, followed his
efforts to dodge, and struck him full as he turned. The leopard
seized his left arm in its mouth, and then bit again and again
as its jaws worked up the arm from wrist to elbow.

Akeley succeeded in throwing the beast, holding its throat
with his right hand and flinging the body to one side. He fell
forward on top of it. Luckily, the leopard was on its side,
with the two crippled paws uppermost, and so could not claw
him. He crushed in the beast's chest with his knees until, as
he told me, distinctly hearing the ribs break. This was the
first moment in that grim fight when Akeley felt that he might
overpower the leopard.

Redoubling his efforts, and using both knees and his free
hand, he actually choked and crushed the life out of the beast.
His left arm was very badly bitten ; and he was also severely

clawed in other parts of the body. It took some weeks for the terrible wounds to heal; but, when camped with him at Londiani, he was nearly well again and just starting out after elephants.

The leopard shares with the tiger the doubtful honour of being one of the greatest scourges to human and animal life in India, even if not in Africa. Though a wicked beast, I have nòt found it providing good sport. To obtain a shot at one, it is necessary to rely on luck more than on anything else. This is because the leopard, like the tiger, has no den or fixed abode. It is a great traveller, and likes to hide in trees or thick bushes. Consequently, they are most difficult to find and kill.

Leopards have more cunning and courage than any other animal I have encountered in my hunting days. The tiger will seldom enter any dwelling that is reasonably barred against him, though lions are known to do so. On the other hand, the leopard will try to force its way into any building where it can detect the slightest odour of its favourite prey. Failing to reach it, the beast will walk up and down all night in the vicinity.

A most persistent devil of destruction is the leopard.

They are very partial to eating dogs, and will go to almost any extremes for such a meal. I have known them break into houses to seize a pet dog, even in broad daylight; and they are generally successful, for the attack is so sudden, swift and unexpected.

An instance of this impertinence, happily unsuccessful, occurred in Nairobi when I was there. While Mr. Sandiford, the Acting Manager of the Railways, was sitting at tea with his family in their bungalow on Railway Hill, his daughter entered her bedroom to get her tennis racquet. She hurried back a moment later, and quietly informed her father that a full-grown leopard was curled up asleep on her bed. Sandiford seized his rifle and went to investigate. On opening the door of the room, he saw the leopard had just awakened and was sitting up on its haunches and yawning. He shot it dead.

The Sandifords kept a number of dogs and cats, and there is little doubt that this beast had been attracted by them to the house. It had made its entry, unobserved by anybody, but had failed to locate its prey. Finding the bed in Miss Sandiford's room comfortable and to its liking, it calmly settled down

for a quiet afternoon's nap. Just forty winks, and then on
again with the dog-hunt—there can be no other possible explanation for its unusual behaviour.

I lost Jess, my Great Dane bitch, to a leopard when hunting
in the Sotik country. Jess was stretched at my feet outside
my tent, which was brilliantly illuminated by a powerful lamp,
while I sat and smoked before the camp fire after dinner.
I had no idea that any wild animal might approach, and had
taken no precautions beyond having my rifle handy to my
chair. When out on safari it is never wise to part with your
rifle. I sat there in contemplation of the eerie African night,
and listening to the strange whispers from the bush. In the
far distance, I heard the fiendish cackle of a hyena's laughter,
followed soon by the vocal scales of a hunting lion.

All at once I thought I saw something pass in front of me
in the gloom, a little to the left of the camp fire. For several
minutes I bored the darkness with an intent stare, but could
see no more movement. I decided that my imagination had
been playing tricks, and slowly refilled my pipe.

Before I could put it in my mouth, I was startled to hear
a loud squeal of anguish beside me, and looked down hurriedly.
I saw a large leopard dash off with Jess in its mouth. I had
neither seen nor heard its attack, and Jess was a big and heavy
animal. She had been with me for two years, and was seldom
caught napping when in camp or out hunting. But the leopard's
attack had been so swift and silent, that poor Jess never had a
fair chance.

The beast found some difficulty in dragging her away rapidly,
and I was able to shoot. My bullet hit the beast in the hind-
quarters, and it dropped the dog to attack me. Another bullet
in the chest raked the body, and it went down to move no more.

I ran swiftly to my poor dog, but she was too badly hurt
for any hope of saving her life. Reluctantly, I fired a merciful
bullet into her brain. Poor Jess, it was a rotten end !

Sam Pike, a veteran European engine-driver on the railways
and who had served from construction days, told me of a curious
experience which he had with a leopard. In company with
some other drivers, he occupied a comfortable bungalow in a
clearing in the forest, situated on a hillside overlooking railhead
at Escarpment.

Shortly after darkness had fallen, the inmates of the bungalow
heard a persistent scratching noise at the front door. They

A GOOD SPECIMEN OF A BLACK-MANED LION

thought it must be one of their dogs, anxious to get inside the house. One of the men went to the door and threw it wide open. He was shocked to find himself confronted by an exceptionally large male leopard. The animal was as startled as he was, and promptly turned about and bolted off into the forest.

Pike grabbed up his rifle on seeing what had happened, and courageously gave chase. The forest was so thick, and the night so dark, that he soon lost all trace of the beast. Abandoning the fruitless search, he retraced his steps to the bungalow. A sudden gleam of moonlight disclosed the leopard, crouching on the roof of the house. Before Pike could take aim and fire, a cloud obscured the moon and rendered a shot impossible. He heard the leopard jump down and rush off into the forest.

A few nights later, this same beast returned to the bungalow for its prey, and repeated its former tactics. This time Pike was ready for it, but taking no chances. He listened carefully to locate the sound of the leopard's movements, and then fired at this spot through the shut door. As all was still for some time after this, he cautiously opened the door and peered out into the moonlight. The marauder was dead, lying on its side only a few yards from the house. On weighing, the carcass tipped the scales at 133 pounds.

Leopards used to be very plentiful about Nakuru, especially close to the lake. They became such an unmitigated nuisance to the few European residents of Nakuru, and so great was the devastation they caused among the livestock, that it was decided to wage war upon them. Every night dogs, cats and poultry had been killed by these brutes. Often they killed for the sheer lust of slaying, not for food. A leopard will scorn nothing that is meat, and often will create great havoc in a poultry-run, or among flocks of sheep and goats. Their tastes in food vary considerably, but they have a special preference for dogs or pork. Often they prey on wild pigs.

The hunt was organized by G. McL. Tew, the Superintendent of the Railway Police ; and he told me the story of what happened. Three other Europeans and a stalwart Sikh policeman volunteered to accompany Tew, and one afternoon they set out on their little private war with the leopards. Between Nakuru and the lake is a wide grassy plain, covered by scattered and stunted bushes. It is easy for a leopard to hide in such a region, and nobody expected much luck.

The habits of the leopard are all in its favour. Comparatively speaking, few are killed by sportsmen who hunt them, though they greatly exceed lions in point of numbers. If seen during the hours of daylight, the chances are that you will merely get a momentary glimpse of the brute while it is in the very act of dropping from the bough of a tree on which it has been sunning. Wonderful climbers always, the leopard is as much at home, if not more so, in the trees as on the ground. They are also past-masters in taking cover in long grass or bush country. To look for a leopard is rather like searching for a flea on a rhinoceros—the chances of success are about equal in both cases.

At night you may often hear their coughing call ; but, in daylight, will seldom see them unless attacking you. Then, you mostly see them too late for safety or comfort.

The sportsmen passed through the long grass in extended formation, shouting at the top of their voices in the hope of disturbing a slumbering leopard and getting a shot at it. Harnam Singh, the Sikh policeman, easily drowned the noise of the others by his lusty shouts. Tew said that he had every appearance of thoroughly enjoying his share in the hunt. Finally, he noticed that the Sikh was lagging behind the line of attack, but paid little attention to this, being far too intent on keeping his eyes watchful for any movement in the grass to indicate a leopard's presence.

After a time, Tew became conscious that the Sikh was yelling louder than ever ; and now there was a note of extreme terror in his vocal efforts. He turned round to see what was the matter. The Sikh was running toward them at top speed, with his turban dragged off his head, and a big leopard perched on his shoulders. The brute's body clung round the back of the man's neck like a woman's fur, and its paws clutched at Harnam Singh's khaki uniform.

The others all ran back swiftly to the man's assistance, while the Sikh rushed to meet them, yelling wildly. He came bounding along with huge leaps, shouting in abject terror as he came. The leopard was having a rough ride on his shoulders. No one dared to shoot, for fear of hitting the Sikh instead of the leopard.

On seeing the other four men, the beast appeared to take a sudden dislike to so much human company. It slipped off its perch, flinging Harnam Singh to the ground in doing so, and slunk off out of sight into the tall grass. Everyone was so much concerned with the Sikh's plight that not a single shot was fired at the leopard. The injured man was hurried back to Nakuru, where his slight injuries were treated and dressed. They were mostly claw scratches, for the beast had not used its teeth at all.

Thereafter nothing could induce Harnam Singh to go out on a hunting expedition! He served under me for two years at Kisumu after this incident, but I only had to mention the word leopard to see his big body shudder violently and his face go ashen-grey.

CHAPTER VI

MAN-EATING LEOPARDS

CASES of man-eating leopards are a rarity. I only know of two instances where they have taken up this deadly work.

When I was in Kenya in the early days, a man-eating leopard appeared at Nyeri ; and, later, another at Meru. In both cases, these brutes caused widespread terror among the natives of the two districts before being slain.

It was recorded that the Nyeri leopard killed and devoured seven native children. It never attacked at night, as is customary, but during the hours of daylight. In all cases, the victims were small boys guarding the village flocks and cattle. Sometimes this man-eater took a native herd-boy ; at others it was quite content with a sheep or goat from the flocks. Two old warriors finally killed this brute with spears, while in the very act of taking its last victim. It proved to be a large male, very old and emaciated, and with teeth worn down to mere stumps.

The man-eater of Meru, however, displayed a marked preference for native women. It killed one poor woman at work in the fields by biting through her throat, after first felling her to the ground ; and then devoured most of her body. It next sprang upon, and badly lacerated, another woman ; but was driven off in time to save her life. This scourge was finally trapped and shot in the very locality in which it had committed most of its outrages against human life. It was also a very old and thin male, with teeth much worn down.

In each instance, the reason for the beast's action was quite obvious. These two leopards, finding their hunting powers failing them, had fallen back on the most helpless of all creatures : defenceless women and children.

An old Masai Chief once told me of a most peculiar adventure which had befallen him. It tends to prove the queer individual freakishness which must always be taken into account when dealing with all kinds of wild animals. He was sitting under a bush with three companions, resting and eating their food. Absolutely without any warning, a leopard sprang out upon the old man, clawed him severely on the head and hand without using its teeth, and instantly disappeared again. The Masai's scars were convincing testimony to the truth of his story. Quite unmistakably, they were the claw-marks of a leopard ; but I could not find any marks made by its teeth.

When with the Roosevelts, camped at Saigai-Sai Farm on the shores of Lake Naivasha, Edmund Heller set a large steel trap with a big thorn-bush drag. It was intended to catch a jackal or serval cat : no more than that. In the morning, when making our rounds, we were staggered to find a handsome leopard caught by one toe of a fore-foot in this trap. The beast had dragged it into a bush, and now hid there and growled savagely at us. Heller shot at the brute and registered a hit, but the leopard charged out at us several times, snarling fiercely and dragging the trap after it. Two more shots ended its life. When the carcass was weighed in camp, it tipped the scales at 126 pounds.

The interesting feature of this incident is that the beast had been so lightly caught, the trap not being large enough to hold the entire paw. The thorn-bush acted as a heavy drag, which prevented the leopard from going very far ; and yet always yielded somewhat when the beast pulled to free its foot. Most other animals, thus caught, would have either broken the trap or else pulled loose, even if it entailed the sacrifice of a toe or foot.

A hyena, similarly trapped, would most certainly have wrenched itself free ; but the leopard, though a far braver and more dangerous beast, has less fortitude than a hyena. Leopards and their kind are very sensitive to physical hurt. This specimen was characteristic of the tribe : a bully and treacherous sneak-thief. While courageous in attack, they are arrant cowards when made to suffer bodily pain.

Sir Alfred Pease told me that, on one occasion, he was watching for lions outside a Somali boma. All at once, a leopard leaped clear over the thorny zareba and close beside where he was hidden. It came lightly back over the hedge, a few seconds later, with a sheep in its mouth. No sooner had it landed outside the zareba, than a pack of hyenas rushed forward to seize the prize. The leopard put up a good fight, but got the worst of the exchanges and abandoned its kill to the savage hyenas. A single hyena would never dare to attack or interfere with a leopard ; but a number of them will often combine to do so, and generally win the fight.

Lord Delamere also told me of a strange experience with one of these spotted cats. He was out hunting when he heard a leopard attack some baboons in a rocky kopje. There was a tremendous commotion at once, for the other baboons immediately hastened to the succour of the one attacked. They finally succeeded in rescuing it from the beast. That same evening, a leopard was seen in his camp and shot dead. It was very old and thin, and obviously starving. It had been frightfully bitten and torn, all of the injuries being similar to those such as only baboons can inflict. The leopard must have died of the wounds before long, even if not killed by that bullet.

Selous told us on the s.s. *Admiral,* when journeying out to Mombasa early in 1909, that he had seen a big fight between a giraffe and some leopards. The giraffe was a cow and accompanied by a small calf. She broke the poor thing's back in her strenuous efforts to protect it from the savage attack of these leopards. When one compares the size of the two animals, it is evidence of the latter's courage and savagery. A giraffe's kick is terrific ! Selous said that he drove off the attackers, but had to kill the calf as its case was hopeless. The mother giraffe was full of fight, and put up a most spirited defence before he intervened and saved her life.

Just after the Roosevelts had landed in Kenya and started their hunt on the Kapiti Plains, Kermit Roosevelt and Sir W. Northrup McMillan were beating up a ravine in search of lions. Instead, they put up a leopard. They saw it slink forward ahead of them through the grass and bushes, and then lost sight of the beast. Concluding that it must be hiding in a large thicket, they started to beat in the hope that the beast would show itself. It did not wait to be driven.

Without warning, it sprang out of cover and charged Kermit Roosevelt. He stopped it with a bullet in the fore-part of the body, when only six yards from him. It turned at once and raced back to cover, while Kermit again fired and crippled it in the hip. Both wounds should have proved fatal, and would have knocked all the fight out of most animals ; but this leopard was an exception.

Meanwhile, the beaters had pressed forward heedlessly, and

one got too near to the thicket. The leopard dashed out at him at once. It was so badly crippled, however, that it failed to make good the sudden attack. The native turned and ran for safety, with the leopard after him. The sorely wounded beast was fast overtaking the man when McMillan, standing on an ant-hill, managed to get a clear shot. In spite of this third wound, the leopard got the beater down. It then started to worry the man with its claws and teeth.

It was so weak from wounds and loss of blood, however, that the native was able to wrench himself free. McMillan fired again, and once more registered a hit. Back went the leopard through the long grass into the cover of the thicket.

There came a pause in the fight, while the mauled beater was given first-aid and then removed to a point of safety. But the leopard, on its own initiative, soon brought matters to a crisis. Out it charged again, and went straight for Kermit Roosevelt. He saw it coming, and promptly dropped it with a shot into the brain.

No animal could have shown a more resolute and fearless temper, and it was game to the bitter end. This spotted feline had displayed a most unflinching courage throughout the long fight. It proved to be an old female of small size, and only weighed seventy pounds.

Only once have I seen a specimen of the extremely rare black leopard in the wild state ; and only once in captivity. I was riding back to Kyambu from Nairobi and, just on dusk, was nearing the end of my ten-mile journey. All at once, a perfect specimen of a black leopard raced across the roadway ahead of me, within ten to fifteen yards, and disappeared swiftly down a nullah.

As I was only armed with a revolver, and am a very poor shot with this weapon, I decided not to risk following up this unique beast. On my arrival at Kyambu, I told J. O. W. Hope, the District Commissioner, and H. R. McClure, his assistant, about this incident. Both proved sceptical, and insisted there was no such thing as a black leopard. I was quite positive, however, that my eyes had not deceived me as to its colouring.

Early next morning, we all three went out to try and track down the beast. We found the spoor at the point where it entered the nullah, and followed this for a considerable distance. Then we lost it for good and all. I was bitterly disappointed. Hope and McClure were now openly laughing, and kept on chiding me about being "colour-blind." I need not have fretted, for I was to be completely vindicated within the week.

Four days later, Hugh H. Heatley, the owner of Kamiti Ranch, rode into Kyambu and joyfully announced that he had caught a handsome black leopard in one of his traps. We rode home with him, and found he had actually trapped a beautiful male specimen. It was genuinely black all over, with the spots just faintly showing. I understand he donated this rare animal to the Zoological Society in London, and that it reached Regent's Park hale and hearty.

I heard afterwards that there had been a pair of these unique black leopards haunting the edges of the Kikuyu Forest. In so far as I am aware, the others were never killed or captured. It is possible, of course, that Heatley's specimen was the same one that I saw ; and it may have been one of the above pair.

When trekking down the Nile through Uganda, in 1910, I had a most nerve-racking experience with a leopard in my tent at night. It was an adventure which, for many years thereafter, occasioned me frequent and horrible nightmares. In my sleep, I have often lived over again that ghastly scene, awaking wet through with perspiration and fighting hard against an imaginary leopard.

I had camped for the night at the deserted post of Wadelai, a desolate place bound up with the stirring history of Emin Pasha and Sir Samuel Baker. It had been a particularly exhausting day after elephants, ending in my failure to get the big bull I wanted. I retired to bed soon after dinner, being intent on making an early start next day and in having another try to kill that grand old tusker. I slept with my tent-door wide open ; and a large camp-fire burned brightly before the entrance.

I awakened suddenly in the middle of a vivid and horrible nightmare. Rightly or wrongly, I have always blamed this on the tinned lobster consumed at dinner that night.

I dreamed that I was walking along the railway track near Nairobi, and came face to face with a large black-maned lion in the darkness. I was unarmed. As the lion stood still and stared at me, I picked up a few flints from the ballast and threw them at him. My aim was true, for I heard the thuds as my missiles struck the tawny body ; but the lion did not budge. After a few moments, he began to advance slowly toward me.

At this stage of my dream, I woke up with a shout of terror. I sat up under my mosquito-net, and looked around me. The rays from the bright camp-fire illuminated the interior of my tent clearly.

I saw the head, shoulders and forelegs of a large leopard thrust under the wall of my tent, while the baneful and brilliant eyes stared boldly at me. It was motionless, the advance halted by my sudden shout and movements. My rifle was always kept handy under my bed; and, with a rapid thrust of my hand, I tore loose the mosquito-net and reached down for my trusty weapon. I could not find it, despite frantic efforts.

All this time—a matter of a moment or two in reality—the leopard remained perfectly still, staring fixedly at me. I held its eyes with my own, while continuing the frenzied search for the rifle.

Failing to get my hands on the gun, I pulled myself clear of the enveloping net, grabbed my pillow and struck wildly at the leopard's head. It swayed from side to side, and then came to a gentle halt. Again and again I struck at it savagely, all the time shouting to my native followers to come and drive off the beast. The leopard made no attempt to attack, nor am I conscious of hearing it growl or snarl. It neither advanced nor retreated. I do not know how many times I registered on the head of the beast with the pillow, for I was in a frenzy of fear.

Then I heard the natives running up to my tent, and the sound of them beating all round it with heavy sticks. At that moment, Hamisi bin Baraka, my brave and trusted gun-bearer, ran boldly into the tent with my second rifle levelled for swift action. Behind him was my faithful personal servant, Sefu bin Mohamed. The latter carried a hurricane lantern and a big stick, and the rays of the lamp clearly illuminated the brute's head and fore-quarters.

That leopard was my bath towel!

It had been hung up to dry on a rope running along the side of my tent. My nightmare, combined with the flickering lights from the fire, had created this ghastly illusion.

I tried to laugh: but could not. I was incapable even of speech. My pyjamas were soaked with sweat; it poured down my face and body in rivers; my teeth chattered a loud tattoo; and my whole body shivered as with ague, while my legs would scarcely support me.

Staggering to my camp-table, I poured out an unusually generous tot of whisky and swallowed the spirit neat. It was only then that I was capable of uttering a single word. I turned to Sefu and Hamisi, and smiled weakly. They were both grinning broadly, obviously restraining themselves from a burst of hilarious mirth.

" The joke's on me," I stuttered. " Get back to bed, now ; I'm all right ! "

They departed, laughing heartily. Presently, I could hear my native porters shouting with ribald merriment ; but I found it no laughing matter. The shock of that midnight experience had been much too vivid and real for me to find any particle of humour in it. I strove to woo slumber, but it was impossible. So I sat beside the camp-fire all night, waiting hungrily for the dawn.

I did not go out after that bull elephant next day. My nerves were too badly frayed to face such risks !

CHAPTER VII

JUST LIONS: SAD AND GAY

I HAVE often been asked which is the most dangerous animal to encounter in hunting. Invariably my reply has been that, "in my own experience," it is the elephant of Africa. That qualification is essential. Strangely enough, there exists the widest possible difference of opinion among really expert big game hunters as to the relative dangerous qualities possessed by the major wild animals. Few hunters of any genuine note can be found in agreement upon this subject. It is quite impossible to be dogmatic in regard to this highly controversial matter, for so much depends upon individual circumstances and the element of luck.

I have known intimately many of the most famous big game hunters of the past half-century in Africa, and have often discussed this problem with some of them. I have seldom found any real agreement between their personal view-points. Each judged the animals in the light of his personal experience with them. There is no other basis on which to form an honest opinion.

Personally, I would put them in the following order : elephant, tiger, buffalo, leopard, rhinoceros and lion. Many will thoroughly disagree with this view ; but who can say, with any possible degree of certainty, that the other man is wrong ?

Despite the fact that Selous, Stigand, Cunninghame and Leslie Tarlton often told me that they believed the lion to be the most dangerous of all big game, I have not found this to be so in my personal experiences with this beast.

I can speak only from my own actual knowledge. Yet Tarlton is known to have killed more lions than any other man, and still thinks them extremely dangerous. Perhaps I have been unusually fortunate in my encounters with this animal, and less so with elephants and other beasts. To be frank, however, I would far rather face up to an infuriated lion than an elephant.

With lions I have seldom known any really serious trouble. But that does not imply, by any manner of means, that he is not dangerous. He most certainly is, and can be.

As a general rule, however, it may be accepted as a fact that a lion or lioness is never really dangerous except on three specific occasions. Firstly, when wounded and followed into thick cover ; secondly, a lioness with cubs ; and, thirdly, an old and toothless lion, who has become too enfeebled to hunt natural food and so has turned man-eater. The human prey is always easier to get and tackle than any other creature. It also happens, sometimes, that a lion has acquired a taste for human flesh and likes it as a luxury diet.

When first I arrived in Nairobi, very early in 1904, there were seven graves of Europeans in the little cemetery, all of whom had died as the result of encounters with lions ; and only one of a man killed by any other beast, a rhinoceros.

Many of the fatalities caused by lions are due to quite inexperienced or foolhardy sportsmen following up wounded beasts into dense cover. Soon after I went to Nairobi there occurred just such a tragedy on the Athi Plains.

Stewart, an Army officer on leave, wounded his first lion on the edge of the reeds lining the banks of the Stony Athi River. He was so excited that he quite forgot to reload his rifle after hitting the brute twice. He followed it into the tall grass and reeds, with his rifle empty. The wounded beast had not gone in far, and Stewart walked right into it. The lion sprang out and knocked him down, mauling him severely before his plucky gun-bearer could drive the beast away from his master. Stewart died a few days later in the hospital at Nairobi.

A brother of Lord Grey of Fallodon also met his death tragically at about this same spot, and in much the same way. Soon after Stewart's death, Grey was out hunting lions near the Stony Athi and put up a small troop of them. He made the error of riding between them and their refuge point. Having passed in front and a bit to the flank of the troop, he dismounted to take his shot. Instantly one of the lions turned aside and charged straight for him. He fired twice, and wounded the beast each time ; but it got him down while he was trying to reload. He was terribly mauled, and never had a chance of recovering.

Man-eaters are more of an exception than a general rule. When they do take to preying on human beings, they usually

COLONEL THEODORE ROOSEVELT, SIR FREDERICK JACKSON, F. C. SELOUS,
AND A. SANDIFORD ON COW-CATCHER OF LOCOMOTIVE

THE CHANIA FALLS ON THIKA RIVER

haunt native villages, in the same way as a tiger, and attack the old and decrepit, the women or children. Then there is a reign of terror in that particular area. This method of obtaining food requires less arduous stalking to fill their bellies. The classic story of the man-eating lions of Tsavo is well known, and in that case they centred their attentions on the huge encampments of railway coolies constructing the railway. They also created a ghastly reign of terror. These particular lions, however, were extremely bold and cunning; and not forced to man-eat by infirmities. When a lion does take to man-eating it is generally a frank confession of old age and incapacity in hunting natural food.

The Uganda Railway reached the spot where now stands Nairobi, the capital of Kenya Colony, in June of 1899. At that time—thirty-four years ago—there was not even a native village visible, and the spot was merely a camping-place for the caravans passing between the coast and Uganda. When I saw it first, four and a half years later, it was not so much a budding frontier township as a scattered railway centre. It was a very different Nairobi to the town of to-day. When I returned there in 1929, after an absence of twenty years, I was staggered by the changes that had then taken place and the handsome new buildings already erected or being built.

When railhead reached this spot, the name Nairobi was applied only to that part marked by the junction of Swamp and N'gara roads. This was the actual site of the original Nairobi caravan-camp. It was a bleak, swampy stretch of landscape, devoid of human habitation, and the home of teeming thousands of wild animals of almost every African species.

Lions were very plentiful, especially in the papyrus swamp extending from where now is the Norfolk Hotel to the hill above Ainsworth Bridge, and even as far as the present suburb of Parklands. It was then quite common to see a lion thereabouts, and quite a number were killed within the limits of what is now the modern town of Nairobi. It all sounds very incredible; but it is true. Even in early 1904, it was not unusual for a resident of the town to complain of a lion having been on the veranda of his bungalow during the night, grunting and growling, while trying to effect an entry.

At one of the first meetings of the East African Turf Club, one of the events on the card was ruined by a lion chasing a

E

zebra across the " straight " during the progress of a race, and making its kill behind the grandstand. In early 1904, another lion hunted and killed a zebra on the new racecourse ; and, in the following year, one killed and partly devoured a zebra in my front garden in the centre of the growing township. One can quote such instances in plenty.

Life in Nairobi, in those cheery pioneer days, never lacked the unusual. Kenya is always full of surprises ; and there were plenty in those early times.

One dark night in the middle of 1909, the popular Principal Medical Officer, Dr. A. D. Milne, cycled right into a black-maned lion on Railway Hill. He was returning, about midnight, to his own house after attending a dinner party at a friend's bungalow, and bumped into the lion as it crossed the road just in front of him. It was a toss up as to which was the more surprised by the unexpected collision ! The lion bolted off into the long grass, and was not seen again ; while " Daddy " Milne ran off in the opposite direction to get a rifle. Neither was hurt —except in their feelings ; but the front wheel of Milne's bicycle was badly buckled.

Such episodes as this but added zest to life in that infant Nairobi. It provided a subject for conversation for weeks to come ; and there were few amusements in Nairobi, in those pioneer days, except gossip and big game. It made a curious cocktail !

I killed my first lion—or rather, lioness—in the then main street of Nairobi. This was early in 1904, and just outside the town's wood-and-iron post office. Noble, the postmaster, was very annoyed with me for waking him up. I suppose he had just cause, for it was midnight and lion-hunting on your doorstep is rather startling.

Walking down the street one night when visiting my sentries at their posts, a native policeman reported that a lioness with two small cubs had just gone in under the raised floor of the post office. Leaving him to keep watch and report further movements, I ran off to my nearby bungalow and got my rifle.

When I returned to the spot, the policeman said the lioness and cubs were still under the building. I sent him, and also a few interested native spectators, behind the building, with orders to bombard the lioness heartily with stones. She soon broke cover under this intensive barrage, and I killed her as she stood out in the open street. It was an easy shot, for there was a very bright moon.

I sent off the trophy to my bungalow in the care of some of the natives, with orders to hand over the carcass to Hamisi, my gun-bearer, for skinning. Then I considered the matter of the two orphans. I felt they were my responsibility now, seeing that I had killed their mother.

They had not yet shown themselves. I rather wanted them as pets, so crawled on hands and knees under the building to get them. They were spitting and snarling at me, but I managed, after a prolonged rough and tumble, to secure both. I crawled out with my prizes firmly held by the scruff of the necks. They were jolly little balls of wool, and could not have been more than a month old. But they had most vicious tempers for such infants. They snarled, spat and scratched vigorously all the time, but I held on grimly until they desisted ; and then carried them back to my bungalow in triumph.

One was a male, the other a female. I named them Jack and Jill respectively. Jack died a couple of days later of some silly infantile ailment ; but I succeeded in rearing his sister, and she became a great pet.

My second lion was also killed in Nairobi. Somewhere about midnight, I was returning to my bungalow in the railway town, after attending a dinner party on the Hill. I decided to pay a surprise visit to my Indian guard on the headquarter offices of the railway. Instead of surprising my sentries, it was myself who was surprised.

Garbed in dinner clothes and patent-leather shoes, I was not carrying any firearms. When I got near the first sentry's post at the General Manager's office, I was astounded to hear him banging on the side of the iron building with the butt-end of his rifle. At the same time, I could hear him shouting, fearfully : " Shoo ! Shoo ! "

If ever mortal man sounded thoroughly frightened, that Punjabi policeman's voice gave a true indication of the state of his nerves. I ran toward him at once, though far from feeling comfortable in my own mind. As I got closer, I saw the sentry suddenly abandon his post and swarm up a nearby lamp-post.

" Why are you making all that damned row, you confounded idiot ? " I demanded, angrily.

" *Simba*, sahib : very close ! Eating a zebra, sahib ! " came the astounding reply through chattering teeth.

I did not believe him. Why should I ? I advanced to see
what really was the cause of his unsoldierly conduct. Sure
enough, there was a large tawny-maned lion devouring a zebra
within fifty yards of the sentry's post. In the moonlight, he
looked simply colossal !

For several minutes I stood rooted to the spot, staring at
this unusual sight. I was confident that he would not abandon
the banquet to attack me. It certainly was an awe-inspiring
sight ; but the " gallery " might have enjoyed the spectacle
with far greater relish if provided with modern and powerful
weapons. My sympathies were certainly with the Indian sentry.
His rifle was a very antiquated and utterly worthless Martini-
Henri. As a means of offence or defence, it was far more orna-
mental than useful. Besides, how can you walk about your
post " in a smart and soldierlike manner " if a lion is having
his supper a few yards from your beat ?

I might just as well not have been there for all the interest
the lion evinced in me. This was just as well, for the Punjabi
policeman occupied the only lamp-post in the vicinity.

Evidently the lion had chased the zebra into the outskirts
of the town from the Athi Plains, brought it down and was
now eating his hard-earned supper. Judging by the sloppy,
tearing sounds he was making, he could only just have killed.
He was a noisy feeder. I saw him deliberately tearing large strips
of flesh from the poor zebra's corpse, and then slowly digesting
the toothsome morsels. All the time he was grunting loudly.

Warning the man to remain where he was—clinging like a
frightened monkey to the topmost pinnacle of the lamp-post,
I hurried off to the bungalow of my friend, Dr. Stewart, of the
Railway Medical Service. There I hoped to borrow his .350
Rigby-Mauser rifle ; and, thus armed, return to tackle the lion.
To reach his quarters, I had to pass within thirty yards of the
lion's supper-table. He paid no heed to my passage.

Stewart would not believe my story when I awakened him.
I cannot blame him. The hour was after midnight, and I had
dined out obviously. He accused me sternly of having dined
well but not wisely, and declared that the lion scene was pure
imagination due to alcoholic stimulation in excess of regulation
doses. I insisted that I was perfectly sober.

It took me some time to convince him that I was in deadly
earnest and not just inebriated. He loaned me his rifle, but
flatly refused to accompany me back to the lion's banquet.

He said that he was warm and comfortable in bed, and the lion—always supposing there was one—had probably eaten his fill and departed to sleep it off. I did not stop to argue the point any further. I wanted that lion ; now more than ever.

The beast was still there on my return to the spot ; so was the sentry. My injunction to him to remain where he was had been unnecessary : nothing would have induced him to come to earth. I could see the lion licking his chops over the last mouthful of zebra, and his belly was much distended. He had eaten well.

My first shot wounded the lion in the shoulder, but did not kill. He growled savagely and stood up above his kill, looking most majestic and impressive in the moonlight. A moment later he was bounding off through the grass toward the European cemetery.

I did not know how " sick " he was, but could hear him grunting and growling as he disappeared from my range of vision. Unwritten laws for all sportsmen decreed that I should follow up and kill. Distasteful as the idea seemed, especially remembering that dinner clothes are not ideal garments in which to lion-hunt at midnight, I knew there was no other alternative. Stewart's ribald, mocking laughter still rankled deeply. I set off in pursuit.

He came to bay not far from the cemetery wall, and now stood boldly silhouetted against the skyline. He was broadside on, offering a splendid target. I crept closer, slowly and cautiously. Once or twice, I thought he was going to bolt again ; but he changed his mind and stood watching me. Thirty yards distant, I took steady aim and fired. I saw him reel to the bullet, topple, and then go down on his side. I stood still and waited, ready to shoot once more ; but he did not move again.

Leaving him where he had fallen, I hurried back to Stewart, awakened and told him the glad news. Then I made him eat his words. He apologized most handsomely, sprang out of bed and offered to accompany me back to my kill. Routing out his native servants to help in skinning the beast and to carry back the fine trophy, we set off again. It was dawn before the work was done, and we returned in triumph to Stewart's bungalow. It seemed worth it to forfeit a night's rest.

For years I treasured that lion trophy, killed in a dress-suit, and carted it about with me to many parts of the world. Then the moths devoured it. Now I only have the memory of that midnight adventure.

When in Nairobi in 1909 with the Roosevelt Expedition, an old lion made itself a perfect nuisance and was continually being met as it prowled about the outskirts of the township or in Parklands suburb. A few days after we had returned from the hunt in the Sotik, R. J. Cunninghame was dining with V. M. Newland, Leslie Tarlton's partner, at his house in Parklands. On his way back to the Norfolk Hotel, he met this lion unexpectedly face to face. The beast did not attempt to attack, although credited with being a man-eater. Cunninghame whipped out his revolver and had a couple of shots at the brute. He did not know whether he hit it or not, for the lion disappeared hurriedly. He did not see it again.

A number of other people reported having seen this lion, but I never heard of anyone, European or native, being attacked by it. In the absence of evidence to the contrary, that lion must be acquitted of the charge of being a man-eater. Popular rumour, as is so often the case, was false.

Major C. J. Ross, the Assistant Game Warden, made a number of most determined attempts to trap or kill this old lion ; but met with no success. He sat up night after night, for he was insistent on ridding Nairobi of " this public nuisance." He never even got a glimpse of it, let alone a chance to shoot. Others were equally unsuccessful. I maintained a lonely vigil on several nights, but never saw anything resembling a lion.

Finally, it disappeared to pastures new. I presume the old beast found itself getting far too unpopular to make it worth while to prolong the visit to the capital. Everyone was much relieved when it left.

When camped for a week-end holiday on the N'gong Road, close to Nairobi, I went out for a stroll after tea. There had been no word of any lions being seen hereabouts, and I had no thought of danger. I had not even troubled to arm myself.

I had not walked more than a few hundred yards from the camp, and could still hear my native followers singing and talking, when I suffered a rude shock to my peace of mind.

The bush was exceedingly thick, and it was difficult to see any distance from the path I followed. I came to a halt in a small clearing, and was watching some monkeys at play, when I saw a large bush-lion spring out from the undergrowth just in front of me. He saw me at once, halted and turned to stare full at me.

Not liking his looks and being foolishly unarmed, I rapidly

shinned up the nearest tree. When I had reached what I thought was a safe height—Marcuswell Maxwell had not then proved that lions do climb trees—I blew my whistle shrilly to summon Hamisi to my aid with a rifle. I knew that, when he heard it, he would realize that I was facing danger and needed help urgently.

The lion stood perfectly still, calmly inspecting me in the tree-top. I whistled and shouted with all the strength of my lungs, for I did not like the look in the beast's eyes. The savage light in those glittering eyeballs sent cold shivers down my spine, even though I believed myself safe in the tree. Without a sound, the lion walked slowly up to the base of my refuge and stood staring up at me thoughtfully. He seemed really puzzled by seeing a human being in a tree. It was a most unpleasant feeling, being watched that way.

As he had approached steadily, I experienced the sensation that my tree was dwindling to the dimensions of a small bush, while the lion was growing to the size of a mammoth elephant. The illusion made me feel horribly uncomfortable about the pit of my stomach!

I shouted vigorously for Hamisi, and alternately blew my whistle to attract his attention. My voice seemed to unnerve the lion, for he wheeled about suddenly and bolted back toward the thick undergrowth.

At the same instant, a bullet droned past my tree and I saw Hamisi running toward me with my rifle. Hurriedly I climbed down and seized hold of the weapon, much as a drowning man clutches at a piece of floating wood.

For several minutes we stood still, listening intently for sound of the lion's movements, our eyes peering at the thick mass of matted bush and creepers. We could see and hear nothing. That old lion could jolly well keep his hide, for I was not going to follow up in such country. It would have been positively suicidal.

We returned to camp at a jog-trot. Hamisi was soon the hero of the hour, and I could hear him telling the other natives that he had actually killed the lion while charging full at me. Thus had he saved his master's life. The absence of the skin of the lion seemed to pass unnoticed by the credulous Wakikuyu porters.

I had not the heart to contradict his heroic tale.

CHAPTER VIII

TERRORS OF THE NIGHT

THE epic story of the man-eating lions of Tsavo and Kima, in the early construction days of the Uganda Railway, has been told by Lieut.-Colonel J. H. Patterson in his thrilling book,. *The Man-Eaters of Tsavo.* I need merely state that his grim narrative well repays reading, and is perfectly true. I have heard confirmation of the details, times without number, from both Europeans and Indians who worked at Tsavo during that reign of terror.

The terrible tragedy of poor Ryall's death at Kima, when he was taken by a man-eater from a railway carriage in the middle of the night and killed, is also graphically related by Colonel Patterson. I have heard the amazing story from the lips of the other two actors in that ghastly night of horror—Parenti, the Italian Vice-Consul at Mombasa, and Huebner, an Austrian merchant of that port. Nobody knew better than these two men the real facts of that dreadful episode.

Poor Ryall's body rests in the cemetery at Nairobi, among those other graves marked with the simple epitaph : " Killed by a lion."

Benjamin Eastwood, who was then Chief Accountant and later General Manager of the Railways, told me another most astounding story of a man-eater's persistence in pursuit of human prey marked down for a meal. The incident occurred in the very early days of British East Africa, before even the railway had reached Nairobi.

A caravan from the coast to Uganda had camped near the Stony Athi River for the night, intending to make the Nairobi caravan-camp next day. The European in charge slept with his tent-door wide open, for the night was very sultry. There was an Indian sepoy, armed with a rifle, on guard over his tent ; and a large fire blazed in front of it.

A man-eating lion crept up unseen by this sentry, entered

the tent, seized hold of and dragged forth the sleeping man. The European struggled to free himself and shouted loudly for help. Contrary to custom, this lion had omitted to first kill or stun its victim. The sentry and native porters rushed to his aid, and the man-eater dropped its prey and bounded off into the darkness of the night. The injured man's wounds were cleansed and bandaged, and his servants put him in bed in his own tent. The sentry was warned to be very alert in case the lion returned to the attack.

An hour or so later, when the camp was once again quiet and everyone slept, the man-eater boldly returned after the prey of which it had been robbed. Stealthily it entered the tent, without being seen or heard, seized the unfortunate man in its mouth, and this time got clean away with him. It must have killed the European with a blow of its paw, for there was no outcry heard. The Indian sentry was unaware of what had taken place in the tent, and did not even see or hear the lion.

At dawn, the native servant went to his master's tent to dress the wounds and take him a cup of tea. He was horrified to find him missing. The writing was plain on the sand—human blood and lion's pad-marks. The whole camp was aroused and turned out. They followed up the spoor of the persistent man-eater and, at some distance from the camp, found where the lion had devoured its victim. There remained very little of the body to bury.

When stationed at Kyambu, ten miles out of Nairobi, a terrible tragedy occurred near there. A young European, who had come out to Kenya to take up land and farm, went out with a small safari towards Fort Hall to view that area. He camped in a small tent on the banks of the Ruiro River. A few days later, one of his porters came into Kyambu and reported that his master had disappeared during the night. He said that the tent looked as if a lion had broken into it, and dragged off the European. They had made a search, but had not found the man or his body.

I started off immediately to make an investigation on the spot. Late that same day I found all that was left of this poor young fellow. The head and shoulders had not been touched, but the rest of the body had been devoured. I found the remains under a thick bush not very far from his camp. The spoor of this man-eater was followed easily for some distance ; but, though I hunted it until after dark, never got even a sight of the brute. I would have given much to have killed this savage beast.

We carried back the remains of the unfortunate man to Kyambu, and gave them burial near the Government Boma.

The late Lady Delamere, whose husband owned considerable land near Njoro, was returning from a dance at Nakuru at two o'clock in the morning. She was accompanied by Dr. Atkinson, who was a guest at their ranch. They had the train stopped at Lord Delamere's private siding, mounted the horses which a native syce had brought to meet them, and rode off at a walk to the ranch'house. The syce went on ahead with a hurricane lantern to light the way.

A big lion unexpectedly dashed across the roadway between the syce and two riders, and the native dropped the lantern and ran for his life. Lady Delamere and her companion set their horses to a gallop, and raced after him. The lion, meanwhile, stood still beside the road and watched them ride past him, and then bolted off into the long grass. They did not see him again : or want to. The beast was probably just as startled as they were, for he made no attempt to attack.

Lady Delamere told me of this adventure with an amused laugh. At the time she was unarmed and in a dance frock, which is not the best way to meet a lion, face to face, in the small hours of the morning.

Kenya has always been full of surprises !

During the year 1906 I had an unpleasant midnight adventure with a full-grown tawny-maned lion. I was riding into Nairobi from Fort Hall, a distance of roughly sixty-four miles. There was a full and bright moon, and I was hard pressed for time. Late that afternoon a native runner had found me at Fort Hall and delivered a summons to appear as a witness for the Crown in a High Court trial next morning at Nairobi. There was only one thing to do, and that to ride through the night. I had trotted, walked and cantered my Arab pony at intervals, and was making good time. About midnight, we reached the banks of the Thika River. As I slowed down into a walk to cross the river, I saw a majestic lion stand out boldly in the moonlight on the opposite bank. His sudden appearance on the scene came as a distinct shock, and I pulled up my pony immediately.

I was armed only with my Service revolver, and under no circumstances would I ever start trouble with only such a weapon handy. I knew my limitations far too well. Neither did I fancy trying to rush through the river to get past the lion, nor to retire gracefully from his neighbourhood. So I sat my pony and glared at the lion, hoping against hope that he would make himself scarce without undue delay. The beast, however, stood motionless on the lip of the far bank, staring back at me. For some time he made neither sound nor movement, and it looked like a deadlock. Then he lifted his head and gave tongue. The terrific volume of sound was a direct challenge to all; and made me shiver on my saddle.

The roar of the lion, when heard in the still hours of the African night, is always most awe-inspiring and blood-curdling. To call it a " roar," however, is scarcely correct. The sound starts with a prolonged moan, which is quite audible on a quiet night at a distance of fully two miles. This is followed by a series of shorter moans, perhaps eight in all, which gradually grow less in volume until the last is only faintly heard. The more accurate description of the lion's vocal expression would be " a coughing grunt "; but " roar " is certainly the more picturesque. To deprive the lion of the capacity for " roaring " would be to rob him of his alleged most marked characteristic. That would be unthinkable ! Roar, let it remain.

His vocal efforts challenged the peace of the night on the plains, and gave me a rotten sensation. I felt exactly as if a strong current of electricity was running up and down my spine, and longed to be far removed from the vicinity.

Caliph, my Arab pony, liked the look of things even less than I did ; and was strongly in favour of a strategic retreat ! But I simply had to be in Nairobi by daybreak, for I was the first witness for the Crown in a vitally important murder trial before the Chief Justice, Sir Robert Hamilton (recently the Under Secretary of State for the Colonies). I was cited to appear at nine o'clock, and wanted time to bath, change and breakfast before a long and gruelling examination in the witness-box.

Lion or no lion, I had to continue my journey and appear in the High Court at the hour for which I had been summoned. To have admitted that my dilatory arrival was due to having been held up by a lion on the banks of the Thika River was unthinkable. I should never have heard the last of such a story, and the whole of Kenya would have rocked with gay laughter at my expense. That prospect made no appeal, for I am very sensitive to ridicule.

And here was a damned fool lion committing two most

grievous offences against the law—Contempt of Court and interfering with a Crown witness ! What was to be done to end such an impasse ? Seemingly, the lion would not budge : I could not.

For the best part of an hour—it may have been much longer, but I lost count of time—we silently stared at each other across the swift-flowing river. That lion was the most obstinate idiot ever whelped ! It was patent to me that the brute had no intention of going off on his night's hunting adventures or permitting me to proceed on my lawful occasions. Retreat I would not.

Finally, growing impatient, I dismounted and picked up some largish stones. My first throw landed plumb central, with a resounding thud, on the lion's well-rounded ribs. He let out a mighty roar of anger and disgust, but still did not move. Caliph fought hard to break away from my grip on the reins, but I succeeded in controlling him. I tried another stone. It was a better aimed missile, and decided that unrehearsed battle of patience. The stone registered full in the lion's majestic face, and must have gingered him up quite considerably. It was a large stone, with sharp edges.

The animal grunted loudly and savagely, tucked his tail between his legs, and bolted off incontinently into the long grass. Promptly I remounted and kept a sharp look out, anxiously hoping he had gone for good. I was rather afraid that he might be lying up in the reeds or tall grass, waiting for me to cross the river so that he could get his revenge. But I saw no further sign of him. Presently, the deathlike silence of the veld encouraged me to proceed on my way. I waited no longer, but dug spurs into Caliph's flanks, raced through the river, clambered up the opposite bank, and headed for Kyambu at a non-stop gallop. I did not ease down until I had safely passed Kyambu and was on the last lap to Nairobi.

I did not even wait to admire the superb waterfall at the Thika River, which is never more beautiful than when seen with the moon's tender kiss upon it.

I never told a soul about that incident, for I knew the story would travel far and fast, and evoke much mirth at my expense. I was not in the mood to see any humour in the adventure.

Major Hugh Chauncey Stigand was a very close friend of mine from boyhood ; we were at the same Army Crammer's together and served in Kenya side by side. He was outstanding even

THE " BOW AND ARROW " EXPEDITION WITH A LION

among the most noted of hunters, and his courage was of the very highest order. I know of no other man who could have said that he had been severely injured by an elephant, a rhinoceros and a lioness, and yet survived to tell of it.

As a boy he had a passion for physical culture, and had been a show pupil of Eugene Sandow. His truly astounding bodily strength stood him in good stead when the lioness attacked him. To fully appreciate all that follows, the fact that he was endowed with almost superhuman strength and iron courage must not be forgotten.

When travelling by the mail-train between Nairobi and Mombasa, about 1906, Stigand learned that three lions were continually haunting the railway station at Simba (the native name for lion) and always a menace to human life. He decided to leave the train at Simba, and try to rid the neighbourhood of these pests. At dark, Stigand climbed up into a water-tank overlooking the platform, and there waited for the lions to put in their customary appearance. It was a bright moonlit night, and visibility was good for some distance round his post.

He had not long to wait for the lions. An hour passed, and then he heard a movement in the tall grass near his post. Out on to the platform stalked a fine lion, followed by two handsome lionesses. For a moment or two, they stood in full view of Stigand, listening and gazing about them. The night was deadly still ; and hunter and hunted had the stage to themselves.

He killed the lion and one lioness with his first two shots, and severely wounded the other female. She bounded off into the grass beside the railroad-track, but he saw she was really " sick " and had no intention of letting her get away from him. He got down from the water-tank, and quickly followed her into cover. He would have been the first to condemn such folly in another man, but Stigand never hesitated to face long odds and risks though never placing others in jeopardy.

He went after the wounded lioness alone, for he had ordered his gun-bearer not to come to him if he heard any shooting. He was afraid of only wounding a beast, and that it might attack the man. Her trail was easy to follow, for the grass was heavily trodden down by the passage of her body and also blood-smeared. He ignored the supreme danger, and carried on with his mad moonlight adventure.

Stigand told me all that he knew of what followed, when I went to visit him in hospital at Mombasa a few days later ;

and his gun-bearer filled in the gaps of that great story of heroic adventure.

The wounded lioness suddenly sprang out at him from the long grass; and, before he could shoot, had got him down. She seized his left arm in her massive jaws, and began to bite and claw at him. His rifle had fallen out of reach. While his left arm was being badly chewed at the forearm, he managed to get his right free, put the last ounce of his strength into a powerful blow, and hit the lioness a terrific jolt to the jaw. Then he seized hold of her throat with his right hand, and fought to strangle the life out of her. While they struggled on the ground, Stigand fainted from pain and shock.

Just before the dawn broke, the gun-bearer came out of a hut and saw the bodies of the two lions on the platform; but there was no sign of Stigand. He had heard three shots in the night, and then not another sound. He knew Stigand's great daring, and suspected that his master had wounded another beast and followed up to kill it. Hastily rounding up every available man to help, he picked up the spoor of the wounded animal, and followed it into the tall grass.

They found Stigand lying unconscious, with the dead body of the lioness stretched out on top of him. He had choked her to death with his vice-like grip on her throat; and her jaw had been fractured in two places by the sledge-hammer blow of his naked fist.

Stigand told me that he did not recollect choking the beast. But when he was found, his right hand was firmly imbedded in the thick throat of the animal. He had been very badly mauled. They carried him tenderly to the station, did all they could to disinfect and bandage the ghastly wounds, and telegraphed to Mombasa for medical aid.

The next down-train carried Stigand in the guard's van to Mombasa, and a doctor and nurse went up by special train to meet him half-way. He made a remarkably quick recovery, and was soon able to return to duty with the King's African Rifles. Stigand was a man of steel. To his death, however, he carried the terrible scars of his hand-to-hand fight with that lioness, as well as those caused by an elephant and a rhinoceros.

Stigand was killed on Christmas Eve, 1919, when Governor of the Mongalla Province in the Sudan, during the progress of a sudden revolt by the Dinka tribe. An eye-witness of that final tragedy, when Stigand was speared to death by the Dinkas in an ambush, told me that he died fighting to his last breath. He fell riddled with spear-thrusts delivered at very close range, after all his ammunition had been expended. Round his body was a solid wall of dead and wounded Dinka warriors. By his heroic death, he saved his own men from certain massacre. His end was in keeping with his splendid life. Those who knew and loved Hugh Stigand would have expected nothing less from such a very gallant English gentleman.

But to survive a mauling from those three savage beasts of the wilds only to die by the spears of unruly African tribesmen —what a tragedy !

Sir Frederick J. Jackson, a former Acting Governor of Kenya and later Governor of Uganda, told me a lot about the black record of Simba station in the earliest days of Kenya Colony. One story, which he related at Government House in Nairobi, has always remained green in my memory.

Before the buildings had been erected, the Indian station-master and his small staff lived in bell tents. A man-eating lion had been haunting the camp for a week or so, and already had carried off two of the wretched coolies. The babu was badly scared. One day he remembered there was a large galvanized iron water tank on the platform, and had a brain wave. On making a test, he found that it was possible to wriggle through the aperture. He had the tank carried to his tent and placed inside. Having dropped his bedding through the hole, that night he slept safely at the bottom of the iron fortress. His mind was at rest ; fears stilled.

For three nights all went well, and he enjoyed a carefree rest during the hours of darkness. His novel plan seemed quite fool-proof, and his ingenuity in devising it was a great source of joy. His comrades at Simba envied him greatly, for there was not another such secure bedchamber available.

On the fourth night, however, his dreams of security were rudely shattered. The man-eater made an unwelcome appearance at Simba, and for some time prowled round the babu's tent. Finally, the savage brute forced an entry. The station-master was awakened by the lion's efforts to climb up the slippery sides of the tank to investigate the contents. At last, taking a flying jump, the beast landed on top and sniffed hungrily through the hole. It grunted with satisfaction. Within apparent reach was a most tempting morsel of human prey. The terrified babu could plainly see the bulky form of the lion against the white walls of the tent, and flattened himself on the bottom of the tank.

For a time the lion was baffled. Then it thrust a huge paw through the opening and tried to reach the babu's quaking body. Its foreleg was too short, however, and the sharp claws reached no nearer than a foot above the victim. For a time, it struggled to force the leg further in, but failed.

Like the pendulum in Poe's story, the lion's paw swept round and round within the tank, just as if it was stirring a pot of porridge. Its wicked talons were extended, but always just missed the babu by a matter of inches. The wretched man shivered and moaned, and watched that great paw in circular motion above his sweat-streaked face. He was palsied with terror. Each time those cruel claws started a new sweep of the interior, the babu cowered to the bottom, teeth clattering like castanets, eyes almost popping out of his head, and uttering groans of misery. Hour after hour the lion continued the unequal struggle.

Then, for a short time, the beast desisted and sat on its haunches to examine the position afresh. The babu prayed loudly for the man-eater's departure; but in vain. Presently, the stirring process was repeated. Several times the panic-stricken man fainted from sheer terror, only to awaken to further mental torments.

Just before dawn, the lion grew weary of the fruitless efforts to fish up that human body, jumped down to the ground, and made off slowly into the bush. By that time, however, Nature had considerately drawn a veil over the ghastly happenings. The almost demented babu had lapsed into unconsciousness.

When the station-master did not appear to issue orders for the day's tasks, as was customary, the pointsman was deputed to go and awaken him. As this man approached the tent, he noticed that it was badly torn and then saw the clearly defined pad-marks of a lion outside. These signs told the story. Standing still and listening for some minutes, he could hear no sound of life. He crept forward gingerly, and presently peeped cautiously within. His ears were greeted by a deep human moan; and the sound patently came from within the tank.

Hoisting himself up, he peered down through the opening. The babu was stretched out on the bottom, unconscious and groaning. He jumped down and ran back to the coolies to tell them of his discovery, and for a long time there raged a heated argument as to what should be done. Finally, the pointsman carried the day; and they advanced to the tent in a body to view the scene of the near-tragedy. Thereupon arose the problem of how to get the unconscious man out of his stronghold.

It was finally agreed to turn the tank on its side, and then shake out the human contents. This was easier said than done. Despite some very strenuous shaking and rocking, the body of the unconscious man could never be aligned on the aperture. At last, the pointsman climbed through the hole, lifted up the babu's body and pushed it head first out of the tank.

The station-master was unhurt, but paralysed with fright. His black hair had turned snow-white during that night of ghastly terror, and he was a gibbering maniac. They did all possible to revive him. Later, he recovered sufficiently to give a more or less coherent account of what had happened.

The first train through Simba for the coast bore away the station-master of Simba. He abandoned his post and worldly possessions, asking leave of nobody, and vowing nothing could induce him to spend another hour at Simba. He declared his intention of boarding the first steamer out of Mombasa. The destination was of little importance just so long as it took him from the land of lions.

Few will find it in their hearts to withhold their sympathy from this Indian.

The pointsman reported the circumstances to the Traffic Manager, and was promptly appointed temporary station-master. He requested a transfer to some other wayside post, while not declining the step up the ladder of promotion. His request was granted, but entailed reverting to the ranks. He stoutly swore that he would take on any job cheerfully, except that it forced him to remain at Simba.

There was a completely new station staff next day.

CHAPTER IX

LIONS: AND LAUGHTER

IT is curious how lions will often halt and look back at their pursuers. I have known them do so on a number of different occasions, and can only think it is done in a spirit of sheer curiosity and not animosity.

When camped near the Thika River, I was followed by two lions and a lioness almost up to my camp, and in broad daylight. I am sure they had no intention of attacking, but were merely interested in my movements. They kept a distance of just over a hundred yards from me, which was a great relief to my mind. My rifle was in camp, for I had been out shooting guinea-fowl and nothing larger.

Immediately I reached my tent and changed my shot-gun for a rifle, I returned to attack them. By then they had moved off on the plains, and I followed for some distance. Every now and again, one or the other would halt abruptly and turn round to stare at me. A moment later, it trotted on after the others. Several times I thought it possible to bring them to a halt and get a clean shot; but it was not to be. Rather than merely wound, I let them go. The sun had dipped down over the western rim of the plains, and I had no fancy to tackle three lions in the dark.

On another occasion, when in the Sotik, I put up a fine black-maned lion when armed only with a very light rifle. I did not like the idea of using it on this beast, for it was not safe; so I employed my camera only. That lion was the most contrary brute I have ever met. He appeared to like my company and gave me every opportunity of photographing him; but from too great a distance. He would not go away, and would not let me get close enough to take his picture. For two hours or more this tantalizing game continued, but I had the laugh on him in the end. I managed to get a reasonably good snapshot of the beast with a telephoto lens.

By that time he had got bored with me, and was stalking off in a most leisurely fashion to stand under the shade of a tree. His walk was very deliberate, as he turned his back upon me. In fact, his whole attitude was one of studied contempt.

It had been quite an amusing morning ; and I had got all I wanted.

It has been my general experience, however, that lions will act boldly enough whenever there is good cover. Unless wounded or really angered, they are invariably cautious when found on quite open ground. This is particularly the case on the Athi and Kapiti Plains.

During 1909, I paid several visits to Nakuru and stayed at the Nakuru Hotel, then owned and managed by Frouville d'Etienne and his portly spouse. Lions were plentiful all around this little township in those days ; and the more especially on the shores of the lake. The little Frenchman insisted on taking a constitutional every afternoon, and generally walked down to the lake and back after his tea.

On one of these daily strolls, he unexpectedly came face to face with a lion. The meeting was a complete surprise to both, for the lion had been hidden under a big bush and sleeping off the effects of a heavy meal on zebra. They stood and looked at each other, neither moving an inch. The Frenchman was unarmed, and simply paralysed with terror. The lion was just mildly interested, and not anxious to attack. He was not a confirmed man-eater, and had scarcely digested his last heavy meal and so was not the least bit hungry. But d'Etienne was not to know that. How long that strained tension continued I am unable to say ; and the Frenchman could not tell me.

At last, the lion, who was more sleepy than pugnacious, turned on his heel, and stalked majestically away from the man. Once he was out of sight, the Frenchman turned also, and ran as fast as his shaking legs would permit. Later, he staggered into the hotel and collapsed on the ample bosom of his wife. It was some time before we could get any coherent story out of the little man, for he was so badly scared by this adventure that he acted like one demented.

From that day onwards he never ventured outside the limits of the township, but took his exercise by walking up and down the main street or else perambulating the broad veranda of his hotel. He was always accompanied by an armed native as escort wherever he went.   No doubt he found these walks much less exciting and nerve-racking.

It was most unwise to mention the subject of lions in his presence thereafter, for the excitable little man always imagined that you did so merely to imply that he was afraid of the brutes.

" *Sacré bleu !* " he would exclaim, angrily.   " I spit in the lion's face.   Poof !   he run and I walk back here.   *Simba !* Bah, he is only veree big cat, and I fear not ! "

But it required two very large neat brandies to calm his nerves each time the word " lion " was unfortunately used in his presence.   I ought to know, for I paid for some of them !

While the Roosevelts were camped at Naivasha, preparing for the hunting in the Nyeri and Meru districts, we had a visit from Dr. Robert J. Stordy, the cheery principal veterinary officer of Kenya.   When Stordy joined a party, there was never a dull moment for those present.   This old-timer of East Africa was a perfect well of quaint and humorous stories of the pioneer times ;   and his well never seemed to run dry.   After dinner he treated us to a feast of fun and entertained the party prodigiously.

One of his stories concerned a recent adventure of a very nervous trader, well known to both of us.   This man was obsessed with a particular dread and horror of lions.   He feared them like the plague.   Nobody had ever known him even take a shot at one, let alone kill a beast.   This trader had his headquarters at Nyeri, where he had built a very comfortable house.

A man-eating lion made an unwelcome appearance in the district, and for some weeks exacted a heavy toll on the nearby villages and wandering natives.   His continual presence in the neighbourhood made the trader increasingly nervous and most apprehensive.   Every night he barricaded himself into his house and had six armed natives on guard over his premises. Knowing the African native, it can be taken for granted that they slept all through the hours of darkness.

In the middle of one night, he thought there were sounds of the man-eater on the prowl round his house ;   and, at one time, actually on the veranda.   He cautiously opened the window a little way, and emptied his magazine rifle at the spot where he believed the lion to be.   Then he fastened up the window tight and went back to bed.

In the morning he discovered that he had knocked a big

WANDOROBO HUNTERS AND CAVE-DWELLINGS

BLACK-MANED LION IN THE SOTIK

hole in a crate, which contained a piano just imported from London and not yet unpacked. It had only reached Nyeri that very afternoon. It was utterly wrecked, and valueless after his heavy bombardment.

On the following night he again heard sounds of what he thought was the lion. The noise came from the front of his house. He opened the window slightly, and fired a number of rounds at the spot where he saw something moving about. As there came no further sound, he felt confident that he had either killed the man-eater or else badly scared it. With his mind at rest now, he went back to his interrupted slumber.

Shortly after daybreak he ventured outside to investigate. A few yards from his front door was the District Commssioner's mule, stone-dead and riddled with bullets. The official was very angry about this incident, and insisted that the trader must either replace the dead mule by one of equal worth or pay the Government its full cost. The trader was forced to agree. That little mistake cost him about sixty pounds sterling !

On hearing this yarn from Robert Stordy, I sat down and wrote a letter of hearty congratulations to the trader on " killing his first lion." He rose to the occasion nobly, and thereafter silenced all sceptics by producing my letter as positive proof that he *had* killed a lion.

He acquired quite a reputation as a hunter of the district ; but not in the Nyeri district !

R. J. Cunninghame, the famous guide and hunter, knew more than most men about the habits of lion and other African species of game. He had many years of experience behind him. His name was one to conjure with in Eastern and Central Africa, and his services as a hunter-guide were always in big demand. He generally had a stirring tale to tell, if you could ever persuade him to talk ; but it was very difficult to get him to do so. I knew him well and intimately, but always had to drag yarns out of him by arguing some point against my honest convictions so as to beguile him into disputing my rash statement.

We were both stopping at the Norfolk Hotel in Nairobi in 1907, and " R. J.", as he was affectionately known to his friends, had just arrived from a hunting trip in the Lake Baringo area. I was badgered by a very young and green sportsman, just out from London, to introduce him to Cunninghame. Despite constant questioning, the famous hunter declined to be drawn beyond offering some sage advice in crisp sentences. Finally, the youngster was so persistent that " R. J." took refuge in a really first-class method of silencing his tormentor.

" A few weeks ago," he stated, as we all gathered round to listen attentively, " I was hunting towards Lake Baringo, and marching well ahead of my safari. I was alone, and stupidly unarmed. As I walked round a small rocky hillock, I stumbled suddenly upon a large tawny-maned lion.

" I drew back at once, and the lion crouched ready to spring at me. He was twitching his tail from side to side, and growling savagely. Then he sprang. Instinct made me bend down to avoid him, and the beast missed and landed with a thud beyond my back. I jumped round quickly to face the lion. He had done the same, crouched again for a spring, snarling and tearing up great chunks of earth with his claws, and beating the ground with his tail. Once more he sprang ; and I ducked lower.

" The lion again missed me. A third time he rushed, and I threw myself flat on the ground as the huge body sailed through the air. As I heard the thud of his landing, I jumped to my feet and faced about. The lion was staring at me over his shoulder, his expression very sorrowful. Then he shook his great head once or twice, tucked his tail between his legs, and trotted off out of sight. He paused for just one last look at me, however ; it was one of pained disgust."

" Good God, sir ! What a frightful experience ! "

It was the young sportsman who spoke, and his eyes were popping out of his head and mouth wide open. The rest of us strove hard to conceal grins behind hands.

" I was returning over the same route a week later," resumed Cunninghame, without a smile and his voice solemn. " This time, however, I carried a rifle and was taking no chances. At almost the identical spot I found that old lion quite dead, with his skull shattered against a large flat-faced rock. Odd, wasn't it ? "

" How the deuce d'you account for that ? " asked the young sportsman eagerly.

Cunninghame winked at me ; and I chuckled openly now.

" Practising low jumps on the rock, I guess," explained Cunninghame, quietly. And he rose, and hurried away.

His departure was the signal for a roar of hilarious laughter, in which the butt of the jest joined good-naturedly.

At the conclusion of the Sotik Expedition, I was ordered

to take my column of troops back to my station. We were marching across the Loieta Plains, on the way into Naivasha to entrain for Kisumu, and I had out-distanced my men. I had been walking fast, the sun was exceptionally hot, and I was feeling tired after marching since before dawn—a matter of seven hours.

Noticing a large bush close to my path, I decided it was an admirable spot at which to rest awhile and allow my men time to overtake me. I walked over to it, dropped down in the very welcome shade, placed my rifle ready to hand, and took a cooling drink from my water-bottle. As my safari was not yet in sight, I stretched myself on my back and relaxed my weary body.

I must have fallen asleep, for I have no recollection of anything further until abruptly awakened by the lusty singing of my porters as they trailed across the plain toward me. The noise startled me into wakefulness, full and immediate. As I sat up, I heard a strange rustling movement in the bush behind me, and thought it was a snake. A moment later, there was a sound of the crackling of twigs trodden on by a heavy body. I grabbed up my rifle, alert and ready to act, rolled over and faced the danger-point.

I was dumbfounded to see a big black-maned lion stalk out majestically from behind the bush where I had slept. I stared at him with wide eyes, too astonished either to move or utter a sound.

He stood perfectly still for a moment or two in full view, gazing thoughtfully at my approaching safari. Then he stretched himself luxuriously like a big dog, yawned prodigiously, grunted deeply, and turned to look once more at my porters. A moment later, he had trotted off into the tall grass and vanished from sight. I could only stare after him, paralysed into immobility by sheer astonishment. Even if I had willed to do so, I was incapable of firing a shot at him.

Sometimes surprise is greater than fear in clogging a man's nerves and brain-action!

I do not know to this day what had actually happened, and can only presume that the lion had been asleep on the opposite side of the bush when I arrived and had not been disturbed by my movements. I found the place where his body had rested, and it was quite warm. That was a sure sign that he had been there for some time.

Obviously he had been unaware of my presence, even as I had been blissfully ignorant of his until he disclosed himself.

He was scarcely an ideal bed-companion ! There are both good and bad lions ; but I would rather keep both types at the business end of my rifle.

Until I knew to the contrary, like so many others, I had always believed there were no lions on the Kavirondo Plains. I found out my mistake in 1905, during the Nandi Rebellion. My column had come into Muhoroni for a rest, and we camped there over Christmas week. I went out for a stroll near the camp after tea, and was unarmed. There was no reason to suspect any danger thereabouts. I was accompanied only by my game little fox-terrier, Mickey Doolan.

On reaching the banks of an almost dry stream, about a mile from Muhoroni, I halted to watch Mickey Doolan amuse himself by chasing imaginary rats with immense enthusiasm and praiseworthy zeal.

Abruptly, the long grass on the far bank parted, and out stepped a graceful young lioness. I was very much taken aback by this wholly unlooked for apparition. Mickey Doolan expressed his annoyance at this rude interruption by barking furiously, his hair bristling with rage. I looked at the lioness, and she stared back at me. I have often wondered which of the three of us was the most startled—Mickey Doolan, the lioness or myself. The answer to that conundrum can never be known.

Then, as quietly and suddenly as she had appeared, the young lioness faded back into the tall yellow grass, and vanished. I rubbed my eyes in bewilderment, wondering if my lunch, perchance, had disagreed with me. After all, I had only swallowed a small bottle of lager beer !

Her departure was too much for Mickey Doolan. Before I could call him to heel, he had rushed pell-mell, and barking loudly, into the bed of the stream and was half way across to the other side. Brave, but foolish little dog ! I whistled and called to him without avail, and then set off in pursuit.

I adored Mickey Doolan. His mother had been killed at my side during an affair of patrols in the South African War ; and only three days previously had presented me with a litter of four grand pups. We drowned three, and raised Mickey Doolan by hand ; but it was not an easy task. He had been my inseparable companion ever since. To think of him falling a victim to a hungry lioness was more than I could bear.

The lioness crashed off through the grass at full speed, with Mickey Doolan in hot, noisy and joyous pursuit. His eager barks indicated that he considered his unusual quarry much better sport than field-rats, real or imaginary. My heart was as heavy as lead as I ran fast after him, and repeatedly urged him to come to heel. He was the most obedient dog I have ever owned, normally ; but not this time.

Finally, Mickey Doolan abandoned the hunt and returned to my side. He was wagging his tail vigorously, and I thought there was a distinct grin on his intelligent face. I may have been mistaken ; but he was obviously mighty proud of himself, even as I was of his courage.

I was so overcome with relief at getting him back safely, that I knelt down and hugged him tight to me. What I said into his ears does not concern anyone else. The words were sacred as between dog and master.

I doubt if there ever lived a more game, more splendid, or more loyal dog-friend than Mickey Doolan. I have always thought him to be without peer. That opinion seemed to be universally shared in Kenya, for everyone liked my dog. You could not help doing so. Sefu, my personal servant, and Hamisi, my trusty gun-bearer, worshipped him almost as much as I did. They were the only natives of Africa whom I have ever known to show any genuine affection for an animal.

When I told my brother officers in Muhoroni about this incident, they were distinctly sceptical. Had a lion *ever* been seen or heard in that area, asked one of them. And there came an emphatic chorus of : " *No*—absolutely never ! " I let it go at that, and swallowed their good-natured chaff.

A week later I was vindicated, and this time had a European witness to confirm my experience.

I left Muhoroni by hand-trolley for Kisumu, some forty miles distant, having been invited to a New Year Eve's party by S. S. Bagge, the popular and charming Provincial Commissioner. The European Permanent Way Inspector had invited me to accompany him on his hand-trolley, for he wanted me to shoot some game-birds for him en route. The weekly mail-train connecting with the steamer for Uganda had left Muhoroni a bare half-hour ahead, and we knew that there was a clear line to our destination,

Less than three miles out of Muhoroni, and as we were descending a steep gradient, I suddenly saw something yellow in the middle of the track about a quarter of a mile ahead. We were travelling at a good speed, and I could not clearly distinguish the nature of the obstruction. When about two hundred yards or less from the spot, two young lionesses rose to their feet. They had been stretched out on the permanent way, enjoying a sun-bath. Now they slowly climbed up the bank to our right, watching us intently over their shoulders.

I did not dare to shoot at them with my shot-gun, for I only had small bird-shot in the breech. I told Sefu to hold Mickey Doolan tight and not let him get away, as he was already eager to give chase; and then urged the native trolley-boys to redouble their efforts. They required no such urging, for they were now working at top pressure. We dashed past the two lionesses and started to ascend the up-grade. Luckily for us, the two beasts made no attempt to molest or follow us. They stood still on the top of the bank, and watched us with evident curiosity. Soon we had reached a safe distance, and halted to look back at them. The lionesses had now gone, and we did not see them again.

I have never heard of anyone else having seen lions in this part of Kenya. I fancy they had come down from the Sotik country for a change of air and diet; or else planned a pleasant holiday in the salubrious climate of the Nandi Escarpment.

They did not appear to have heard there was a war on in that territory !

CHAPTER X

TOLD ROUND CAMP-FIRES

AFTER several years of big game hunting in Africa, the ordinary delights of the sportsman are apt to grow wearisome. Just to pursue and kill, if taken in large doses, is bound to react.

Adventure means much to all red-blooded he-men, but too often it is come by far too tamely and easily. Variety in your sport and pleasures is essential to enjoyment. That is why, perhaps, there have been so many novel departures from accepted canons within the past quarter of a century.

Novelty was introduced by Carl G. Schilling, A. Radclyffe Dugmore and Cherry Kearton in the substitution of the camera for the rifle. This was followed by the W. D. Boyce Balloonograph Expedition from Chicago, organized with the object of photographing wild game from a captive balloon. It proved a costly failure, for the altitude effects on the gas made the attempts to ascend abortive; but it was the first balloon in Kenya. Prior to that, Blayney Percival and others initiated the thrilling sport of riding down lions on horseback.

In quick succession there followed the " Buffalo " Jones party of cowboys to lasso dangerous game, which proved a really unique and remarkable adventure; the Paul J. Rainey's party to hunt down lions with a pack of hounds; the Stewart Edward White " bow and arrow " venture, which signalized a return to primitive man's methods and was successfully achieved; and, finally, the shooting and photographing of wild game from motor-cars and aeroplanes.

In those golden days of the past, such frills to hunting were unknown; at least, when I lived in Kenya. Then the sportsman was content to rely upon either rifle or camera, or both, for his sport and adventure. I am old-fashioned enough to think nothing can improve upon the methods employed by Selous, Neumann, Jim Sutherland, R. J. Cunninghame, Major

Stigand, Major Powell Cotton, Abel Chapman, Sir Alfred Pease and that gallant host of other real experts. The danger to both hunter and hunted was then balanced much more evenly.

Soon after my first arrival in Kenya, a small party of good sportsmen had gathered at the Norfolk Hotel in Nairobi. They were discussing various methods of getting more fun out of hunting lions than possible through the usual means. It was the Chief Game Warden, A. Blayney Percival, who first suggested that a trial might be given to riding down lions on horseback.

The proposal offered a novel and, possibly, most exciting departure from customary methods. It was certainly likely to furnish more thrills for the hunters than the hunted, and the dice would be loaded heavily in favour of the lions. The plan tickled the imagination of all present, and it was decided to test out the idea.

Percival, G. H. Goldfinch (who later joined the Game Warden's Department), and Lucas, a settler at El Donyo Sabuk, were the first to attempt to put the plan into practice. It ended in a terrible tragedy.

They put up and chased a lioness, wounded her and followed up into the long grass. Goldfinch was first attacked, and was badly bitten through the thigh. Lucas dismounted and fired at the beast to save Goldfinch. Immediately she left her first victim and attacked Lucas, got him down and mauled him terribly before Goldfinch could crawl to his aid. As soon as Lucas had wriggled clear of the brute's head, Goldfinch shot her dead at close range. Percival had been hunting down a lion elsewhere, and was not in sight.

Somehow, the two severely wounded men managed to mount and ride back to El Donyo Sabuk, where Percival joined them as soon as he heard of the disaster. The gashes of the two men were dressed and carefully disinfected, and then both were carried into hospital at Nairobi. Despite every possible care, gangrene poisoning set in and Lucas died in fearful pain a week later. Goldfinch, however, made a remarkable recovery but was lamed for life.

Nothing daunted by this tragic accident, Percival and many others continued to hunt down lions in this sporting manner ; and killed a great number. It became a popular pastime among the most daring hunters in Kenya ; and to anyone who desires a really sporting adventure, I can commend it.

Fitz Schindelaar, another old friend of mine, was killed some years later in much the same way as Lucas. It was a sheer accident, and occurred when he was hunting lions with Paul J. Rainey's hounds. He was one of the most daring hunters in Africa and, until that day, had always seemed to bear a charmed life.

Fitz was an Austrian, and arrived in Kenya soon after I got to Nairobi. He was one of the most likable men you could meet, and I do not think he had an enemy throughout the length and breadth of Eastern Africa. That says a very great deal, for it is a region where tempers are short and easily frayed ; too easily for the maintenance of the peace. Quite minor grievances often assume undue magnitude ; and many a staunch friendship has been wrecked over the very simplest and most childish misunderstandings. Medical opinion holds that this peculiarity can be attributed to living at high altitudes under an equatorial sun. Be that as it may, both men and women are often most unreasonably sensitive in those countries.

Poor Fitz was trying to draw a lion out of cover after it had been brought to bay by the hounds. The lion suddenly sprang out upon him, mauled the pony severely and then dragged the rider to the ground. Fitz was terribly mauled in the abdomen, and his condition was quite hopeless. They rushed him to the nearest hospital, but he died in agony a couple of days later.

Fitz sleeps his last in the cemetery at Nairobi, beside those many others over whose graves stands a cross with the tragic words : " Killed by a lion."

The " Buffalo " Jones Expedition made history. Never has there been an adventure in Africa so thrilling or amazing. Means, one of the cowboys, told me about their experiences, at the Adventurers' Club in Chicago, some time after his return to America.

They roped a full-grown lioness in the Rift Valley near Mount Longonot, and with no weapon more deadly than a cowboy's lasso. It proved a long and exciting fight, and the lioness charged repeatedly before she was finally roped, thrown and securely caged. She was the only animal they captured which was not released afterwards.

Means told me that, several times, they actually got the rope over her head ; but she slipped it off with astonishing swiftness. Finally, Loveless, the other cowboy, followed her up into cover and threw his rope so that it rested on the long grass just above her head. He then fastened his end of the rope round a tree, went forward with a long stick, and gradually pushed the noose over the head of the beast. Promptly she charged him, but the rope tightened round the neck and pulled her up short. The other cowboys then took a hand, and roped her securely.

Those American cowboys are entitled to extra full marks for that unique achievement. It has never been equalled, let alone excelled.

Another American expedition, headed by Stewart Edward White, the author, went out into the Rift Valley from Kijabe and killed lions, eland and other wild animals with bows and arrows. Their success with this novel method of hunting animals was phenomenal, and their skill as archers does them immense credit. Whatever else may be said about this adventure, no one can deny that it was really sporting. That is more than can be said for many other shooting and photographic expeditions into the heart of Africa within recent years.

The Sotik country of Kenya is famous for being a really first-class lion country, as well as being the habitat of rhino, buffalo and elephant. On one memorable morning there, I saw a troop of no less than fifteen lions on the Loieta Plains. They comprised males, females, partly grown beasts of both sexes, and cubs. Leslie Tarlton had reported having seen an even larger troop in the same area; but both instances are exceptional.

J. Alden Loring, the naturalist with the Roosevelt party, is not likely to forget one experience which he had with a lioness in the Sotik. He had a very narrow escape from being mauled or worse. If it had not been for his companion, Lieut.-Colonel Edgar A. Mearns, another member of the Expedition, the incident would probably have ended fatally for Loring. Mearns was a wonderful shot and always remained cool under every circumstance. Undoubtedly, he saved Loring's life.

The latter had wounded a lioness with a light automatic rifle. Loring had been told that such a weapon was useless for killing or stopping big game in Africa, but insisted on testing this for himself. He put the first bullet through the heart, but it did not stop her for a second and she continued to charge straight at him. He hit her four times altogether, and each bullet should have proved a mortal wound. But the calibre of his rifle was so slight that the shock of the bullets striking the lioness only served to make her real mad. Both Loring and Mearns assured me later that she was the angriest beast they had ever seen!

Then Mearns shot her through the neck with his heavy rifle, and she fell over dead at Loring's feet. Mearns had aimed so as not to spoil the skull, for he wanted it for the Smithsonian Institute in Washington. Loring told me, with a hearty laugh, that Mearns seemed to think far more of the beast's skull than of his companion's life.

Colonel Mearns had an utter contempt for danger, and his accuracy with rifle or shot-gun was astounding. I knew his aim to be deadly, for I seldom ever had seen him miss his target. On more than one occasion I have seen him bring down a large bird on the wing with a rifle; and with ease.

One of the first men I met in Nairobi, on my arrival there at the beginning of 1904, was Captain Ewart S. Grogan. He had made history, a few years previously, by being the first European to walk over the Cape to Cairo route; just recently, he was one of the passengers on the first Imperial Airways machine to cover the same ground when inaugurating that service. It was a happy thought to have invited him.

He told me of a most picturesque meeting he had with a lion on that historic journey. He had killed a zebra for bait and, just before the dawn, went out from his camp to see if it had functioned as desired. As soon as Grogan approached close to the kill, he saw a number of vultures perched on trees at a short distance from the carcass. Then, in the faint light of a new day, he saw a lion pulling at the zebra's body. It was a grand old beast, and was leisurely gnawing at the ribs of the bait. Just behind it sat four jackals in a row. In the background were the limitless plains, streaked with mists gradually evaporating in the heat of the rising sun. Just out of reach of the lion's tail was a solid circle of immense vultures, craning forward their bald necks, chattering and hustling each other.

The more daring quartette of jackals sat within the magic circle like graven images of patience, while the lion, in all its might and matchless grandeur, calmly chewed and crunched the tit-bits of the feast. It was magnificently indifferent to the expectant eyes of the encircling scavengers.

After watching this unique scene for some time, Grogan told me that he was in two minds about killing the lion. Finally,

however, he fired and got it with the first shot. The jackals
bolted to cover at once, while the vultures rose, with a noisy
clattering of wings, and took to the air.

When travelling out to Mombasa early in 1909 with the
Roosevelt Expedition, we had the great pleasure of the company
of Frederick Courteney Selous. After leaving Aden, we used to
gather in a group round Colonel Roosevelt and Selous, while
they entertained us with many amusing stories of their past
adventures. It was all very fascinating, and we listened with
bated breath to their thrilling reminiscences.

While Theodore Roosevelt talked of his early days on the
cattle ranches of the Western States of America, Selous unfolded
for us strange tales of his many-sided activities in the real
pioneer days of the African hinterland. Roosevelt out-rivalled
Bret Harte : Selous was a master story-teller. We all sat at
their feet bewitched, day after day, hour after hour, and styled
ourselves " The Arabian Nights Club." Membership was
unlimited, and all passengers and ship's officers were made
welcome. There was only one rule : " Don't interrupt to ask
fool questions ! " That rule was rigidly observed.

Selous had a fascinating style of narration which was pecu-
liarly his own. I have never heard his equal. Where an ordinary
hunter spoke of killing just a few lions, Selous talked in dozens ;
and the same was the case with elephant, buffalo, rhino and
all other major game. Moreover, as he told his story, he had
a habit of imitating the animal actors in his drama of the veld
and in a marvellously realistic manner. His rapt audience could
visualize their presence and movements. Selous was always
most vivid and accurate in detail, and possessed a remarkable
degree of penetrating observation. Each animal's habits and
characteristics were known to him like an open book ; and he
gave us the full benefit of his vast knowledge.

Major " Rattle " Barrett, the international polo player, was
on board also, en route to Kenya for a shooting trip. He told
me later, in Nairobi, that he had acquired more helpful knowledge about the game from those daily sessions with Selous on
board ship than from any book on shooting. I can well believe
him.

Another of our fellow passengers was a very cheery young
settler from El Donyo Sabuk. He was an inveterate leg-puller,
and not a day passed but he sprang some surprise on his ship-
mates. He was a regular member of the " Arabian Nights

WANDOROBO HUNTERS AFTER ELEPHANTS

Club," and could always be found at the feet of Colonel Roosevelt and Selous when we were in session.

Once, after Selous had related one of his interesting lion adventures, the young settler, without a smile on his face, broke a thoughtful silence and told us a really preposterous story. We all listened with mingled feelings of admiration and amusement, for he certainly displayed a vivid imagination.

" I was out after lions near the Thika River, and had not seen any," he stated gravely. " On nearing a thicket of Acacia trees, I saw a leopard fighting fiercely with a rhino in a small clearing. They were savagely tearing at each other. I stood still to watch the unusual duel, with my money on the old rhino every time. At last, the leopard sprang at the shoulder of the rhino and landed almost on its neck. Away crashed the latter through the bush, carrying the cat on its back. That leopard must have had a pretty rough joy ride !

" I hurried after them, anxious to see the end of that scrap and to know who won. It was some time before I came up with them again. The rhino was dead, with its frontal horn wedged securely in the forked branch of a big tree. I think the beast must have been strangled, for its feet were clear of the ground. It may have broken its back or neck, but I don't know for sure.

" We searched all about the spot for any signs of the leopard, but found no trace of it. This struck me as odd, so I ordered my gun-bearer to climb the tree and look out over the bush for the beast. When he had climbed up to some height, he shouted out that he could see the dead body of the leopard among the thorny branches. I can only presume that the rhino tossed the brute up there, was unable to brake down on its wild charge, and so got hung up in the branches."

There was a prolonged silence, broken presently by a low whistle from Selous. Then Colonel Roosevelt's voice cut crisply into the silence.

" I think you're mistaken," he remarked, without a hint of malice in his voice. " Your explanation of the rhino's death must be wrong. What you should have said is that the rhino was trying to climb the tree after the leopard, slipped and got its horn tightly jammed, and thus broke its neck."

We all joined heartily in the merriment, and none more loudly than the young settler.

" I guess you're right, sir," he grinned. " I hadn't thought of that ! "

One of the first people to greet us on the platform at Nairobi railway station on our return from the hunt in the Sotik country was Selous. He was going on to Mombasa by the same train, and embarking there for England. He had just completed a two months' shooting trip with McMillan, of Juja Farm ; and had been accompanied by Greswolde Williams and Will Judd. The latter was a famous professional guide and elephant hunter, and a good friend of mine. To everyone's great regret, he was killed a few years ago by a wounded elephant.

In answer to Colonel Roosevelt's anxious enquiries, Selous spoke with irrepressible sadness and a tinge of bitter disappointment in his voice.

" No, Colonel—no luck at all this trip. Not even a solitary lion ! "

He told us of his experiences during those two months, while we waited to see him depart for Mombasa. He had not even had a chance of a shot at a lion either in the Sotik or on the Mau Plateau ; yet Williams had killed thirteen, and then been mauled by a lioness that had charged full at him in a most determined fashion. His gun-bearer killed her as she stood over Williams, and thus saved his master's life.

" Will Judd had a most astounding adventure," continued the gentle voice of Selous. " We saw a couple of lionesses, and at once galloped after them. That was on the Mau Plateau, and after Williams had been mauled in the Sotik. Judd was about eighty yards behind me, riding a rather good type of mule. Suddenly I lost sight of one of the beasts, but continued to gallop after the other. The first lioness, apparently, had halted and crouched down behind a thick bush. She let me pass without hint of her presence ; but when Judd came abreast of her on his mule, she sprang out at him.

" She was about ten yards or so from Judd, when he first saw her, and coming straight at him. He fired from his hip, never for a moment expecting to do more than possibly turn her charge. As he fired, his mule bucked him over her head and he landed in a sitting position on the ground. He was almost touching the lioness, which was stretched out flat on the ground.

" Judd sprang to his feet hurriedly, picked up his fallen rifle, and got ready to defend himself against any further attack. But the lioness did not move. Judd advanced cautiously to examine her ; and, to his amazement, found she was quite dead ! His chance shot had sent a bullet through her right eye into the brain. She must have been killed instantly. There was not even a mark on her skin, only one eye shot cleanly out of her head. Judd is very proud of his unique trophy."

" By Gosh ! " exclaimed Colonel Roosevelt. " What a most remarkable incident. No wonder Judd is real proud ! "

" He *is !* " agreed Selous, with a smile.

He rose to say good-bye, for his train was just about to start. It was a very keen disappointment to Colonel Roosevelt not to get the two weeks' shooting trip with Selous, which both had planned ; but the famous white-bearded hunter had been forced to curtail his visit to Kenya and return to London on urgent business affairs.

That was to have been Selous's last hunting trip in Africa. But he returned to Kenya as a captain in the 25th Battalion (Legion of Frontiersmen) of the Royal Fusiliers, commanded by my old friend of Boer War days, Colonel " Jim " Driscoll. This fine old soldier is still living in Kenya, growing coffee just outside Nairobi. I saw him there in 1929, and he was just the same charming and cheery soul as he had always been. Serving in the same battalion as brother officers were many other noted big game hunters—Cherry Kearton, James Outram, Alan L. Black and several more.

Selous died as gloriously as he had lived. When leading a patrol of Royal Fusiliers against the enemy, he was shot dead through the brain. It was a short and sharp fight, during the campaign in German East Africa, in 1917 ; and expressions of the deepest regret for his death were afterwards received from the Germans. Selous joined the Royal Fusiliers at the age of sixty, and was awarded the Distinguished Service Order for a very gallant action just about a year later.

He died exactly as he would have wished—facing the enemy. All who knew and loved him—and their name is legion—will never cease to mourn his death, and yet be proud to have known this very gallant gentleman-adventurer. They know that he would not have asked a better epitaph than : " Killed in action."

Until you have been stalked in reality by a lion or lions at night, when defenceless and riding across the plains, you cannot appreciate all the horrible sensations you endure in the process. I had such an experience during 1909, when camped with the Roosevelts at Saigai-Sai Farm on the shores of Lake Naivasha.

I was then stalked by four lions in the inky darkness and

during a torrential downpour of rain. Erhan, my Arab pony, was a valuable racing stallion and could not travel faster than at a walk owing to the slippery surface of the rain-soaked ground and the innumerable ant-bear holes. Foolishly, I had not taken any weapons with me on that ride, and was accompanied by an unarmed Masai syce.

We could hear the grunts of the lions on either side, as well as the distinct sucking noise made as their pads were uplifted from the liquid mud. It was a most confoundedly unpleasant experience, and one which I never want repeated. I have seldom felt so abominably nervous and uncomfortable in my life, before or since.

It is all very well to stand up to a sudden attack from a wild beast; but to be followed, hour after hour, by an unseen but vividly heard danger, and when you have no means of defending your life, sets all your nerves on edge. The former is swift action; and you take risks automatically, almost subconsciously. You do the right thing just at the correct moment by sheer instinct, and are really only half aware of what is actually happening. With the latter, however, you are faced with an ever-present dread. Worse than all else, you have ample time to let your imagination run riot.

Every now and again, the lions would utter a long-drawn and menacing moan; but they kept a respectful distance of a hundred yards or, possibly, more than that. It was much too dark to judge accurately their positions, but do not think it could have been much over a hundred yards. As a matter of fact, it seemed a much shorter space in the deadly stillness of the night.

Imagine, if you possibly can, riding across a flat plain, covered with liquid mud and fast-flowing rivers of rain water, in the pitch darkness, with a tropical deluge soaking you to the skin and unarmed, while two lions on either flank stalk you step by step. Such an experience, I can swear, demands a most vivid imagination to picture the actual sensations. I know, from having actually faced the ghastly horrors of it.

Never once did they attempt to attack, but merely stalked along and grunted deeply at intervals while keeping abreast of me. However, that terrible nightmare ended at last. On reaching the railway track, the lions abandoned the pursuit and retired silently into the thick pall of darkness behind me. The relief to my mind was immense.

I have used the word " stalk," for it more closely expresses my real sensations than any other word ; but they may have been merely lonely, and desired company on that walk through a bleak, wet and cheerless night ! It was a companionship that I would have much preferred to have foregone.

As soon as I reached the railway, I trotted to the Rift Valley Hotel in Naivasha, while my Masai syce held on to Erhan's flowing tail and ran at his heels. I arrived wet through and very badly shaken, for it had been a most hair-raising adventure.

An outsize in double brandies did much to steady my nervous system, but the glass beat a merry tattoo on my teeth as I poured the neat spirit down my throat. Until next day, I could not even speak about it. I spent the entire night in tossing about on my bed, vividly living over again those beastly hours, hearing again those ghastly noises, and knowing fear.

Lest this adventure be viewed with any suspicion or open doubt, I may state that Leslie Tarlton was stalked by the same four lions, and at much about the same place, some three days later. He also was riding in from Saigai-Sai to Naivasha.

He assured me that, though his bag of lions even then exceeded three figures, this was by far the worst experience he had ever had with them.

I am sure he spoke the plain, unvarnished truth !

CHAPTER XI

SOME OF MY LIONS

IF it were not for the millions of ticks and jigger-fleas, both the Athi and Kapiti Plains would be ideal hunting grounds for the keen sportsman. They are vast, calm lakes of grasslands and rolling plains, with very little in the way of bush, scrub or trees ; and are well-watered areas.

In my days in Kenya, you could stand on those far-stretching grassy plains and look upon thousands and thousands of almost every variety of wild animal and bird life indigenous to Eastern Africa. Then it was well worth coming all those weary miles from the Indian Ocean to feast your eyes on that unique spectacle —" Nature's Zoo." Nowhere else in all the world was it possible to witness such a novel and fascinating sight. The picture still remains to-day, but the relentless advance of civilization has dimmed the canvas.

You would have to travel far and wide to improve on the view from the summit of the Athi Escarpment. To the west stand out the N'gong Hills ; to the north can plainly be seen the forest-clad Kikuyu Range ; and, on a clear day and when visibility is reasonably good, in the north-east stands up boldly into the blue sky the magnificent snow-capped peak of Mount Kenya. Sometimes the actual peak itself is hidden by floating clouds ; at others, it stands out, clear cut against a brazen sky-line. Once or twice, to the south-west, I have caught a faint vision of the snowy summits of great Mount Kilimanjaro, appearing like a wisp of cloud in the high horizon.

Often, as I have stood there on those vast plains and stared out at Mount Kenya, nearly a hundred miles away, I have recalled the words of A. J. Monson, my old friend in the Secretariat at Nairobi :

> The sky is overcast, the rain
> Comes driving up across the plain ;
> But yonder on Lukenia's heights
> There hangs a haze of golden lights.

Ah ! gleams of gold among the hills,
I pray that, in the midst of ills
When life seems desolate and grey,
I still may see you far away !

The love of the veld, which is so utterly inexpressible, gripped
my soul from the earliest days in the Boer War. Africa, the
mystical and inscrutable, was my first love ; and ever I have
remained true to her. The Arabs have a saying : " He who has
once drunk of the waters of the Nile, will return again to drink
thereof " ; and so with Africa. She has called me back to her
side, time and time again ; and is always calling. Her allure
is just as strong, just as fascinating, just as irresistible, and just
as difficult to stifle as ever it was. Only those who know Africa
can understand how potent is her appeal. All love her.

The veld is so lonely, mournful, wild and mysterious—all
the adjectives you may care to lavish upon it ; and also something else besides which you are unable to express in mere
words. There is some keynote to those plains of Kenya, as
there is to the plains of South Africa, which is most difficult
to either find or define : something subtle, vague and half-
hidden. Lonely indeed they are—terribly lonely in the great
distances, the broad stretches of level plain or rolling downs,
without sign of human habitation. Mysterious they are—in
the mile upon mile of changeless characteristic, the very dupli-
cation of themselves. Mournful they are—in the apparent
emptiness of most that makes a country prosperous. And wild
surely they are—in the savage population of wild beasts densely
packed on the grasslands, in the eternal war on life, and in the
unconquered nature of their vast wastes.

The plains of Kenya are hideous or beautiful, sad or gay in
the vivid sunshine, just as the mood possesses you ; but always,
even unto the worst of their recollection, they are fascinating.
This, because they are so utterly inexpressible. You may have
starved and thirsted on them ; shivered in wet clothes as you
lay in their clinging mud, benighted far from camp, or been
sunbaked on them ; bled on them and suffered pain ; all that,
and still more. But afterwards, when you look back at them,
and time has wrapped a haze of tender memory about their
sterner outlines, you will always recollect the charm, the half-
conscious attractiveness and the indefinable something that was
of their very nature. You will never be able to forget them as
long as you live.

I was camped at Simba, soon after my arrival in Kenya, in search of lions. From the coast to Simba, it is mostly thick bush country ; but at Simba there comes a welcome change to the hill-engirdled Emali Plains. The bush gives way to an open grass-covered plain. To the north of the railroad lie fairly high, grassy hillocks of varying sizes, shapes and colouring. There was always good hunting hereabouts.

I had started out on the first morning, when still dark, to climb to the summit of one of those hillocks and feast my eyes on the masses of game on the plains below me. I knew it would be a thrilling and fascinating spectacle. And now I sat on the top of that hill, and waited for the sun to step up boldly over the eastern rim of the veld. And then it came. Sunrise —with the dew sparkling like diamond points on the long waving grass, the cold breeze fanning my sunburned face, the glorious blue sky overhead boasting of the new day, the golden disc of the sun rising higher and higher in that blue vault and melting my chilled marrow. I could see the scattered, queer-shaped, brown and purple kopjes stretching as far as the edge of the yellow horizon ; and I breathed deep of the splendid, dry and invigorating atmosphere about me. Now the plain was turned to burnished gold. It was beautiful seen thus: an inspiration. God ! it was good to be alive : and there.

Now I saw a wholly unforgettable scene. Thousands upon thousands of wild game of an infinite variety were marching steadily towards what was then the German East African border and is now Tanganyika Territory. Over a thousand zebra formed the vanguard of that mighty host of animals, and were followed by uncountable numbers of hartebeest, wilde-beest, and all the other many kinds of species of both antelope and gazelle. The mixed herd resembled a gigantic army on the march ; and the column, measured from head to tail, must have covered at least three miles of country. It was one of the most astounding sights it has ever been my lot to witness. Such an opportunity cannot be repeated to-day, for the wild creatures have had to make way for mankind's more urgent needs. Ever since that day, I have always looked upon caged beasts with pity ; and my gorge rose at the cruelty of confining these animals, born to freedom, in cages of small dimensions.

At a rough estimate, there could not have been less than twenty thousand animals in that huge, far-flung army of hoofed creatures migrating to new pasturage.

BUFFALO BULL KILLED IN KENYA FORESTS

COLONEL ROOSEVELT'S FIRST BUFFALO ON KAMITI RANCH
R. J. CUNNINGHAME, KERMIT ROOSEVELT, COLONEL ROOSEVELT, EDMUND HELLER
AND HUGH H. HEATLEY

Hour after hour I sat on my lookout and watched the scattered herds feeding on the plain below me. In the noon, the clear sunlight made lakes and lagoons ahead of me clearer and more distinct even than the mirages of the great Sudan desert. In the late afternoon, just as I was about to return to camp, the setting sun threw long shadows across the bare levels. And, that night, I stretched myself on the wide bosom of the veld beside my camp fire, while the bright stars glittered like electric points high up in their indigo setting and the smoke from my pipe curled lazily into the darkness above me. Then the veld had for me its greatest charm.

There could be no pining then for London, for the gay lights of Piccadilly Circus or for the feel of the pavements of Bond Street under your feet. To experience one particle of home-sickness was a sheer impossibility. You thanked God for the peace and the rest. This was Life : civilization but an empty sham.

For a long time, I remained thus. There seemed to have settled down over all my vicinity a profound peace and quietness. Nothing broke the deep silence, except the low-toned mumbles of some wakeful porters. If there was some performer in Nature's orchestra playing his little part in the ceaseless symphony of the night, then I heard him not.

As I rose finally to turn into my tent and retire to bed, I heard, far out on the plain, the fiendish laughter of a hyena, followed shortly by the coughing roar of a prowling lion. Out there in the black canopy of night the relentless law of the jungle was being enacted. Men must eat to live : so must the wild beasts. Then, once again, all was as still as the grave. I undressed, crawled into my blankets, and slept.

In these wide game regions, the lion is always plentiful. He never strays far from his potential larder. He is the lord of the veld ; and his reign is a cruel one. Zebra and large antelope are his favourite dishes, for he is a big eater. They know it. I have often seen a lion over a dead zebra, gorging himself, quite close to the railway track as the mail-train clattered past. The beast did not even pause from the ravenous attack on the carcass to look up at the train.

Time and time again, I have examined fresh kills made by lions, and their method of killing has always been the same. Zebra are found lying on their bellies, the legs spread out and the neck vertebræ broken. The head is always twisted round to the rump. The lion springs clean on to the back of the victim, bearing it down on to the knees by sheer weight, while biting through the neck to crush the vertebræ. One claw is generally pulling at the forehead to bring the neck round to break it. You have only to examine the body of a zebra just killed by a lion, and not yet devoured, to see how it is done.

In killing the larger antelope, such as hartebeest, eland, kudu and wildebeest, the lion's hind legs do not appear to have left the ground ; and the front paws have obviously grasped the victim's head and shoulders. I have seldom found any claw marks on the haunches of any antelope freshly killed by a lion, which must have been the case if it had been attacked in the same way as a zebra. But there was always a broken neck ; and there were terrible claw marks on face and withers. The lion, I suspect, stands up on its hind legs, while holding the victim with front paws until its teeth have splintered the neck bone ; and then the head is jerked backwards to break the vertebræ.

It was here, on this visit to Simba, that I had a very unique insight into the methods employed by lions in killing for their sustenance. I had been camped beside the railway station, of evil reputation, for a week without even seeing a lion. I had heard them roaring at night, but all efforts to locate them during daylight hours had failed. My gun-bearer, Hamisi, was an optimist and insisted that hope need not be abandoned. When I declared my intention of leaving Simba, he strongly advised me against doing so.

Hamisi was the only African I ever knew whose opinion in matters concerning big game hunting was always worth following. In this, he was an unique exception to the general rule. I have never found it either profitable or wise to trust implicitly to the advice of my African trackers. Too often they have told me what they thought I most desired to hear, and with a total disregard of accuracy. Over a number of years, I found that Hamisi was the only African on whom I could count on being dependable on all occasions. Never once did I find his judgment faulty, and could always rely upon it without any qualms. He was simple directness. To him a spade was a spade, and not a bunch of violets. I liked him immensely for that.

Faithful, lion-hearted, loyal friend and companion through six stirring years of adventure, no man possibly could have wished to have hunted with a wiser or more efficient mentor, or to be accompanied by a more courageous and unselfish servant.

Acting on Hamisi's advice, therefore, we went out again before the dawn. He said he had heard a lion during the night, close to our camp.

The bush country was thick with game of every variety, but there was not even the shadow of a lion. For a long time, after the new day had dawned, I stood and watched the immense masses of animals grazing. It was all very fascinating. I observed that there were sentinels posted all round the outskirts of that teeming congregation of beasts : sometimes zebra, and at other points hartebeest, did duty. While grazing, these sentries continually lifted their heads to stare about them and listen. I could see their nostrils sniffing the fresh morning air, searching for danger-tainted whiffs. At the slightest suspicious indication, they ran in abruptly toward the feeding herds ; and the latter promptly ceased nibbling at the grass, and waited for the signal to bolt or for the " all clear."

Suddenly, Hamisi nudged my elbow gently and pointed to our left front. For several minutes I could see nothing unusual, only a well-marked, sleek young zebra stallion keeping watch and ward on the outkirts of the masses. Then I saw a light movement in the grass, but some distance to the zebra's rear. Instantly, I was all attention.

Several more minutes dragged by, and still I could not make out what was moving so stealthily through the grass toward the animal sentry. If it had not been for Hamisi's lynx-eyes, I should never have seen even the grass waving gently. I looked into his face, my eyes questioning silently.

" *Simba !* " came the laconic whisper.

I started to crawl toward the lion, every once in a while lifting my head gradually to see what was happening ahead. At times, I halted to watch developments. By now, I was far more interested in the lion's stalk than in stalking the lion. Now the zebra was obviouly suspicious. He ran forward and backward at intervals, staring about him and sniffing the air, and ears cocked to listen intently. He had picked up a faint whiff of tainted wind, and was keenly alert. After a time, however, he seemed to be satisfied there was no real cause for alarm. He resumed grazing. But his mind was not at peace for long, and he kept on lifting his head to look, sniff and listen. He was still uneasy, and was not leaving matters to chance.

Then the lion engaged my attention. I could see now that it was a young lioness, and not a maneless lion as I had thought. She was crawling on her belly, just like a cat stalking a sparrow, and creeping closer and closer to her prey. We kept on hands and knees, and followed her. Slowly we gained ground. I could see she was far too intent on her own attack to pay heed to us, even if she had either seen or heard us.

For two hours by my wrist-watch we stalked that lioness as she, in her turn, stalked the zebra. At times, we paused to watch first the zebra and the lioness. I could see the zebra was still very disturbed and acutely suspicious. He stood still for a long time, listening, watching and sniffing the wind ; and made no attempt to feed. The lioness was now within sixty yards of her prey, every move forward being carefully considered before taken.

I was tremendously excited and thrilled, and would not have changed places with any man on earth. Never before, or since, had I witnessed a lion in the very act of stalking its prey ; and felt that I gazed upon a page of the book of Nature seldom seen by human eye.

Finally, the lioness got within twenty yards of the zebra, and was favourably placed up-wind. Following her wise example we crawled to within ten yards or so of her. Neither animal had yet seen us.

The zebra was now standing close to a small acacia tree, pensively staring round the countryside. He was still a trifle suspicious, but fear was abating. The lioness was crouched down low to the ground, behind the tree, tense and quivering with eagerness to spring. Not even her tail moved. She seemed to be waiting and watching for just the psychological moment to hurl herself through the air on to the zebra's beautifully marked back.

I was almost tempted to warn that poor stallion of his impending fate, and shoot the lioness dead where she crouched. It would have been simple to have done both by one act. But here was the law of the wilds being enforced before my eyes with a deadly ruthlessness. Kill : or be killed. It had been ordained that the zebra should die. I held my fire.

It all happened in a split second, and too quick for me to follow the swift movements of attack. Almost before I was aware that she had made her fatal spring, the lioness was round the tree and on the back of the zebra. She landed perfectly, just in the right spot for her deadly work to be performed most effectively. She was stretched out on the stallion's back, right paw clawing savagely at the centre of the forehead, left well dug into the shoulder, mouth biting viciously into the neck to reach the bone, and tail arched like a cat's. Her hind legs were motionless on the zebra's back, steadying her hold.

Now the blood was pouring down the zebra's face, shoulders and neck. I could hear the lioness growling fiercely, and the wretched victim was neighing shrilly. The thunder of the panic-stricken flight of the herds across the plains sounded like the roll of drums.

The weight of the young lioness and her sudden attack had brought the zebra on to his right knee, left leg extended, and hind legs bent to support the extra burden imposed on them. The mouth of the lioness was almost buried in the poor brute's neck ; and life would soon be ended for that zebra. The herds were safe, their sentry having paid forfeit by sacrificing himself on the altar of duty.

Handing my rifle to Hamisi and taking the camera from him, I ran round the tree until I stood broadside on at a distance of about twenty feet from the pair. The lioness seemed not to have seen or heard my sudden advance to the centre of the stage. I focussed the camera and took my photograph.

As the shutter clicked, the lioness looked up sharply at me. She growled angrily : a stern warning. It was a distinct and menacing threat, but she continued her gruesome work. I dropped the camera on the ground, snatched my rifle from Hamisi, and sent a bullet crashing into her brain. She tumbled off the back of the poor zebra, and did not move again. The stallion was so severely mauled that his case was quite hopeless. I put a humane bullet into his head.

Hamisi stared at me, and I grinned back at him. Neither spoke a word. The wonder of that scene had dammed our vocabularies, and words would not flow from our lips. Silently we shook hands, and then laughed outright. The laughter was an immense relief to our taut nerves, and brought us back to earth again. I went over to examine the dead lioness. She was quite young, and under three years of age. The clearly defined spots on her hide told me that, for after three years they disappear entirely.

Then I remembered my camera. I was using plates, and had dropped it rather unceremoniously. A careful examination

showed it was undamaged; all seemed well. Leaving Hamisi
to mark the lioness's body, I trotted back to camp to obtain
help to skin her.

That night, in the station-master's office, I developed the
negative. I watched the process expectantly and fearfully, and
slowly the picture shaped itself before my eyes. I shouted aloud
in my joy. I had got it.

Hamisi, no doubt, wondered why I made him a present of
one hundred rupees. I felt it was little enough for what he had
done for me.

A year or two later, I had a most anxious time with a lion
in the Sotik, for he put up a most determined fight for his life.
Late in the afternoon, when out shooting for meat to feed my
porters, I saw a good lion at some distance from me. The
trophy looked too good to be ignored. I followed him and was
soon within reasonable range. He was a large brute with a fine
black mane, and in the pink of condition. Just as I was about
to fire, he went off at a fast trot and disappeared into a clump
of small bush and long grass. I advanced toward him, cautiously.

A moment later, out he came with a rush and dashed away.
It was getting late and I was far from camp; and I lost my
temper completely. It is a fatal thing to do. I tried a rather
long shot, and hit him in the body. He now disappeared into
the long grass, growling savagely. My loss of self-control and
my Irish impatience had left me dirty, very dirty work to do.
Keeping a watchful eye for possible developments, I went after
him. I could both see and hear where he was, but he declined
to offer a good target. I knew it was madness to follow him
into that thick cover.

Halting where I was, with rifle ready, I considered the problem
thoughtfully. I had to get him, and soon. A wounded beast
could not be left to suffer, so I had to kill him. But the situation
bristled with pitfalls, and was far from pleasant. Hamisi now
suggested that he should burn out the brute from his cover.
I agreed. He worked round behind the beast and set fire to
the grass. It was soon burning fiercely, and the wind driving
the flames and smoke toward the lion. Now he would soon be
forced to break cover and show himself. I kept my sights on
the spot where I knew the lion to be, finger on trigger, and
eagerly awaiting the critical moment.

The flames spread rapidly, fanned by the strong evening
breeze, and every instant I expected to see the beast charge out

at me. Suddenly, with an angry roar, he came bounding toward me in huge leaps. I fired full into his chest, raking him. As it did not stop him, I let him have the second barrel. Still he came straight for me, though I had now hit him three times in the body. Meanwhile, Hamisi had rejoined me and extended my second rifle. I made the exchange rapidly, got my sights on and fired full in the lion's face. My bullet crashed through the frontal bone into the brain, and the great tawny body fell with a thud at my feet. He was dead.

Those had been anxious seconds, and I was tingling all over. At one moment I had thought it impossible to stop him, and that he must get me down. As it was, I had only saved myself from a bad mauling by a matter of a second or two. I measured the distance between his body and where I stood—six feet!

When periodically stationed in Nairobi, I often slipped out on Sundays and hunted lions on the Athi Plains. Sometimes I was in luck; at others, far from it. Chance plays a big part in success with big game shooting.

One such morning I shall always remember. Hamisi alone was with me. It was a very hot and tiring day, and we had drawn blank. At noon, I decided to halt and rest awhile, and have my lunch. At that very moment, Hamisi whispered hoarsely: " *Simba, Bwana!* *Simba watatu!* "

I was in no mood at that moment to give battle to a lion, and certainly not three at once. I was dead weary, hot and fed up; and now to find my path to the only available bit of shade for miles around barred by three fool lions! The combination of annoyances had upset my nerves and frayed my temper. I wanted lions, and was hunting them; but was not in physical condition just at that moment to tackle three. I knew it.

Quickly I decided to let them go on their way, and save their hides; and stood motionless to watch what happened. The three beasts moved back slowly, and finally allowed us to proceed to the small ridge crowned by that lonely tree. I wanted that haven of rest more than the lions. Arrived at this vantage-point, I had a good look round over the plains. Instead of three lions, I now counted six of the brutes. There was only one maned-lion among them; and he did not look much of a trophy. Yet lions are vermin, and should be killed whenever possible. But six . . . !

All of them now stood in a crescent formation, not more

than one hundred and fifty yards away. They were walking about uncertainly in a narrow circle, eyeing us suspiciously, lashing their tails to and fro, and growling angrily at intervals. They did not seem to be in a hurry to move off, and I could not have my lunch until they did. I was rather surprised at their behaviour. It was not according to Cocker!

The maned lion now came forward for about thirty to forty yards, and stood staring rudely at us. His attitude was more puzzled than menacing. This was too much for my liking, and so I let rip. Owing to my exhausted condition, my hand was none too steady; and I missed shamefully. My bullet hit the ground over the brute's back. I swore savagely under my breath. I now tried a second shot, and again missed badly; but it served to send them all about their business. All six now turned and trotted away from us. I let them go.

If I could not kill, then I would not merely maim or wound —not even a lion. But I saw one of them halt and turn round, broadside on, offering a splendid traget. I was sore with myself about the two rotten shots, and tried another. It was a rather long one, but registered. The beast went down for the count, and did not move. We waited to see what would happen, but the others trotted on and soon disappeared from view.

We went forward to the kill, and found it was a lioness. We started in to skin her straight away. Hamisi, however, called out sharply that he had seen a maned lion go into a clump of bushes not fifty yards from us. Not liking the look of his cover, I remained where I was but fired two shots into the place where Hamisi said he had gone. The beast did not make his appearance, and there came no growling. With eyes intently fixed on the danger spot and sights levelled at it, I now went forward slowly. Hamisi, busy with the skinning, did not follow me with my second rifle.

To my joy, out jumped the maned lion. He offered a perfect target, and I sighted and pressed the trigger. The sharp click of the striker told me that the worst had happened. I had quite forgotten to reload. For a moment or two, my heart stopped beating. Through my own folly and supreme carelessness, I was now facing an infuriated lion with an empty rifle. I deserved all that was coming to me, though that is not how I felt.

I knew that the only sensible thing to do was to stand perfectly still, and keep my eyes fixed on those of the lion. This sounds all very simple ; but, in actual practice, it is far from being so. I do not know how close that lion came to me ; but do know that, several times, I was sorely tempted to bolt back to Hamisi for my second rifle. Then, to my great relief, the lion turned and slunk back into cover.

At the same moment, Hamisi came running up with my second rifle. Luckily, he had seen my predicament and sensed that I had not reloaded. His look of reproach, as he handed me the charged weapon, stung ; but I knew it was well deserved.

I fired a shot into the bush with the heavier gun, and instantly out came the lion. He was now bristling with fury, and full of battle. For a moment, he stood facing me and gathering himself for a spring. That brief hesitation proved his undoing, for my next bullet hit him full in the chest, raked his body, and knocked him down. He must have died instantly.

Frankly, I did not deserve that lion. Instead of killing him, by all the rules of the game I should myself have been mauled or killed.

My self-contempt for my gross negligence was unutterable. Hamisi's silence was more biting than words ; and he made plain all he felt by quietly taking the rifle from my hands, reloading and handing it back.

CHAPTER XII

NATIVE GAME HUNTERS' METHODS

DURING the years I wandered about Africa, either in my official or private capacity, I learned much about the various methods employed by different tribes in trapping or hunting big game. In many areas I saw cases of gross barbarity. Any means is legitimate in the eyes of Africans to achieve the downfall of their human enemies or the wild creatures. Life is cheap. You cannot expect humane ideals from people who make a practice of taking the sick and dying out in the bush to be devoured by hyenas or other savage beasts. It is considered by many tribes a dreadful thing for one of their relations to die in his hut.

The Wakikuyu, and some of the other tribes of Kenya, defend their territory against aggression from neighbours by digging cleverly concealed staked-pits in the paths or scattered about in the forests.

The royal sport of the European hunter in Africa is well enough known, but little has ever been recorded of the natives' hunting. The African tribesman, from long practice and urgent need, has become an expert in capturing and killing wild animals of all varieties ; and a study of their methods well repays the time devoted to it. Probably, these have altered but little from the days of prehistoric man. Their skill is exceptional ; their courage beyond reproach ; and their casual indifference to death or severe injuries is that of a born fatalist.

Their traps are both ingenious and effective ; while their ordinary hunting, without aid of traps, is equally instructive. From the dawn of Time, primitive man learned to feed and clothe himself by killing wild creatures. He has always been just as much a victim of the law of the jungles as have been the animals themselves. With both it has been ever a case of kill : or be killed.

From time to time, I have felt it incumbent upon me to lodge a strong protest against some of their barbarously cruel traps for both large and small game ; but I knew it to be futile. They have no rifles or ammunition, and their only weapons are spear, bow and arrow, trap or poison. It is impossible to stop them using these age-old methods unless they are allowed rifles ; and that solution is out of the question, for obvious reasons. Kinanjui, the king of the Wakikuyu, answered my protest against the cruelty of some his tribes' traps by demanding rifles so that the game could be shot. Unerringly, he had put his finger on the weak spot in my case.

I had seen some elephant-pits in his country, at the base of Mount Kenya, which were most inhumane. They were large enough to hold the entire body of an elephant, and so expertly hidden that I only found them accidentally. At the bottom of each had been fixed a number of sharp-pointed stakes, spears or arrows ; and, on these, any unwary animal falling into the pit was impaled until such time as the hunters came to despatch the suffering beast.

I found a modicum of consolation in the knowledge that, probably, not one elephant-pit out of every hundred ever accomplished the purpose for which it was designed. The acute sense of smell and hearing of elephants makes it extremely difficult to thus trap them, no matter how cunningly concealed and constructed are the pits ; and it is rare to hear of an animal caught in them. The native of Africa, however, is a super-optimist. The profusion of these pits in the forest-lands of the Wakikuyu is ever a source of danger to the unsuspecting traveller through their country.

When a herd of elephants journeys through the forest, each beast holds the tip of its trunk to the ground ; and, by tapping every few paces, can easily detect the trap before stepping on to the weak superstructure. You may catch an elephant by trickery once : but *only* once. The moment they encounter any ground which is the least bit suspicious, they always tap it carefully ; and then, if still doubtful, will make a wide detour to avoid the hidden danger.

It is only when they are stampeded that they are really liable to fall into one of these pits, for then their ordinary forms of caution are dormant.

The methods employed in hunting elephants do not vary to any appreciable extent throughout Central and Eastern Africa. It is generally the practice either to dig pits, set booby-traps with weighted spears, or wound with poisoned arrows.

The Pygmies, those curious dwarf people inhabiting the Lake Kivu area of Central Africa, mostly employ the poisoned arrow plan. Once an animal is so wounded, these quaint little folk follow up until it drops dead. They will eat the meat of an animal so poisoned ; and, in fact, will eat even putrefying flesh in preference to fresh meat. They have pretty tough insides and are blessed with the digestion of an ostrich, being second only to the hyena as carrion-eaters. Their slogan seems to be : " the higher the meat, the more tasty." What is one man's food, however, is another man's poison !

During one of my visits to Uganda, I learned from an old chief many vastly interesting things about the tribal customs in hunting a variety of animals. He showed me some of his people in the pursuit of game, and also some of the clever traps in general use.

The former kings of Uganda, and a few of their principal chiefs, used to make the hunting of antelope and gazelle a pleasurable pastime. They followed the chase for the pure love of the sport. With the common people, however, hunting was either a profession or else solely a means of obtaining food. The elements of sport did not enter into their calculations at all ; they killed so that they might live.

The tribal elephant hunters were men whose fathers had followed the profession from earliest childhood ; and the tricks of the trade were handed down from father to son. They were trained to observe every single peculiarity of the beast, and were familiar with its haunts and habits. Different modes of hunting the animal were in vogue, and are still followed to this day in various parts of Uganda. The physical features of the country hunted largely dictate the process practised. In some areas, where it is mostly forests, the plan employed is more humane than those used elsewhere.

On the previous day, the Muganda elephant hunters spend their time in most careful preparations. Their weapons are spears with leaf-shaped blades, fully six inches long, and having an iron shank of about a foot in length. These are inserted in a wooden shaft, which is about five feet in length and anything up to two feet in diameter. The weapon weighs about as much as a strong man can lift and manipulate.

After the spears have been sharpened, they are taken to the temple of the god of the chase, Dungu, where they are left all night at the feet of the god. He is propitiated with a gift of

OLD-TIME SHOOTING SAFARI LEAVING CAMP

a pot of beer and a goat. The Baganda, like most African tribes, are intensely superstitious ; and rigidly observe every custom ordained by their tribal medicine-men for appeasing the gods in a variety of public and private matters. Being a god of a tribe in Africa is a pleasant occupation, for their stomachs being well-filled is considered to be of primary importance ; and every care is always taken to see that they want for no luxury.

Teetotalism, apparently, is not regarded as a godlike virtue, for pots of native-brewed beer always form part of any offering made to these heathen deities.

On the morning of the actual hunt, the professional elephant killers complete their final arrangements and partake of a hearty meal. Then they proceed to the neighbourhood of the herd chosen for attack, and climb up trees already selected for the purpose. Here they conceal themselves with their heavy spears, and wait patiently until the herd passes beneath them.

When the elephants approach, the hunters choose one with large tusks and, as it walks beneath the tree, the spearsman draws back his right arm and drops the weapon with all his force. They try to strike the beast squarely between the shoulders. If the spear is driven home to the shaft, the elephant is disabled at the first blow.

If the thrust is successful, the animal sinks down ; and the hunters jump down from the trees to despatch it. If the blow is only partially successful, the spearsman calls to a companion for help. The latter waves a piece of skin to attract the attention of the infuriated elephant. Naturally, it rushes straight at what appears to be the cause of its pain. The whole plan of attack is similar to that employed by the bull-fighters of Spain and Mexico. The aides are merely the matadors of the bull-ring.

When the wounded elephant is close to him, the African matador drops the bit of skin to the ground and, as the huge animal halts to crush it under foot, tries to spear it once again.

Meanwhile, the herd of elephants has crashed off through the forest. At the very first moment of alarm, they were off and did not pause to ascertain the cause. As a general rule, however, the hunters will kill from one to four animals before the herd finally makes good its escape. The spearsmen and their aides work together like a well-trained football team immediately an animal is wounded, for first one and then another has to attract the attention of the beast and spear it as best he can.

Their skill and agility are born of long practice ; and seldom is a native hunter the victim of the elephant.

Some of the other tribes hunt elephants from trees also, but in a much more lazy fashion. This is more suitable to the average African temperament. They employ a booby-trap, in which a weighted spear is suspended from the trees over well-trodden elephant-paths. The animal releases these in passing by striking its foot against a cord, stretched across the path at a height of from eight to twelve inches above the ground. Once a beast is thus wounded, the hunters follow up until it becomes faint from loss of blood or is isolated from the remainder of the herd. Then it is surrounded and speared to death.

Another method of killing these beasts, and employed more generally on the open grass-plains or where there is only small bush, is for three or four men to carry long throwing-spears and approach close to a feeding herd. They crawl along the ground, and so silently that they can get right into the centre of the animals without their presence being detected. The elephants find it difficult to pick up their scent, for their own odour is not unlike that of the African native ; both are highly flavoured and strong smelling.

Once in their midst, the hunters deliberately pick out a big tusker and spear it in the side of the head. The attacker then has to escape as best he can from the now maddened and terrified beasts. This is always a most exciting and dangerous time for the hunters. The spearsmen's assistants help by rushing boldly up and spearing the wounded animal again and again, and thus divert its attention from the first man. In this way, by taking turns in spearing the quarry, they soon kill it.

The plan, of course, requires infinite courage, resource and steady nerves. Only men who can be trusted implicitly to stand by their comrades when an infuriated elephant charges are ever enlisted for this special type of work. Not infrequently, one of the native hunters is either killed or severely injured ; but such mishaps do not seem to deter them from repeating this hazardous form of elephant hunting.

I have seen the Bulemezi tribe commonly employ a novel foot-trap for elephants. A deep hole is dug in the ground, generally in elephant paths, to a size a little larger than a beast's foot. At the bottom of the hole is placed a stout stake, sharpened at the top and notched a few inches down so as to break off easily. The thick end is firmly embedded in the bottom of the trap, while the sharpened end points upward. The trap is then carefully covered over so as to obliterate all traces of any interference with the surface of the ground.

When an unsuspecting elephant treads on the light covering of this hole, its foot sinks in and is firmly spiked. As the beast tries to rub off the stake, it pierces further into the foot ; and then it breaks off where notched. The sharp spike is left firmly fixed in the wound, and lames the animal. It soon becomes isolated from the herd, and falls an easy victim to the hunters who follow up, waiting and watching for a chance to kill it without undue interference from the other elephants. Quite a number of these pits are prepared in each elephant-path, so that one or more animals from a passing herd are certain to become victims.

Most of the ivory obtained by the professional elephant hunters among the tribes of Uganda becomes the perquisite of the king—a kind of civil tax. He rewards the intrepid hunters with gifts of wives and cattle. Both are considered worth their weight in gold, and a man's wealth in the majority of African tribes is measured by the number of wives and cattle he happens to possess.

The chief of the district in which the animals are killed also levies a tax on all the ivory obtained. The system of tribal graft is as perfect as anywhere else in the world, and might make a Tammany Ward politician of New York sick with envy. Ivory is worth anything from ten to thirteen shillings a pound in the local markets ; and a good pair of tusks ought to average from 120 to 160 pounds in weight.

The Baganda do not normally eat the flesh of elephants so killed, but sell it to the neighbouring tribes. The proceeds of these sales are the sole property of the actual hunters, and are free from taxation or any other form of graft. Most other African tribes, however, are very fond of elephant meat. I have only tried it once, and that on New Year's Day, 1910, when with the Roosevelt Expedition marching through Uganda and the Congo to the Sudan. We had soup made from an elephant's trunk, and it was most nutritious. It had a very strong flavour, was very rich and thick, and rather like a super-oxtail soup. It had been boiling all day. Six spoonfuls, however, proved a meal in itself ; and I found it impossible to eat anything else at dinner.

A few years later, I happened to be in a barber's shop in

New York. The manicurist recognized me for an Englishman at once, and tried to be conversational. Finally, she asked if I had ever yet tasted chop-suey, the favourite dish of the Chinese restaurants in New York and Chicago.

" No," I answered quietly, " but I've tried elephant trunk soup, and it was delicious."

The conversation ended abruptly. I presume she thought me such a colossal liar that she could not compete.

Most tribes in the heart of Africa hunt the buffalo. It is killed chiefly for the rich meat, but is also much prized for the tough hide. The latter is employed to make shields and sandals, both of which are very strong, heavy and durable.

The buffalo is generally stalked. The native hunter creeps up close to a herd to inspect it. When he sees a really good animal, he spears it and lies down flat on the ground to avoid the mad charge. Another man then dashes up, again spears the wounded beast, and thus turns attention away from the first spearsman. Three or four hunters will soon despatch a buffalo in this manner.

Sometimes, however, I have seen native hunters employing dogs to run down the buffalo. The duty of the hounds is to assist in keeping the quarry at bay while the hunters run in and spear the beasts. These dogs are very courageous and do their work excellently.

In some districts I have seen foot-traps used for catching buffalo, but somewhat different in principle to those employed for elephants. They consisted of a ring of stout creepers, through the sides of which had been pushed strong thorns from the outside to the centre, but leaving a small open space in the middle. This crown of thorns was fastened to a strong stake or stout tree by a thick cord of twisted creepers, and then the foot-trap was laid over a shallow hole in the path leading to the usual wallow or watering-place of the buffalo herds.

When a beast stepped upon this ring, its foot slipped through it, the thorns penetrated the upper part of the foot or fetlock, and the animal was held prisoner. The more it tugged and kicked to free itself of the obstruction, the more firmly was it caught in the trap. Presently, the owner of the device came along, found the buffalo and promptly speared it to death. Any attempt made by the beast to escape its impending doom was futile, for the rope of creepers was strong enough to hold the most powerful buffalo ever calved.

The Wakikuyu use the same type of deep and staked pit for buffalo as employed for elephants.

In hunting hippopotami, most natives use a spear or harpoon ; though a few tribes also employ booby-traps or pits. The Baganda do not eat the flesh, and therefore seldom hunt them. Their most common plan is to erect a spear-trap on a path generally used by the hippopotami in going to or from the water. The beast falls into this cleverly concealed pit and is impaled on the spear-point. The Baganda take so little interest in the fat and flesh of the hippo that they rarely go near these traps, so that any poor beast thus impaled generally dies a lingering death. It is a heartless act of cruelty ; but the African is a savage by instinct and custom.

On some of the Sesse Islands, and at other groups, in the Victoria Lake, I have often seen the natives out in their frail bark-canoes when engaged in harpooning schools of hippo in the water. They use long lines, with floats, attached to the harpoon so that, when an animal is struck and sinks, the hunters can track it until the quarry is killed. This humane plan is not dictated by any sense of mercy, but devised to enable them to get their beast or recover their harpoon if the throw has been bungled.

Round the shores of the Albert Edward Lake, I have come across native traps for hippo which were entirely different from any employed elsewhere. They had built a stout scaffold of logs over a customary hippo path, and made a real booby-trap. It was loaded with a heavily weighted spear-head, which was released by the animal in passing under the scaffold. Once so speared, it was easily killed by the native hunters.

Like the Wakavirondo of the Victoria Lake, these tribesmen are extremely fond of the fat of the hippo. They use it mostly for greasing their bodies and anointing their woolly hair, while the meat is much prized for eating.

The Wandorobo people, who live in the forests or rock caves round Mount Elgon and elsewhere in that region of Kenya, are by far the best and most ingenious hunters in all Africa. They are a very primitive people, and support themselves almost entirely by their prowess in hunting game.

They carry a harpoon-shaped wooden handle, which is fairly heavy, and also a large quiver of darts with iron heads as sharp as needles. The heads of the darts are smeared with a deadly poison obtained from a mountain tree, and each is carefully wrapped up in a piece of skin carried expressly for this purpose. The slightest scratch from one of these darts proves instantly fatal ; but the Wandorobo always eat the meat of any animal killed with this deadly weapon.

On getting close to the game pursued, the Wandorobo hunters take out two darts from the quiver, remove the skin covering, and fix one with great care into the heavy harpoon-handle. This is then carried in the right hand, while the spare dart is held in the left. They enter the bush in a state of complete nudity, and creep forward stealthily to within a few paces of the nearest animal hunted.

The naked hunter delivers his blow with all his strength, and then immediately dives through the cover to avoid a probable charge. If elephants or buffalo are being hunted, the herd generally stampedes as soon as one is wounded. The hunter then inserts his second dart in the handle, and follows up the wounded beast. I was told by one of my Wandorobo hunters that the most deadly spot at which to aim is that part of the stomach where are the small intestines, or roughly about the flank of the animal.

These Wandorobo hunters are famed throughout the equatorial belt of Africa for their great ingenuity in hunting ; and, without any doubt, are far and away the most proficient trackers in all Africa. It is probable that a 'Ndorobo hunter is without a peer in this difficult art. I have tried many men of various tribes, but have never found one who could touch the skill of a 'Ndorobo.

When out hunting with two of these wild cavemen one day, we came across a fine but small herd of eland. I wanted meat for myself and porters, and fired at the biggest bull. It was a long shot, because they were so restless and I was pressed for time. I only succeeded in wounding the beast. Much crestfallen, I saw the herd, including the wounded bull, gallop off out of sight. That promised a long stalk, and always getting further away from my camp and, consequently, a greater distance to carry back the meat. But I had to go on now, and could not let a wounded animal suffer. I cursed myself for the rotten shot, and followed up.

We went at a run, my two Wandorobo trackers in advance. We were soon travelling over hard and rocky ground, in open country. It was impossible for my eye to follow the spoor, though I tried hard enough to do so. I soon abandoned the attempt and trusted to my cavemen trackers. I knew they would not fail me. Nor did they. Abruptly, the leading tracker turned swiftly to the left, and we followed without questioning. He was now running fast, head bent down to the ground and body doubled, with a forefinger extended like the nose of a pointer-dog. He ran on rapidly, never once pausing or at fault. It was as much as I could do to keep at his heels.

Half an hour later, he brought me straight to the wounded eland bull, which had left the herd and gone off by itself. The beast was standing out in the open, broadside on to me, and patently in great distress. One merciful bullet ended its pain.

Now, I had seen no tracks or blood spoor to indicate that this wounded animal was in solitary flight from the point where the 'Ndorobo had turned off to the left. It was one of the most marvellous feats of tracking big game which I have ever seen. Everything was against the man, yet he made no mistake.

I gave that 'Ndorobo very full marks indeed ; and a handsome present of rupees !

CHAPTER XIII

" COW-PEOPLE " WHO THRASH LIONS

THE Banyoro people of Uganda are among the most quaint and interesting tribes in Equatorial Africa. Generally, they are spoken of as the " Cow-People," because they are very powerful clansmen whose wealth, health and religion are all intimately connected with the peaceful domestic cow.

These people have many strange customs and beliefs. It is considered, for instance, a positive degradation for any man of the upper classes of the Banyoro to dig or till the soil, and nothing will induce them to become agriculturists. Milk and meat are their staple forms of diet, but they buy cereals and other products of the land from the neighbouring cultivators. Like the Masai of Kenya, they are esssentially a pastoral race.

I spent a considerable time among these strange tribesmen when in Uganda, and have a high regard for their personal bravery and charming courtesy. The only wild beast these " Cow-People " really seem to fear is the leopard. Their chief weapon, both of offence and defence, is a long stick ; and, armed only with this simple stave, they willingly go out to face a lion which is attacking their precious herds of cattle.

They will tackle a lion quite fearlessly, and drive him away from their neighbourhood. All they do is to round up the beast and thrash it unmercifully with long sticks ; and then " the king of beasts " tucks his tail between his legs and beats an undignified retreat.

I had often heard them speak of this custom, but frankly had not believed it could be true. Although I knew them to be brave beyond all question, for I had seen them face up boldly to a wounded elephant in full charge when out hunting with me, yet I also knew them to be inveterate thieves and barefaced liars. As thieves they are very subtle, and always conceal their sins by the most shameless lying. One of their favourite mottoes is : " Keep a grave face, even though you laugh behind your back ! "

In January of 1910, I paid a visit to the *Mukama*, or the King of Bunyoro, and spent the best part of a week encamped near his chief residence. He accorded me a most royal welcome. The king was a tall, distinguished looking native, with a most intelligent type of face. I was told that he ruled with a rod of iron over a large and unruly kingdom. He had come to the throne through the customary bloody warfare, for on the death of the ruling monarch his sons fight among themselves until only one survives. As these dusky sovereigns have many wives and large families, the fratricidal war of accession is both prolonged and bloody.

I invited him to lunch with me one day, and he accepted with alacrity. The guest of honour arrived at my camp, dressed in a multi-coloured ceremonial robe and spotlessly clean, but was followed by a large retinue of white-gowned courtiers. My heart sank within me, for my stores of provisions could not stand up against such an invasion of hungry mouths. I need not have worried, however, for the king commanded them to sit down outside my tent and wait until we had finished our meal. They were permitted to watch their ruler eat and drink heartily of everything offered—customs of the tribe being waived for the special occasion ; but were not allowed to join him at the festive board. It was a relief to my mind. After seeing their king gorge himself at my expense, I had no fancy to entertain his army of courtiers.

The old man was so delighted with my hospitality that he volunteered to show me how his " Cow-People " thrashed a lion with their sticks. I jumped at this offer ; and it was arranged that the affair should take place on the following morning. A lion had been prowling about their herds for some days, and all were fed-up with the beast's sinister attentions. In Bunyoro, the people hunt lions and leopards only on the express order of their king ; and he gives his august command for these frolics whenever the pests are particularly troublesome.

As had been arranged, I went off next morning to the appointed rendezvous, and found fully a thousand Munyoro assembled to hunt down the obnoxious lion. The king himself was noticeable by his absence, but I welcomed this as it gave me a free hand to go where I listed and see all that happened. Some of the tribesmen already had gone forward to track down the lion to his lair. Now we only awaited a report from them as to his actual whereabouts.

We had not long to wait, for word was soon brought back that the scouts had definitely located the beast. Immediately the large army of Munyoro went forward, making a wide sweeping movement to encircle the quarry in his lair. Beating down the scrub and tall grass as they advanced, they shouted and sang at the top of their lungs, while the war-drums beat with monotonous rhythm. There was no attempt at concealment, and the whole throng acted like a lot of schoolboys out for a picnic. Slowly the vast crowd narrowed their circle, and gradually the lion was enclosed in their midst.

With the exception of a few petty Chiefs, who seemed to be privileged to bear spears, the Munyoro were armed only with long sticks or big wooden clubs. I have never seen anything quite like that astounding lion hunt. It was an amazing spectacle, quite unique and worth travelling many thousands of miles to see.

Above the din could now be heard the angry growls and savage snarls of the thoroughly frightened lion. He had discovered, after several vain efforts to break through the encircling throng of natives, that his foes had surrounded him completely. He voiced his furious resentment in no unmistakable fashion. Time and time again, he made a desperate attempt to evade his impending fate, rushing hither and thither, but always being beaten back into cover again by the hearty showers of blows. The Munyoro wielded their sticks and clubs with real spirit and keen enjoyment ; obviously they did not believe in half measures.

Occasionally the lion tried to leap over the heads of the solid human wall confining him in an ever-narrowing circle. They were always too quick for him, and he was driven back under a terrific onslaught of sticks. The end was not long postponed.

The hedge of sticks and bludgeons pressed forward relentlessly, and now the front ranks of the Munyoro were within ten yards or so of the lion. The beast made one final effort to escape, and sprang straight at the horde of human beings in one sector of the circle. He was met with a deadly battering from sticks and clubs, and fell stunned at their feet. They rushed at him like a pack of wolves, and beat the lion's body to a pulp. I doubt if there was a single bone unbroken.

Only two or three men had been slightly mauled by the claws of the enraged beast. They did not seem to mind, and refused my proffered medical treatment with a laugh of derision. They ran and joined the others, who were all dancing and singing in triumph round that pulped carcass.

The " king of beasts " whipped like a cur and clubbed to death by " Cow-People," could there possibly be a more shameful death ? I had it in my heart to pity that poor lion.

Seldom has an animal been known to escape from such a massed thrashing by the Munyoro.

The ordinary villagers in Uganda hunt the smaller antelope and gazelle in their spare time, not for the sport but only to stock their larders with meat. I have often seen them at work, and found it interesting. There is always a leader appointed over the hunters, and he maintains a special pack of dogs solely for this purpose. He corresponds to our M.F.H., and employs several whippers-in for the hounds. Before the day chosen for the hunt, nets are erected so that the game can be driven into them ; and both men and dogs take part subsequently in a drive over a large tract of country where antelope and gazelle are known to be abundant.

The dogs used, as also in the case of the Nandi tribe in Kenya, are a small type of lurcher, yellowish brown in colour. They are very fast, and splendidly trained for the work required of them. The leader of the pack has a bell attached to his collar, so that the hunters may know whereabouts the pack is working.

On the morning of the day selected, the leader blows his horn to call together the huntsmen and as a warning to all others to keep clear of the game paths in the vicinity. They hunt in the open glades of the forest belts, using nets of about four feet wide and twenty feet long. These are fixed to stout stakes, which are driven into the ground so as to keep the nets upright and firm. They join together as many as are necessary to enclose the area to be driven, and arrange them in a semicircle.

A large number of natives act as beaters, following up behind the dogs and driving the game into the nets. Here the animals are quickly speared or clubbed to death by men, stationed out of sight, behind them. The nets are strengthened wherever there happen to be cross-paths which the game are likely to use. They are made of strong twine, prepared from aloe leaves, which are shredded and worked into meshes by the hunters themselves.

The beaters shout at the top of their lungs, and the dogs yelp sharply like a pack of foxhounds giving tongue. It is by no means uncommon for as many as fifty or more antelope and gazelle to be killed on one day in a game-drive of this type. On a number of occasions, I have seen even larger bags made.

The African native process of making strong rope and string is interesting. All Africans, and the boys particularly, are experts in preparing traps for snaring game, birds and small mammals. Seeing how limited are their means for keeping their larders filled with meat, other than by these methods, it is not surprising that they are so skilful. The making of snares and bird-traps has become second nature to these primitive people.

If you have never tried to make string from the bark of trees, you can take a leaf out of the notebook of the African aborigine. They are experts. String, or *mugie*, is used by the natives for many different purposes, and is generally manufactured either from the bark of certain trees, such as the aloe, or else obtained from the tendons of animals. The process of making never varies, only the material employed.

The first step is to peel the rods ; the second, to chew the stripped bark ; and, lastly, to roll the masticated fibre thus obtained into a yarn of the requisite thickness. Two such yarns are then rolled, the one immediately after the other ; and, as they are formed, are again rolled in the reverse direction into a two-strand rope. The same form of string, in different sizes and qualities, is used for the making of snares. Custom ordains that string used for certain purposes must always be made by the males ; and for others, only by the women. The men, however, must make all string and rope employed in trapping wild creatures.

The tendons of which string is made are chiefly obtained from the domestic animals, such as either the ox, sheep or goat. A very small amount is secured from the wild game snared or killed ; and, occasionally, some tribes obtain their requirements of this necessity by barter with the Wandorobo hunters.

The method by which the tendons are extracted from the carcass of an animal by the Wakikuyu people shows considerable ingenuity. After the beast is skinned, the tendons are taken

AN UGLY WART-HOG

up singly and placed in a cleft stick ; and this is gradually worked backwards and thus separates the flesh from the ligaments. They are then dried in the sun and carefully preserved, being only split up and twisted into thread as required.

The cord made by the Wakikuyu is always formed in two strands, each consisting of a single yarn. Each yarn is made by rolling the fibre between the right palm and right thigh, in a direction downwards and outwards. Immediately afterwards, the two yarns are twisted together by a return movement of the hand, which is now directed upwards and inwards. The string is thus made in varying degrees of thickness. I have never seen anything in the nature of, or as heavy as, hemp-rope. When thick rope is required, wild vines are roughly twisted together or else strips of bark are used. You can find this material employed in the making of suspension bridges over rivers or for snares to entrap elephant, buffalo or other large beasts.

The Nandi tribe in Kenya, who are really cousins of the famous Masai, use spears and hunt *en masse*. When a large body of game has been surrounded by hundreds of Nandi warriors they shoot at them with bows and arrows, or else run in and spear as many as possible before the animals break clear. These people greatly love meat ; and after every such hunt, there is always a big feast to celebrate the filling of their larders.

I have seen boys of many tribes throughout Africa, and even as far south as Rhodesia, catching rats in traps that have been baited with melon seeds. They cook the rodents with all the fur on and without cleaning. I asked one native why this was done, and he assured me that to do otherwise than cook the rat entire would be to spoil its delicate flavour when eaten. It struck me as a most revolting practice.

The older native boys soon learn the art of making effective game-pits and other types of traps. To prepare a game-pit, it is customary to build a long artificial hedge of thorn-bush and tree branches, which may extend for a mile or more. In various points, they leave a funnel-shaped gap. At the mouth of each of these a pit is dug, and then carefully covered over with thin pieces of stick, while on top of this are placed dry leaves and a little earth. The concealment is perfect. The game is then driven up to the fence, and run along it in search of an exit through which to escape from their pursuers. Naturally, they bolt through the first hole found, which happens

I

to be the funnel, and thus fall into the pits in large numbers. They are then clubbed to death or speared.

On a number of occasions I have ruthlessly destroyed traps of a similar character made by the Mashonas on my ranch in Southern Rhodesia. After a time, they learned to leave my land free of their traps and snares. Instead of a pit, however, the Mashonas suspend a noose or heavy log over the gap. On running through the opening in the hedge, the poor beasts were either strangled by the noose or else imprisoned under the log.

Often I stumbled across simple and ingenious snares set by the Mashonas on my land in Southern Rhodesia, all of which were almost identical with those employed generally by the tribes much further north. I sternly forbade their use and always destroyed any found. The cruelty of many of these snares was repulsive ; and I much preferred to see the small numbers of game roaming freely over my ranch. I never shot them myself, and would not allow them to be hunted by others.

The most universal form of snare, and used commonly by the Pygmies, Nandi, Muganda, Mashonas, Matabele and other tribes throughout Africa, is a pliant stick bent so as to act as a strong spring. A piece of stout string is tied to the end, fashioned into a noose and then suspended over a recognized game-path. The bent stick is so delicately fastened down that it is released the moment an animal puts its head through the noose, and thus swings the captive off its feet. It is soon strangled.

Other traps for small game or birds are operated on the same principle as the ordinary brick-traps in use in many parts of Europe. A large slab of flat stone leans over a game-path, being held in position by a light stick. An animal clumsily bumps into it, the support is knocked away, and the stone falls down on it. It either kills or imprisons the beast. Periodically, the trap-setter visits his snares ; but the game, if not killed outright, may linger for several days before being found and despatched.

Another favourite type of trap, and used for birds, is a small cone-shaped cage made of stout reeds. It has a small opening on one side, and this is placed next to the ground. In the mouth of this aperture is suspended a noose made by a hair pulled from a cow's tail, and the bird puts its head through this in trying to reach the corn-bait within the cage. The moment it withdraws, the noose tightens round the neck and holds it fast. The more the bird struggles frantically to free itself, the tighter becomes the noose until the victim is strangled.

In the forests of Uganda, especially close to villages, I have often found pits in use for trapping wild pig or the small antelope and gazelle. They are dug down for six feet into the ground, and are about four by three feet. Stakes are placed at the bottom, so that the animals are impaled on falling into the hole. They are so cleverly hidden that even the trap-setters have to exercise great care to avoid being themselves caught. In fact, when travelling through the native hunters' territories, Europeans always have to keep a sharp look out to dodge these dreadful pits. Often I have only just escaped, by a narrow margin, from such a ghastly fate.

When journeying through Uganda in 1910, I came across a most ingenious spring-trap in the forests. A remarkably fine waterbuck had just been caught and was still struggling to free itself, while being slowly strangled to death. I put it out of its misery. Much as I would have liked that wonderful head of horns, I left it to the rightful owner. There is an unwritten law throughout Africa that the traps are the sacred property of the person setting them, and under no circumstances must they be pilfered.

The native of Africa is never humane, and his primitive methods of stocking his larder are often horribly brutal in their callous cruelty. But he seldom lacks meat to eat.

CHAPTER XIV

INDIAN AND AFRICAN BUFFALO

THE Asiatic buffalo, like his African cousin, makes his home chiefly in swampy country. They are generally to be located near large bodies of water, where can be made the wallow so essential to their existence. Neither species is a weakling and both can be highly dangerous and even fatal to the hunter.

During my service in India, I was invited to join a shikar party beyond Gaya in the region of the Son River, a tributary of the Ganges. I accepted gladly, for my host proposed to hunt tiger, buffalo and rhinoceros.

There were twenty-six elephants in that shikar host, each howdah carrying two or more Europeans. Some of the sportsmen were old hands at the game : others novices. I classed myself unreservedly in the latter category.

We found our first herd of buffalo in heavy jungle, a part of the lowland where grass grew about fifteen feet in height. It offered a good hiding place for any kind of wild beast ; and was, I may emphasize, a particularly dangerous spot in which to go out hunting for big game.

Twice we caught a fleeting glimpse of a tiger, so brief a view in such a tangle of jungle-growth that nobody had a chance to shoot. In fact, the jungle was so thick that without our elephant mounts it would have been quite impossible to do any hunting at all. A sportsman on foot could have seen only the cane-like grass around him and a little patch of blue sky overhead. Against a dangerous wild animal of any species in such surroundings, the dice were heavily loaded against the man.

Then it was that I understood why we employed trained shikar elephants, and eschewed hunting either on foot or on horseback as they do in Africa. Such methods would have been absolutely suicidal in this type of country.

Failing to get to grips with the buffalo herd on the east

bank, we crossed the river. It was a splendid sight to see our huge elephants walk right down the bank into the water until almost submerged. The Indian shikaris and mahouts stood up on the small patch of hide showing above the water. In this way, the large animals walked or swam across in single file, straight as an arrow's flight.

We had no sooner touched the opposite bank than the mighty spread of a buffalo's horns showed up clearly above the grass. Unfortunately, however, the beast bolted before any of us could take aim. The shikar party was promptly divided into two parties, each to act as beaters for the other. Thus re-arranged, we had not gone far, possibly a quarter of a mile, into the long grass when a rush and deep grunt warned us to be prepared for " action front." Our elephants halted imme-diately ; and, a moment later, a rhinoceros broke cover. The totally unexpected again ! Two of the party fired, and the ungainly beast went down. He did not rise again.

We thought that the day would pass without getting any buffalo, for the firing must have driven them further afield. In the distance, we could see the sun-helmets of the second party coming slowly toward us. I turned to my companion in the howdah, and remarked : " Poor sport for us, old chap ! "

I spoke too soon.

Scarcely had I uttered those words than there came the sharp crack of a heavy rifle from our front. By this time we were out of the long grass into much shorter growth. The mahouts halted our elephants, and we all held our rifles ready while our eyes searched ahead.

We could see the grass waving and hear the crash of some big body rushing toward us. Suddenly, a huge buffalo bull, really magnificent to behold, broke out of cover into full view. Blood and red froth was streaming from its nostrils, and its eyes glared savagely. Without a moment's hesitation, the mighty beast, with its formidable eight-feet sweep of horn thrust forward, rushed at the line of our elephants with a thunderous bellow of anger and the lust to kill all in sight.

I fired, the second my sights came on. My elephant, antici-pating a fight and crouching to resist the foe, threw me off my aim. I missed by yards. Then the two huge beasts met with a terrific shock, and I was jerked off my feet. It was all I could do to hold myself in the howdah as the elephant swayed about violently.

My companion now came to the rescue by putting a couple of heavy bullets behind the shoulder of the buffalo. Even then it did not go down, but staggered back to gather space for another infuriated charge at our elephant. Blood was gushing from mouth and nostrils, and eyeballs were glazing over ; but still it delivered that final ferocious attack. As it hit the bleeding side of our elephant, the buffalo fell with a mournful bellow. It must have died at the very moment of impact.

My companion and myself were put out of action for the day, for our elephant was so badly cut about by the buffalo's cruel horns that we were forced to return to camp. And there bad luck still pursued me, for I found a telegram awaiting me from my Adjutant. It recalled me from leave to attend a signalling course. From the sublime to the ridiculous !

Given a steady nerve and a good rifle, or a light one with a high velocity, the only necessity remaining is an ability to shoot quickly with some feeling of confidence in your aim. In the dense Indian jungle, nearly always your quarry is tackled at close range ; seldom greater than thirty to sixty yards. But hunting Indian buffalo on foot is no sport for the inexperienced sportsman. It is far too dangerous.

Largely due to the fact that the African buffalo is rapidly being exterminated, except in certain regions of Uganda and a few other limited areas, they are not often encountered. In my early days in Kenya, the shooting of buffalo was strictly prohibited in the Ukamba Province ; and, in other regions, only two specimens were allowed to be killed on each game licence. These two facts, quite naturally, cramped the style of most sportsmen.

On the few occasions on which I did encounter them in my wanderings through Africa, they caused me moments of acute anxiety. I would class them high up in the list of dangerous animals to be hunted. Abel Chapman, an experienced veteran, always thought them the most dangerous beast of all. And in this view he was strongly supported by Sir Frederick Jackson, a famous big game shot of the earliest days in East Africa and Uganda.

My first intimate meeting with an African buffalo in the wild state took place in the bamboo forests near the base of Mount Kenya. I was hunting in that area with John Egerton, who had recently arrived from South Africa and was anxious to get a couple of good buffalo trophies. We were accompanied by some first-class Wandorobo hunters, but their efforts signally failed to produce results for a matter of five days. We began to despair of our luck.

On the sixth morning, however, two Wandorobo trackers rushed into our camp and reported having located a small herd of three bulls and five cows. They said the animals were feeding in the forest, and within five miles of us. We set off to give battle at once. After a trying march under a blazing sun, we came in sight of them.

Two of the bulls had very massive horns, but not one of the others offered really good trophies. Before advancing, I gave Egerton concrete advice as to the best spot at which to aim to kill, and cautioned him to be extra careful in stalking up to the herd. Nothing daunted, he started his stalk. We had arranged that he was to take the biggest bull, while the next best must take his chance with either of us. I really did not want to kill one, except only in self-defence.

The herd was extremely restless and suspicious. For quite some time we could not get near enough for a safe shot. They were continually moving away from us, but we followed up. At long last, they stood still and glared morosely in our direction. We crept closer, taking advantage of every bit of cover and keeping a sharp note of any changes in the direction of the wind. My companion got within reasonable shooting range, and lifted his rifle to the shoulder to aim. I covered my bull also. Whether it was due to inexperience or excitement, I am unable to say, but Egerton, who really was a first-class shot, fired at the bull's massive shoulder and missed. The bullet went home in the ribs. Wasting no further time, I let drive at my target and killed the second big bull.

The now thoroughly enraged and startled herd took command of the situation. I stood my ground, prepared to shoot again at Egerton's bull, but the beast gave no opportunity to do so. The next instant he was almost upon us. I was far too busily engaged to see what Egerton was doing, for I was striving to get a bullet into that charging buffalo's shoulder. He was in much too direct a line for this possibility, and I was euchred.

He thundered past me, so close that I could have touched him with outstretched hand. Why he did not gore or trample me under foot, I do not know. I could see the blood frothing at mouth and nostrils, and the huge head was lowered for a deadly charge ; but he ignored me. Almost as soon as he had started,

he had disappeared from view into the bamboo forest. A
second later the rest of the herd thundered past in his wake.
As they came, I saw them divide and pass each side of where
I stood behind a small tree. It was a great relief to my pent-up
feelings.

Once they were out of sight, I looked round for Egerton.
Until that moment my mind had been paralysed into a blank
by the acuteness of the danger; and I had been only half
conscious of what was taking place about me. Every second I
had expected to be tossed skywards, or else knocked flat and
trampled under those galloping hooves. I could not have moved
an inch, even if so minded. Brain and muscles were numbed by
dreadful anticipation of a ghastly death.

For several minutes I could not locate my partner in this
unpleasant adventure, and feared the worst had happened.
Then I saw him step out from behind a large bush, calmly
lighting a cigarette.

" Close call, that ! " he drawled. " Rotten damned shot of
mine, old chap. I'm most infernally sorry to have let you
down."

I merely nodded in agreement. Then I chuckled. That
broke the tension, and soon we were both laughing heartily.

Leaving one of the 'Ndorobo trackers to mark the dead bull,
we followed up the tracks of the stampeding herd. We had to
despatch that wounded beast somehow, and soon. Time was
pressing, and we were far from camp ; but we could not leave
a wounded beast to suffer unnecessarily.

We had not gone more than a mile when we spotted them.
They had come to a halt in an open glade in the forest, and the
wounded bull was now surrounded by the remainder of the herd.
I could single him out by reason of his immense spread of horns
and massive head, for they showed clearly over the backs of
the other animals. He was still snorting angrily at intervals,
and uttering sharp bellows of pain. We held a consultation
with Hamisi, and finally it was agreed that I should try and
deliver the death-shot while Egerton covered me.

Keeping careful tab on the changing wind and making no
noise, I gradually crept closer. At last, I could plainly see
the vulnerable shoulder of the bull, and took most careful aim.
My bullet went home, and he crumbled as if pole-axed; and a
second shot, as he tried to rise, killed him.

At the instant that I fired, the rest of the herd charged

OL-ONANA, *LAIBON OF THE MASAI*

MASAI WARRIORS ON ATHI PLAINS

home at us. It was an awe-inspiring sight, but I had no time to admire it. Again I pressed the trigger of my rifle, but no shot rang out. Remembering now that I had stupidly forgotten to reload, I thrust out a hand for my spare rifle; but Hamisi had remained with Egerton. Then the herd was upon us. I did the only thing possible, and jumped behind a small tree. It seemed to me very much smaller than it was in actual fact.

As I reached this scant cover, two shots rang out in rapid succession from my left rear. I saw the young bull stagger and come down on his knees; and then roll over on his side. One of the largest cows did likewise. The remainder thundered past me on either flank, without even touching us. We let them go. I think both of us had had enough for that day, though neither would openly admit the fact. Hamisi was more honest, and bluntly counselled a return to the camp.

The memory of those widespread and cruel horns, so uncomfortably close, was not conducive to a desire for a repetition of the experience. Even if so minded to get another buffalo, the game laws precluded it, the hour was late, and we had no real ambition to do so. We remained there long enough to get our trophies, and then hurried back for the others. It was long after dark when we staggered into our camp.

Egerton was delighted with the day's results, as well he might be. His last two shots were as good and plucky as anyone could have desired, and had made full amends for his indifferent marksmanship earlier in the day.

I had been told by many experienced hunters that the African buffalo could never be despised. This encounter certainly added point to their advice. I have learned never to underestimate an adversary in hunting wild game; and it is only an arrant fool who does so.

It so happened that I was with Colonel Theodore Roosevelt when he got his first buffalo trophies in Kenya, all at the Kamiti Ranch. The owner, my old friend, Hugh H. Heatley, protected a large herd of them on his estate. Only the favoured few were allowed to shoot one or, possibly, two; and he had invited the ex-President and his party to be his guests. As it was well known that this was a particularly fine and large herd, with some exceptionally good heads, Colonel Roosevelt was very delighted at this invitation.

On that particular morning, the herd remained in the cover of the papyrus swamp. Heatley volunteered to ride back and forth on its edge, mounted on his white pony, in the hope of drawing out the herd to charge him. He had every appearance of enjoying this risky performance ; but I was not anxious to change places with him. Finally, while Colonel Roosevelt, his son, Kermit, and Cunninghame stood ready for a charge, Heatley succeeded in drawing the herd into the open plain. There were fully a hundred of them. I sat my pony in the background, eagerly watching the course of events. I longed to have a cinematograph camera with me, for it was a really magnificent sight.

For about a mile from the edge of the swamp, the country was dead flat and devoid of all vestige of cover. Heatley knew the herd to be really dangerous, and already there had been a number of narrow escapes on his ranch from unprovoked attacks by single bulls or small parties of the buffalo. He had told us that, sometimes, they were very truculent; while, at others, behaved perfectly reasonably. One could never bank, he had said, on how they might act. On this day, once drawn into the open, they contented themselves with either grazing or just staring about them.

I watched the Roosevelts start their stalk for two or three beasts which stood apart from the remainder. At about two hundred yards range, the first shots rang out crisply. Two bulls were wounded ; and then the whole herd galloped across the hunters' front, parallel with the swamp. Colonel Roosevelt fired at a large cow, and hit her heavily in the shoulder ; but she managed to make her way slowly toward the swamp, and disappeared into that cover.

My attention was now held by the main herd. Headed by the two wounded bulls, they turned in a short circle and drew up again in a solid phalanx facing the hunters, with heads lowered and eyes watching every movement made. It was not nice country in which to be charged by a really large herd of buffalo, and I was rather nervous as to what might follow. I considered the advisability of trying to draw their attention to myself. The Roosevelts, with Cunninghame at their shoulders, stood their ground motionless and did not attempt to shoot.

There came a distinct movement of uneasiness among the herd. A few moments passed, and then the unwounded mass turned about swiftly and resumed their flight. After hesitating for a short while, the two injured bulls followed them slowly.

The shot cow was soon found on the edge of the swamp,

just inside the papyrus grass. One more bullet finished her. After a long and trying chase, the two wounded bulls were also killed. It had been a most thrilling morning.

On another day, we put up about a dozen of them outside the swamp. They were grazing on the open plain ; and stood to watch us for quite a long time, and then advanced for a distance of about two hundred yards. It looked as if they intended to charge. When they had satisfied their curiosity, however, the buffaloes turned about, sauntered back into the shelter of the papyrus, and were quickly lost to view. We breathed more freely. As dark was falling fast, there was no chance to get at them.

I think we were all surprised to find them in the open, and in such an amiable frame of mind. It was most unlike a buffalo. They seemed to have quite forgiven us for our attack upon them only a few days previously.

To be charged by an enraged buffalo is far from being a pleasant experience. He is an enormously powerful beast, with massive horns which rise into great bosses at the base. Sometimes these meet to cover the forehead with a frontlet of horn.

The list of white hunters who have been killed or gored by buffalo is a long one, and includes a number of notable game hunters, while accidents to African natives at the hands of these ferocious beasts are of constant occurrence.

If Africa is a land of many varieties of wild life, it is also a land of pests—poisons, diseases, deadly insects and noxious plants. Until you have known contact with the Buffalo Bean, however, the list of horrors is far from being complete. I had one most unpleasant experience with this dreadful creeper when out hunting. I am not likely to forget it.

I was after *bos caffer* and got stung by the Buffalo Bean. I had the misfortune to bump into some of this creeper before I was aware of its proximity. In fact, I had never seen or heard of it before. It is an innocent looking plant—a creeper with a russet-coloured, woolly little pod. Only those who have known the torture that this can inflict can fully appreciate all I suffered.

The woolly appearance of the pod is due to a coating of almost infinitesimal and imperceptible hairs. At a light touch, they are detached and, floating broadcast, alight on any object near at hand. In this instance, I was the unsuspecting victim. I did not detect their presence immediately, as the irritation takes a little time to have full effect. I was pretty well coated all over the arms, legs and neck before I became aware of the dreaded presence of these hairs ; but I did not know what was really wrong.

I had walked past the creepers for some distance before the fun began. First, I felt a slight tickling sensation on my arms ; then others at the back of my neck and bare knees ; and, finally, the spreading torture left me bewildered as to where to scratch next. From soon after sunrise until noon, this intense irritation continued ; and no matter what I attempted in the way of alleviation, all failed to give relief.

Finally, in despair and almost driven demented, I appealed to Hamisi for help and advice. He suggested that we should halt, make camp and then apply hot ashes to the afflicted portions of my body. I abandoned my hunting for the day and camped beside a river ; and soon my porters had a big fire roaring. As soon as I could, I tried the remedy suggested by Hamisi. Even the prospect of a burnt skin seemed preferable to the torture I endured.

I had the red-hot embers brought to me, stripped so that Sefu and Hamisi could rub them well into the skin, and hoped for relief. By the time this operation was completed, I must have looked like a fakir of India. I was covered with white ashes from head to feet.

The counter-irritation had a slightly distracting effect, but did not last long. It was not until some hours later that the itching worked itself out and I was able to get some troubled sleep. It had left me exhausted physically and mentally, but a much wiser man. I should know that creeper if I ever saw it again, and give it a very wide berth.

For several days thereafter, I had occasional reminders of this unplesant experience, for the hairs of the Buffalo Bean seemed still to cling to my clothing, despite the thorough washing and stout beating to which it had been subjected.

I think that I would rather face up to a charging buffalo than suffer from this creeper's terrible irritation.

CHAPTER XV

THE FEROCITY OF THE BUFFALO

KAMITI RANCH was famed throughout Kenya even before the Roosevelts bagged their first buffalo there in 1909.

An old Army friend of mine, accompanied by his wife, arrived in Nairobi to shoot in 1906 and found me stationed there. They were both tremendously keen to get good buffalo heads, but their time was limited and the Government would not let them shoot any of the species in the Ukamba Province. They put their difficulty before me, and begged my aid. I wrote to Hugh Heatley on their behalf, and received the desired invitation to bring them out to his ranch on the Kamiti River. He gave them permission to shoot one good bull each on his private buffalo reserve. We lost no time in accepting this generous offer.

On the day after our arrival, Heatley took us out to the papyrus swamp on his estate. There was no sign of any buffalo grazing in the open, and we discussed the best plan to adopt. Heatley agreed to ride through the edge of the reeds, and try to draw out the herd in pursuit of him. His two guests, with the gun-bearers and myself in support, were to take up their stand and await developments. Just as Heatley approached the edge of the swamp, however, the buffalo herd made a brief appearance and as quickly retired under cover. Heatley returned to us, dismounted and handed over his pony to the care of a syce. We changed our plan of attack to meet the new conditions.

Now we advanced in extended order toward the point at which the buffalo had retired into the papyrus. I was on the extreme right of the line, the lady next, then her husband, and Heatley on his left. We went forward slowly, ears and eyes very much on the alert. As there were over a hundred beasts in this herd, our four rifles would be facing rather long odds.

When within eighty yards of the edge of the reeds, suddenly
I saw the head of a big bull emerge above cover and stare
thoughtfully at us. I whistled softly to the lady to warn her,
but she had already seen her target and the rifle was to her
shoulder. I followed suit, to cover her in case of emergency.

Her shot rang out sharply, and the big bull's head vanished
from sight. We halted at once, waiting anxiously to see what
might happen. I fully expected to see the herd rush out from
cover and thunder down upon us in a massed charge. I did
not relish the prospect at all. But nothing happened, much to
my surprise. There came no sign of movement in the papyrus,
and we could not hear a sound. Again we went forward slowly,
rifles held ready.

We had approached to within fifty yards when another abrupt
movement in the papyrus brought my rifle to the shoulder, with
the sights on the spot. The big bull's head showed up just
about at the same place. Again the lady fired, and the massive
head dropped back into cover. There followed another anxious
period of waiting for the inevitable charge ; but it did not
come. We started to walk forward once more, tense and
perplexed. My nerves were jumping badly. We had not
covered more than ten to fifteen yards when again that huge
head of spreading horns thrust itself into full view above the
reeds. The lady's rifle spoke sharply on my left, as if in stern
reproof of such levity on the part of this buffalo. For the third
time, exactly the same thing occurred. I was very puzzled to
account for this strange performance.

My nerves were frayed, and I glanced over my shoulder for
an instant at the sportswoman. She was calmly reloading her
rifle, and appeared to be quite unperturbed. Admittedly, it was
more than I was ; but this was not my first encounter with the
ferocious buffalo. The whole situation struck me as unpleasantly
suspicious.

At a signal from Heatley, we advanced again very cautiously.
For a fourth time, the bull's head showed distinctly against the
background of papyrus grass. A sharp report from my left, and
it dropped back to the lady's shot. I was reminded of a Punch
and Judy show, but this entertainment had more kick and added
thrills. It was all so unreal that, by this time, I was feeling
rather sick at the pit of my stomach. What had Fate in store
for us ?

Now we were all within a ten yard radius of the rim of the

swamp, momentarily expecting to see the whole herd charge full tilt at us. Heatley and my friend closed up on the sports-woman, and all four stood facing the danger point with rifles to our shoulders. I glanced up from my sights for a brief moment, and saw nothing but that tense tangle of reeds and feathery-topped papyrus. While we stood and waited, with hearts pumping fast, the minutes seemed interminable. Nothing happened. I was so intent on watching the reed-bed and listening for signs of the anticipated charge that I did not hear Heatley approach my side. When he spoke to me, I jumped as if a fire-cracker had exploded unexpectedly behind me.

Quickly we discussed the situation in low tones, while keeping an anxious eye on the spot where that bull buffalo had been. Heatley confessed that he liked the look of things as little as I did, but suggested that, while the lady and her husband covered our advance, he and I should try to get action instead of that grim uncertainty. We made known our plan to our companions by signals. They nodded their heads in agreement, and we went forward to the rim of the swamp.

I cannot say that I relished our task, but there seemed nothing else to be done. If Heatley was ready to take the risk, then so must I do so. Silently and stealthily, we advanced. Not a movement came from the cover; and, finally, we reached the edge and thrust our way boldly into it. I expected to find myself rubbing noses with a bull buffalo, or more than one. It was an unhappy prospect. At the sight which met our eyes, both forgot the urgent need for caution and silence.

" Well, I'm damned ! " shouted Heatley, relief, triumph and astonishment struggling for mastery.

His loud exclamation brought our companions running to our side ; and we all danced and shouted in joy, quite forgetting that the herd might be close at hand. We all felt very childish, and with good cause.

There, stretched out on the bed of the swamp, was not one bull as might have been expected. There were four giant bodies. They had fallen within a yard or so of each other, two being practically on top of the others. The lady's marksmanship had been extraordinary, for each had been killed instantly. Her joy and our amazement can best be imagined. We danced round the four bodies, holding hands and whooping gleefully. Then, calming down, we offered our expressions of unbounded admiration to the Diana of the Chase.

Now we tried to reconstruct that amazing scene. Obviously there had been four bulls close together. When the first was killed, the others had been inspired with curiosity in turn and had poked up their heads to see what was occurring. It had proved their death warrant.

The lady bore off her splendid trophies to Nairobi, both she and her admiring husband being delighted with this unique success. I have never heard of a similar incident ; and it is, most probably, without parallel in the annals of big game shooting. It all sounds incredible, I know ; but facts are facts.

I have hunted buffalo in various parts of Kenya outside of the Ukamba Province, on the banks of the Nile, and elsewhere in Africa ; but I do not think more than twenty have fallen to my rifle, if as many as that ; and I have seen about an equal number killed by others. In almost every single instance the task was a pretty lively experience.

A buffalo is always a most uncertain tempered beast, and dislikes intensely to have his privacy disturbed. You have not got too good a chance with an infuriated solitary bull ; but if a herd charges you, the chances are very much against your escape from severe injury or death. He is nearly always a most determined and ferocious attacker when molested.

Once, in the Sotik country, I had a very narrow escape from a solitary bull which I had wounded badly. I had not been able to get a fair shot at him. Finally, much against my better judgment and set principles, I risked a difficult shot. I hit him, but not in a vital spot ; and he charged home at once. As there was no vestige of cover available, I took to my heels. On that particular day, I acted most unwisely throughout ; everyone of my usual precautionary measures was scrapped and past experiences forgotten. Afterwards, I came to the conclusion that an imp of mischief must have sat on my shoulder, mocked and made me act like a crass idiot. Either that, or else I was distinctly off colour for hunting that day.

It was a long and most exhausting chase, for the bull could easily out-distance me. I had recourse to many doublings in my tracks, and was fast getting winded. When I was just about done and unable to continue my flight, I heard a sudden heavy thud behind my back. I halted, steadied my nerves, and looked round. The beast was lying on his side, motionless. I returned cautiously, and put a bullet into the brain to make sure of his death. If he could have lasted just another minute

MASAI WARRIORS—ONE WEARING LION'S-MANE HEAD-DRESS

MASAI WARRIORS IN WAR-PAINT

or two, the final curtain might have been very different. I was incapable of running another fifty yards.

At times, he had got so close to me that I could feel his hot breath fanning my neck. This served only to give me added strength for another burst of speed. That run for my life was a horrible nightmare, the more so as I was alone and Hamisi was not handy to come to my help. When I told him about it later, he merely shrugged his shoulders and grinned. I felt like boxing his ears; instead, I cursed him roundly. He knew I was only letting off steam, and grinned the more broadly.

A year previous to this, I had been hunting in a swampy area at the foot of Mount Kenya. Soon after leaving camp at dawn, we picked up the trail of a solitary bull buffalo; and followed it through the edge of the swamp for some distance. The animal had grazed a great deal, but also had been travelling fairly fast. Probably, we followed him over a greater portion of his night's wanderings, as well as, later on, over the ground traversed by him during the early hours of this morning.

The sun was high in the brazen blue dome above us, and the heat was scorching, when we arrived at a dense bamboo cover through which the fresh spoor led. My hopes fell, for I knew that, under such conditions, the bull would be lying down, most probably, and resting. My chances of finding him feeding in the open were remote indeed. Still, I was not going to throw up the sponge after trailing him thus far. One is never actually licked until the final knock-out is delivered; and this was not yet. I continued tracking him, but now moved forward much more warily.

After going some distance through the thick cover, I heard the rush of the bull as he dashed away from me, thoroughly alarmed by some slight noise I must have made. For some time now I had been fearing that this might happen, and so was not taken by surprise. I could not tell how far the thicket extended; but, just on the bare chance, I ran forward for a short distance. Almost immediately, I came to the edge of an open glade and saw my quarry dashing madly across it.

I tried a snap shot as he was about to enter that far patch of new cover. Not for a moment did I imagine that I had hit him; but, just as a matter of form, advanced cautiously up to the place where he had disappeared. To my surprise and great relief, Hamisi picked up a fallen leaf with a single large splash of fresh blood on it. We followed the tracks, found more blood, and then once again came up with the bull. He was now standing broadside on to me, offering an easy target. Taking very deliberate aim this time, I fired at his shoulder; and he dropped dead to the bullet.

On examination of the carcass, I found that my first bullet, which was fired from directly behind him, had simply grazed the outside of his right ribs, not even cutting the skin along its line of flight; had missed the portions of it overlying the intercostal spaces; and then had entered the foreleg and lamed him. It was a very lucky fluke, and I did not deserve that trophy. It was really unpardonable to have taken such a snap shot at him, and my only excuse is that I completely lost my temper at seeing him escape from me after such an arduous chase. And that is no excuse at all! A hunter should *never* lose his head or temper.

Although, as a general rule, a head shot at any animal other than an elephant, hippopotamus or crocodile, is to be strictly avoided, yet it does happen now and again that the sportsman must take that chance or lose his quarry altogether. In such a case, I consider the head shot is legitimate. The hunter, however, must remember that he must aim at an imaginary line drawn between the eyes; or else, if the beast is standing with the nose elevated, at the top of the cartilage of the latter.

It was once my good fortune to bag a bull buffalo with an exceptionally good horn measurement, in Uganda, in just this way. He was not killed outright; but must have escaped me altogether if I had not risked that shot.

I was returning to camp after failing to get a good bull elephant, which had got clean away from me. Accidentally, I came across the tracks of a buffalo, fresh enough to invite me to follow up. After a time, I saw a single bull out in the open, at the edge of the forest. He was grazing, and appeared to be without suspicion of any danger or that a human being was near at hand. Halting immediately, I sent some of my trackers to make a detour and drive him toward me; and then advanced to the edge of the forest, and stood motionless. I had not been there many minutes when Hamisi nudged me and pointed to our front. The buffalo had started to advance toward us; and now I could see him, close in front of where we stood, but offering no decent target. Then he halted abruptly in his measured walk, and stood staring directly at us. I sighted and fired instantly, for I knew my beaters would soon arrive on the scene and startle the beast into full flight.

I hit pretty close to the fatal spot in the head, but failed to down him. He dashed away, and I followed immediately. I was feeling rather angry with myself for having risked that head shot, and then missed by a matter of less than an inch. I did not expect to see that bull again.

A short distance away, however, I saw him rolling over and over down a hillside into a low valley. On reaching the bottom, he struggled to rise again to his feet but seemed to find this difficult. I was now close up to him, and sent two bullets into his shoulder. The second one settled it, and he collapsed on his side. He was dead.

After running for some distance after being hit the first time, he must have become giddy from the effects of the wound in the head and, as he fell on the edge of the steep slope, rolled down to the level ground. It was a great piece of luck getting that splendid trophy.

A couple of days later, I had the unenviable experience of being charged on the same morning by both an elephant and a buffalo ; fortunately for me, not both at the same time. I say " charged," though that is not strictly correct. They both almost ran over me, though neither had the slightest intention of fighting me. Both provided a most remarkable instance of how wild animals, on occasions, are apt to run headlong into the very danger which they are striving to sidestep. Should they be suddenly startled, and so lose their heads and make a blind rush, most wild creatures are liable to bolt at you instead of in the opposite direction.

I was in the open when the tusker, a solitary animal, rushed straight at me. Obviously, there was not the slightest intention of charging me. I gave him both barrels, and then was left quite defenceless as Hamisi was not accompanying me that morning. I had to sidestep that wounded elephant to avoid being accidentally trodden under foot. It was a near thing : too near to be in any way pleasant. Rapidly reloading, I went after him ; but he fell over dead before I had to expend another cartridge. Both my shots had registered in a vital spot.

The buffalo charge occurred later in the morning. The previous incident with the elephant had rather upset my nerves, and the buffalo completed my discomfiture.

I had gone back to camp to send out men for the elephant

ivory ; and, now accompanied by Hamisi, went off again to hunt down another pair of good tusks. I felt it incumbent upon me to make sure that my nerves had not been too badly strained. As in the hunting-field or in aviation, it is fatal to quit the game after a bad smash. The only sound thing to do is to continue at once. Thus only can you be reasonably confident that your nerves are not shattered, and you can still ride or fly as straight as ever.

Soon we had picked up the trail of a solitary buffalo. After following the spoor for some distance, we found the form in which he had been lying down. The open hoof-marks leading therefrom indicated that he had galloped away in considerable alarm. He must have got our wind before we were close enough to hear his precipitate rush to safety. We had heard nothing of his movement.

A stern chase of this description is always likely to be a protracted one, for a solitary buffalo, who may have been hunted often during the course of his life, is usually very cunning and leaves very little to chance. If a buffalo is alarmed early in the day, before he has had time to lie down and chew the cud, and is then pursued, it is quite possible to come up with him again. But if seriously alarmed after they have had time to perform this very necessary function, normally they may be followed in vain until late in the evening. The probability is that you will never come up with them.

In this particular instance, the bull kept to the thickest cover he could find, and the hunt was both long and wearisome. At last, however, we emerged upon a large patch of very open forest-glade, beyond which I made up my mind not to go. I was frankly fed-up.

Here, to my complete surprise, I saw the buffalo, a really magnificent bull, slowly retracing his steps but rather at an angle to us. Why he had thus changed his route, it is quite impossible to say or even guess. He did not look as if he was seriously alarmed ; and I knew of no other shooting parties in the immediate neighbourhood. It is possible, however, that he might have been disturbed by native hunters or had run into one of their concealed traps. That is only surmise, for I shall never know the real cause of his unusual conduct.

I dare not fire at him from so great a range. I guessed him to be about three hundred yards or more away, and so waited until he should come within a hundred yards. Suddenly, and without any warning whatsoever, he lowered his great head and charged straight at us. I fired at once at his nostrils, hoping thus to rake him through the chest. I heard my bullet strike with a dull thud, but it did not stop him. My two Baganda trackers bolted at once, but Hamisi shouldered up to me with my heavy rifle. He never bolted from anything, and would never dream of deserting me in a moment of peril. Never had hunter a better or more loyal gun-bearer. Always when most needed he was at hand, automatically slipping my reserve rifle into my hand and taking the spent one. I never had to glance round, so smoothly, expertly and quickly was the exchange always made by Hamisi.

The wounded bull rushed blindly past us within a few yards distance, and I fired my second barrel into his shoulder as he galloped past. But I had not made sufficient allowance for the great speed at which he was travelling; and hit too far back. Hamisi exchanged rifles with me in less than a second. A bullet from the heavier weapon in the beast's hindquarters knocked him over flat, and brought the long chase to an end. Another one into the head killed him. It had been warm work while it lasted, and I was greatly relieved in my mind to see him laid low for ever.

Whether my lighter bullet, which had hit him on one side of the chest, could have affected him enough to enable us to come up with him again, had he elected to bolt in another direction, I do not know. I rather doubt it. Undoubtedly, he would have given us much labour and immense trouble to despatch had he acted otherwise than as he did. He was a grand old bull, with a really fine spread of horns.

I have often heard it claimed that there are very few buffalo remaining in Africa. I do not believe it to be correct. There are still quite a large number of survivors of the old herds, but every year sees them growing appreciably fewer in numbers. In Uganda the buffalo are just about holding their own. In Kenya they are not easy to find, and therefore many people think they have been nearly completely exterminated.

A buffalo is a really serious proposition to tackle. If you study an African buffalo's gigantic proportions, especially the immense head and massive shoulders, you will appreciate at once that he can prove an uncommonly nasty customer when angered. He is not an animal with whom one cares to take any liberties; and he will never permit you to do so with impunity.

You do not have to look for trouble with a buffalo, for he generally brings it to you at once.

There are really few forms of shooting with a rifle which can prove more exciting, and from every point of view more sporting, than the pursuit of this grand animal in India or Africa. It demands all the hunter's powers of endurance, and all his knowledge of the habits of the quarry tracked down. Large as the beast is, and consequently easier to hit, the shooting of a buffalo in the wrong spot is only senseless cruelty for it so often escapes. At the best, it will suffer great pain for a considerable time, and only too often will die a lingering death of agony in solitude. Sometimes, when so left to die through force of circumstances, their last hour is rendered the more terrible by the scavenger beasts attacking and devouring the poor beast while still alive and defenceless. Knowing this, all hunters should use every possible effort to finish the work they have begun.

Unlike other wounded animals, a buffalo is not easy to track down ; and, unless killed off quickly, the chances are you will lose it altogether. Thus you have condemned it to a most brutal end.

When hunting buffalo, it is always well to make an early start from camp so as to reach his known haunts as soon after dawn as is possible. A mud wallow, swamp, forest or salt-lick generally provides the best hunting area. The natives will always be able to tell you where you can locate buffalo, if any habitually frequent their districts ; for they are very fond of the meat.

Speaking generally, I have found it best to follow any spoor which shows obvious signs of having been made during the previous evening or night, provided always that it is picked up early in the morning.

I was hunting buffalo on the Mau Plateau of Kenya, early in 1904, being accompanied by a friend from Johannesburg. We left camp as the first hint of a new day flecked the sky with pink. It was bitterly cold, and a drizzling rain did not add to our comfort. Within a mile of our camp, we picked up quite fresh tracks ; and, after following these for some time, we came up to the herd. They were lying down, chewing the cud, in rather long grass. Unfortunately, we disturbed them without being able to get a shot, and off they dashed into the Mau Forest. We followed up for the best part of that day, but never got the ghost of a chance to kill any of the big bulls. When it was growing late, and feeling very weary, we decided to abandon the hunt and go back to camp.

On our return journey, when at no great distance from our tents, we came across tracks which my natives insisted were very fresh ; and Hamisi agreed with them. Late as it was, we followed up the spoor. We were all under the impression that we had found the tracks of another herd, which had passed that way only a short time previously.

The trail led into the forest and eventually brought us to the very spot at which we had found the herd resting earlier that day. We had, late in the afternoon, merely been following a spoor made by the same herd, probably before that tracked in the morning hours. So cold and damp had it been that the grass cut by the sharp hooves of the buffalo remained perfectly fresh and unwithered during the entire day. If there had been a blazing sun, of course the blades of grass would have shrivelled rapidly. The spoor made by the same animal will vary in appearance very greatly and according to whether exposed to the sun or being in the shade.

We had thus been led into a mare's nest by our native trackers'. and our own, failure to read the signs correctly. It served us all right. We got back to camp very late, footsore and dog-tired, and without a single trophy to show for our strenuous labours all day.

That is all in the game !

CHAPTER XVI

A LION AND BUFFALO BATTLE

THE greatest difficulty in tracking down dangerous animals is that the sportsman is almost entirely at the mercy of the varying changes in the direction of the wind. Where the spoor leads there must he follow, whether up or down wind; and sometimes, for several days together, he may experience the keen disappointment of hearing the animal, having got his wind, dash off out of rifle-range. He will not get a chance to fire even a single shot. This is a risk, however, which must be faced; and it is one which no skill or knowledge of jungle-craft can overcome.

It is essential in hunting buffalo in the forest areas, as it is indeed in the pursuit of every variety of game, that the hunter's movements should be as noiseless as possible; and, under no circumstances, should he utter a word louder than in a low whisper. When he knows the game is near, he should approach as silently as feasible; and take his time. Many a real good trophy has been lost irretrievably through an attempt to rush the final stages of pursuit.

Personally, I always would prefer to tackle a single bull buffalo than to try and get one in a herd. Be as careful and experienced as you may, the fact that there are cows in the herd makes it incumbent upon the hunter never to shoot until he is positive that he is aiming at a male beast. Usually in a small herd there is only one bull worth getting, and the chances are that the first animal presenting a target is not the one you would wish to kill.

In spite of every possible precaution, some cows deceive you into thinking that they are big bulls, both by their darker colour and big spread of horns. Even the most expert hunter may incur the self-reproach of having killed a cow in the honest belief it was really a bull. To be sure of the sex of your selected target, you must either see the animal's head from the front or else view the whole herd in the open ground. A full-grown cow buffalo looks a very big animal, and her horns frequently equal the dimensions of a bull's.

Very fine heads, however, have been shot in a herd; but these herd bulls are generally animals in the prime of life, whose horns really bear no comparison in size to those of an old solitary male. The herd on the Kamiti Ranch was an exception to the general rule, for there were a number of grand heads among the bulls. But you do not often encounter such a big herd congregating habitually in one particular spot. The days of the really large herds of buffalo ended many years ago.

I have always found the best spot at which to aim is just behind the shoulder, and a little below the centre of the side. In a broadside target, this shot generally proves fatal. If you happen to hit an animal in advance of this particular spot, and break the shoulder-blade, he will soon be at your mercy. He may travel a short distance, if the bone has only been perforated, but this will soon break under the great weight of his body.

A shot fired at right angles with the body, far back through the ribs, is quite useless and never fatal. It merely inflicts a cruel wound, which may cause intense suffering and the lingering death of the animal. At all costs such a shot should be avoided, for it will seldom give you your trophy. The wounded animal may be followed up for several days and eventually killed, but the chances of ever catching up with him again are always remote.

A bullet high up through the loins, thus perforating the liver, is nearly always fatal; but is not so rapid in effect as a shot placed well behind the shoulder. In the former case, the animal may travel far, fight hard and take much lead before being despatched; even if followed up at once, as unquestionably he should be. A wounded beast will often lie in wait for the attacker, or else double back and charge from your rear when least expected. It uses great cunning and is always ferocious, being determined to kill the pursuer at the first possible moment.

The loin shot should be taken at a spot about nine inches below the termination of the dorsal ridge. If no better target presents itself, such as when an animal is standing broadside on and with all its body, with the exception of one hindquarter, hidden by cover, the best plan is not to delay in the hope of a better shot offering. Fire to break the hip-joint, and then the beast cannot escape you.

Should the animal be standing in full view and facing you, a shot in the centre of the chest is nearly always fatal. It is quite as rapid in effect as one behind the shoulder. If, on the other hand, the bull is standing or moving away, with only his hindquarters visible, the best shot is straight under the root of the tail. A bullet from a powerful weapon will then rake the whole body and penetrate the vitals. I am glad to be able to say that only once have I been forced to use this shot on a buffalo, and then only to prevent the escape of a sorely wounded beast. If there had been another alternative offered, then I should have taken it. In such cases, even if the aim be not quite accurate, one or other of the hip-joints or hind legs will be broken almost certainly. A buffalo with a broken leg or hip cannot travel very far or fast, and can soon be finished off if followed up at once.

A shot fired diagonally behind the ribs, in a line to the opposite shoulder, is a very deadly one. Several times I have proved it to be so.

If only the head of the beast is visible—poked up over cover and staring at you, with nostrils well elevated—a shot in the cartilage of the nose, plumb central and slightly above a line drawn between the nostrils, will penetrate the brain and drop the bull dead on the spot. It was this deadly shooting by my friend's wife on the Kamiti Ranch which accounted for the four bulls, as already related.

In following up a wounded bull, which common humanity and real sportsmanlike instincts require you to do immediately, I have always found it best to shoot a heavy bullet at a proper angle through the forehead, either between the eyes, behind an ear or behind the horns. It will brain and kill instantly.

The one thing to avoid, if practical, is to come upon a buffalo suddenly so that the animal can charge before you have a fair chance to use your rifle. A buffalo charges at very high speed and, unless he can be seen from some distance, has the winning trick in his own hands. The hunter's ability to defend himself is very small in such an eventuality.

Considering that a wounded buffalo traverses the densest cover which he can find, and that the pursuer cannot possibly tell whether he is travelling rapidly with the intention of holding on for a long distance, or whether he is hidden in some thicket near at hand, caution is extremely advisable. It is quite possible, and often is the case, that the wounded beast is hidden, with lowered horns, waiting to charge out upon the hunter as soon as he is within a few yards.

As a wounded buffalo sometimes will travel for many miles, and often make good his escape, it is obvious that every minute wasted in unnecessary precautions is to be deplored ; but great circumspection in following up the beast is always essential.

When hunting alone, along the banks of the Nile, I shot a buffalo through the lungs, which wound ordinarily proves fatal. In this particular instance, unfortunately, it was not so and he got clean away from me. I followed immediately. The light-coloured frothy blood on his spoor offered indisputable proof that I had hit him through the lungs. As long as there was light, and time to get back to my camp before midnight, I went after him. Several times, at long intervals, I came up with him ; but was unable to get another shot. Darkness finally forced me to abandon the pursuit.

Before dawn, Hamisi and I started out after him once more. We picked up the spoor at the spot where I had halted on the previous night. I quite expected to find the bull lying dead ahead of me, but we followed his track for a very long distance without even getting a glimpse of the beast. I found where he had grazed heavily during the night, or else early that morning. When, at last, we reached the spot where he had rested to chew the cud, his hoof marks proved that he had gone off with long strides from the form. It indicated that he had got our wind or had heard us, and had departed quite vigorously. I never set eyes on him again, though I spent four days trying to locate and kill him.

As all signs of bleeding had ceased, and he was travelling so strongly, I have always hoped that this bull fully recovered from the wound and did not die a slow death of lonely torment. I had done all that could reasonably be expected to finish him ; and had even offered a reward to any local native who brought me word of his actual whereabouts, but all my efforts had failed. Time pressed, and reluctantly I had to give him best. I did not mind losing the trophy, but hated to think that I had been the instrument of causing this beast unnecessary suffering.

While tracking down a kudu with an exceptionally fine head, near Tsavo, I had the incredible fortune to be an uninvited spectator during the final stages of another titanic battle to the death between two great savage beasts of the wilds.

My attention was suddenly attracted by a furious commotion in the bush, a short distance ahead of my trail. Advancing silently and cautiously, my ears were assailed by a succession of fierce snarls and deep grunts, a few angry bellows, and then the deep-throated roar of a lion. I could now hear a terrific struggle in progress, and broke into a trot to reach the scene of the conflict as soon as possible. Hamisi trotted close to my elbow.

We arrived at the edge of an open space in the dense thorn-scrub, and came abruptly to a halt. So astonished was I at what met my eyes, that my rifle was not even remembered. I felt unable to do anything but stare, with eyes starting out of my head. I could neither move nor speak. Hamisi crept up to my side, and I heard him utter a deep grunt of mingled surprise and pleasure.

Before our eyes, in full view, was a huge black-maned lion and a gigantic bull buffalo engaged in mortal combat. Patently, it was kill or be killed. I would have given a very great deal to have had a movie-camera with me or even a Kodak; but I had left the latter in my camp. What a stupendous opportunity missed! Never again shall I ever again get a sight to equal it; and I had not even a camera.

A camera-lens I would have used gladly on that madly fighting, savage pair of primitive animals; but a rifle—nothing could induce me. I would act as an audience: but shoot I would not. I wanted to see this thing through to a finish, and satisfy my curiosity as to which would prove the victor.

In all my long and varied experience of wild life, I had only once, that time in India, seen anything so thrilling or more wonderful. Then it was a cow buffalo and a tiger: now a bull and a lion.

I do not know how long that fight had raged before I came accidentally upon the arena. It was obvious that I was only watching the final stages. I have no idea how long I stood there, eyes following intently every single detail of that fierce duel. I lost all count of time.

The lion was firmly fixed on the massive shoulders of the old buffalo when I reached the spot. He was fighting, clawing, biting and growling ferociously. The buffalo was using all his giant strength and every cunning ruse to dislodge the antagonist, and get in some deadly work with powerful head and cruel horns.

Once he did succeed in throwing the lion from his back to the ground; and, before his foe could recover, had driven one horn clean through the body and impaled the beast to the earth. They fought and struggled violently, roaring and bellowing savagely. The whole veld seemed to vibrate to their noisy throats. It was awe-inspiring; and swift thrills ran up and down my spine.

Somehow, the lion managed to free himself. Before he did so, however, he had scored the body of the buffalo in the most terrible fashion. Shreds of hide and flesh were hanging down in long strips, blood and dust were everywhere as they waltzed round and round each other, heads always facing, eyes watchfully intent and glaring, and muscles tensely drawn. Both waited for a favourable moment to spring in again to close grips. Round and round they went, wounds completely ignored or forgotten, frothing with blood at mouth and nostrils, bodies torn open and pouring out a steady stream of scarlet life's blood.

Unexpectedly, almost when I thought the lion had had enough and would slink away to lick his wounds, badly whipped, he sprang in like a flash of lightning and once more landed squarely on the broad shoulders of the buffalo. He perched on neck and withers, his tawny body outstretched along the buffalo's back. The agility of that spring was simply amazing.

It seemed to me that now the buffalo's days were nearly ended, and the fight just about finished. The lion would bite into that massive neck, reach the spinal vertebræ, and with one claw wrench round that great head to breaking point; and then the huge beast would be thrown to death with a broken neck. It is the lion's way of killing big animals.

For a brief second only, I fingered my rifle; but quickly banished all thoughts of intervention. The fight was no concern of mine. Jungle laws had ordained it, and no human being had any shadow of right to interfere. Let the victor not be robbed of the honours in such a gigantic trial of strength.

Now the buffalo was down on his knees, but still struggled valiantly to throw off his foe. They fought all over the arena, savagely and with grim determination. Then, with a swift movement the buffalo threw himself over sideways, and for a moment I thought the lion had actually broken his neck. I

was mistaken.   The buffalo rolled over the lion, and rose to his
feet freed of that death-hold.

The lion was at him again almost before the buffalo had
regained his feet.   This time he landed sideways on the shoulder
and neck of the bull, just behind that magnificent sweep of
horns.   He clung there, biting savagely, while the buffalo
moaned aloud in agony.   But the gallant old beast was not
licked : far from it.   He fought back strenuously and struggled
hard to shake off the lion's tenacious hold.   Then, gathering all
his strength in a last supreme effort, he threw himself backwards.
The lion's body was swung over his head in a half-circle, and he
fell on his back beneath that gigantic and heavy body.   His
tawny hide was lost to view, crushed to a pulp beneath that
great bulk of meat and bone.

All round them, the place was a shambles ; blood was everywhere.   For a moment or two neither animal moved : they
appeared to be at death's door.   I waited and watched, wondering
what the final curtain would be.   For a brief instant I
turned to look at Hamisi's face.   It was streaked with rivers of
sweat, eyes staring fixedly, lips parted, and breath coming in
gasps.   He was hypnotized, oblivious to all but that titanic
fight.   My eyes swung back to the two combatants.

Slowly and groggily, the buffalo bull staggered to his feet,
and stood staring down at the gored and crushed body of his
foe.   It remained there on the ground, motionless.   With two
or three savage lunges with those cruel horns into the prostrate
body of the lion, the latter died.   The buffalo stood erect over
the vanquished, swaying drunkenly on his feet.   His eyes were
glazing fast : breath coming in short and strangled sobs.

A moment or two of tense silence passed, and still the buffalo
swayed on his feet.   There was neither sound nor movement,
except that terribly laboured breathing and that gentle rocking
to and fro.   The veld all around the arena was as silent as the
grave ; not even a bird chirped in the nearby trees.   I could
hear my own heart pumping furiously.

In silence life slipped from the buffalo almost like a smothered
sigh.   He crumbled slowly, to fall with a dull thud on top of
his enemy.

We left them there, victor and vanquished, just as they had
fallen.

To have acted otherwise would have been sacrilege.

CHAPTER XVII

GRIM TRAGEDY AT BANGWEOLO

I CHANCED to be in Dar-es-Salaam while Paul Graetz, a Lieutenant in the Imperial German Army, was in hospital after his terrible experiences on the shores of Lake Bangweolo. A mutual friend introduced me to him at the Club. Paul Graetz was typical of the pre-War officer of the German Army, and of his countrymen to be seen in their East African colony ; but was less stolid and more adventurous than others whom I had met. Tall, silent, courteous, face deeply bronzed and terribly scarred from his ghastly mauling, he impressed me as a man of indomitable courage and great strength of character.

In 1909 he had crossed Central Africa from the Indian Ocean to the Atlantic by motor-car. This unique performance for those days merely served to whet his appetite for more. On his return to Germany, he set about planning a new adventure —to cross mid-Africa from east to west by motor-boat. He designed and had constructed for him in Berlin, a special type of motor-launch, in which he proposed to travel by way of the Zambezi River, Lake Bangweolo and the Congo River. His route was most carefully mapped out and every single detail prepared in advance of the start. It entailed a journey of some six thousand miles, often over unexplored waterways.

He selected for his co-adventurers, a French cinematograph operator, Octave Fière, an African cook named James, and four other African natives. Seven was the limit of the carrying capacity of his launch, the *Sarotti*.

At last all was ready for their plunge into the unknown, and they set off gaily from Quilimane, a small port just north of Chinde on the coast of Portuguese East Africa.

I will let him tell his own story, and in his own words, as related to me in the Club at Dar-es-Salaam. It was with some difficulty that I persuaded him to speak of that adventure ; but, finally, he did so, while I recorded his words as he talked. Here, then, is his own version of what happened on that amazing journey :

The tales I had heard of Lake Bangweolo from the Awemba tribe, on my former motor-car journey across Africa, had made me most anxious to explore this mysterious sheet of water in the heart of North-Eastern Rhodesia. According to them, this lake enjoyed a most sinister reputation among the native tribes residing both near and far. They declared that it was studded with islands, on which were to be found mammoth elephants and immense giraffes ; while in its waters were huge sea-serpents and other strange creatures. From the surface, hot springs rose like fountains into the air ; and pestilential winds, sweeping across the nearby swamps, carried death to all who ventured near the lake's shores. I gathered from the Awemba that Bangweolo and its vicinity was no health resort : rather a Dante's Inferno.

These people insisted that no natives, who had ever ventured upon the waters of this lake in their frail canoes, had again been seen or heard of : they had just vanished. Bangweolo was regarded by some local tribes as a sort of Hades, where departed souls suffered continually the most dreadful torments ; while others again believed it was the approach to a Paradise, where the spirits of their dead relatives enjoyed a perfect life under the benign protection of their gods.

After making all due allowances for their imagination and local native superstitions, Lake Bangweolo sounded sinister but worth investigating.

The lake was known to be surrounded by miles upon miles of thick and impenetrable marshes, and the swamps thickly clothed with tall papyrus reeds and rushes. This all rendered any chance of exploring its waters a matter of great difficulty. But the more obstacles placed in my path, the more I looked forward to the adventure. Any expedition into unknown regions would be deadly tame and devoid of all pleasurable thrills if all was smooth sailing. I was perfectly well aware that we should have to endure many severe hardships and swallow many keen disappointments ; but what of that ? No adventure is worth calling such unless it possesses those two characteristics.

The great prize which I hoped to secure, in addition to being

AN EXCEPTIONAL RHINO HORN

PHOTOGRAPHING A CHARGING RHINO (DEAD!)

the first white man to thoroughly explore this sheet of water in the wild heart of Africa, was one or more specimens of a giant buffalo, reported by the Awemba to make its home on the marshy shores of the lake. They had assured me that these colossal beasts were unusually fierce and dangerous. From all I was told, they seemed to be a new species of African buffalo.

We set off from Quilimane with light hearts and filled with hope. Mile after mile we journeyed onwards. Everything went according to plan, and the river journey proved quite uneventful. The *Sarotti* behaved beautifully, and fully justified the care I had devoted to its design. We were a very happy party, and enjoyed every minute of our adventure until we made the difficult passage of the watershed to Fife, over the so-called Stevenson Road. This was no road at all, in the generally accepted meaning of that word. After several weary. weeks of hard labour in a terrific tropical heat, we managed to push the launch on its specially designed wheeled-carriage across the watershed, and reached the banks of the Chambezi River.

Even when the little *Sarotti* once more floated on the waters of this river, our trials were not ended. The next phase of the journey to Bangweolo was full of dangers, unexpected and impossible to guard against. The river had never before been navigated by anything larger than an African's canoe ; it was uncharted, and full of snags and sandbanks ; and the hippo daily threatened our small craft with disaster. These brutes seemed to have a passion for bumping us or else trying to climb on board. As we slowly voyaged down the river, our hearts were often in our mouths.

Comparatively speaking, all went well with us until we had almost reached the shores of Bangweolo. Then disaster, dire and dreadful, overtook and swamped us. Within sight of our goal, we were overcome by a cruel and relentless fate.

At dawn, one morning, the blood-red sun of a new day rose triumphantly over the crest of the dark chain of the Muchemwa Mountains, drenching the countryside in vivid colouring. It bade us rise, and continue our journey down the Chambezi to our longed-for destination. The sun melted the mists on the river's surface ; and at our feet, as we emerged from our tent on the bank, lay our little motor-boat. It was anchored in a small bay formed by a deep bend in the river's course.

A deep peace and stillness pervaded everything ; but in Africa things happen so quickly, that there is seldom any real warning of approaching danger. One moment all is happiness and contentment : the next, you are battling for your life against some wholly unexpected terror. Little did we know, as we stood on the bank of the river and watched the beauties of the gorgeous sunrise, what that day held in store for us. Perhaps it was well that we were unable to gaze into the mirror of life.

As the sun rose in the sky, we embarked on the launch. A few moments later, we were being rowed lustily down the Chambezi towards Bangweolo, for whenever possible we conserved our petrol and oil supplies. For a time, nothing unusual occurred. There was no sign of life, except occasional birds and monkeys, along the river's banks. At last, a convenient place to land and have breakfast was seen, and I ran the launch into the bank. While our servants made preparations for the meal, Fière and I rested while lazily smoking and watching the deft handiwork of James in the camp kitchen. Then he called out that out breakfast was ready. We rose, gleefully, to take our seats at the camp table.

As we stood erect, both were petrified with astonishment. Not more than fifty feet from us, and close to the river bank, stood three mighty buffalo of unusual size. They were staring at us with wondering eyes, and perfectly motionless. They had appeared so suddenly and silently through the reeds and bush that nobody had any warning of their approach.

And these were no ordinary buffalo. They were simply gigantic, and suggested to my mind a type of prehistoric animal.

Silence, deep and impressive, reigned for a brief moment or two. It was like the silence that foreshadows death, when the whole world and life seem to stop breathing momentarily. And then I awoke to the extremity of the danger that threatened us. With almost automatic precision, I unslung my rifle from my shoulder, and Fière followed my example.

I fired the instant my cheek rested on the butt of my Mauser rifle and the sights came on my target. *Bang !* The shot ran out, awakening the bird life. The report echoed through the trees to the distant mountain range, and then came back faintly to us.

The leading buffalo stumbled and fell forward on his knees, rose again, shook his ponderous head in mingled pain and shock, and then galloped up the river bank and out of sight into the bush. The other two followed in his wake.

Meanwhile, Fière stood ready to shoot in case of necessity ; but there was no further need now. Intermittently, through the dense undergrowth, we caught glimpses of the shaggy forms of the three buffalo as they followed the course of the river toward the lake. Presently, we could see only two of them.

What had become of the third we asked ourselves ? We were not yet cut of danger, apparently. Possibly the wounded buffalo would return to attack us ; but equally well it might be that the three were still together, and we could only see two of them. After a short period of thought, I decided that it was probable that the wounded beast had left his companions. That would be a sure indication that he was badly wounded. If this was so, it would be splendid. We should be able to secure that trophy, after a long pursuit. *Bos caffer graetzii* would read well in the natural history records of African fauna, I thought to myself !

The decision to follow up and kill the wounded giant was soon made. Breakfast was forgotten. Leaving James and two of our natives to clear away the untasted meal and pack the launch ready for a renewed start down the river, Fière and I hastened off on the trail of the buffalo.

It was not difficult to follow. Large smears of blood were seen everywhere—on bushes, boulders, grass and leaves. I must have hit that buffalo pretty hard, judging by that bloody trail. The spoor led up the bank of the Chambezi, and patently the wounded animal was headed for the shelter of the papyrus reeds around Lake Bangweolo. If so, we should gaze upon that most mysterious lake before we had expected.

Hour after hour passed, and still we kept doggedly on the trail of the beast. The sun climbed higher into the sky until it stood directly over our heads, scorching us and everything with its fierce rays ; but we were far too intent on our quarry to pay heed to the trials of terrific heat or the rough going. We were obsessed with the lust to kill this new species of African mammoth. Until we had done so, we could know no rest of body or mind. What we had wounded, we must now kill.

At last, after over six hours of fruitless search, nature demanded a temporary halt and rest. The afternoon was well advanced, and we felt ravenous for neither had eaten since dinner on the previous evening. I decided to have the launch brought up to us, and sent back one of our native followers to tell James to come on up the river to the spot where we

had halted. We reclined in the shade and rested, waiting for
the launch to arrive with something to eat and drink.

An hour before sundown, the motor-boat reached us, and
James got busy with the preparation of a much-needed meal.
We watched his work with hungry anticipation. Breakfast,
lunch and tea must be merged into one meal.

While the repast was being prepared, I sent three of our
natives to search further for the wounded buffalo. I felt quite
positive that he must be lying up in thick cover somewhere
in our neighbourhood ; and I wanted this specimen, and was
determined to get it. I offered a liberal reward in cash if they
located the beast for me. With this incentive, they hurried off
into the dense bush.

We had just finished our meal when they came running back
with word that the wounded giant had been found. He was
lying down in the long grass near the river bank, not far from
where we then were. We had hoped for some such kind of
luck, but had scarcely expected to find it so soon. Fière and I
rose excitedly to our feet, and got our rifles ready. We were
only just in time, for a second later the tall grass parted in
front of us, and the buffalo dashed out straight at us.

We both fired simultaneously, so that the two gun reports
sounded as one. Having shot, I sprang to one side to avoid
that infuriated charge of the beast. As I did so, my foot caught
in a tree-root, hidden in the long grass, and I fell forward on to
my knees. This accident proved my salvation. If I had remained
erect, I must have been impaled upon the sharp and cruel
points of the buffalo's wide-sweeping horns.

Snorting with intense anger, the huge animal nosed under
me as I fell forward on the ground. He tried hard to toss me
into the air on those wicked horns, but failed to get a hold of
my body. At last, I sprang to my feet and clung with all my
strength to the horns. I hoped that, severely wounded as the
beast was, he might give way to me or that Fière could get a
chance for a safe shot. For a brief moment or two, which
seemed like hours, the buffalo and I pitted our strength against
each other. The huge beast was· rapidly tiring from loss of
blood, and I made a supreme effort to throw him to the ground
or, at least, hold him so that Fière might deliver the death-shot.
But I was no match for that brute's terrific strength, and there
came no shot from my companion.

It all happened in a brief second or two. The buffalo tried to shake off my grip on his horns and, as he flung his massive head from side to side, the point of the left horn pierced deep into my right cheek. I cried out in agony, and then felt myself lifted bodily off the ground and hurled skywards. I remember nothing further of what happened. It was just as well that Nature had dropped a curtain over that scene and blotted out the ghastliness of it all.

In the meantime, I learned afterwards, Fière had come gallantly to my aid, wholly unmindful of his own great danger. It was some time before he could manage to shoot without the risk of hitting me instead of the buffalo. As I was flung away, he fired; but only succeeded in wounding and making the beast more infuriated than ever. The savage brute turned upon Fière instantly, and tossed him again and again. His body was fearfully torn and gored. Then, as if worn out with his terrific vengeance, the buffalo toppled over dead beside our mangled and unconscious bodies.

I recovered my senses to find myself covered with blood and racked by an extremity of pain. I was stretched out on the bank of the river, with the motor-boat afloat below me, being supported in the arms of two of the native followers. Another man was washing my dreadful wounds with cool water.

" Where is the other *Bwana ?* " I managed to whisper.

The effort was so terribly painful that I almost swooned again.

" The others are bringing him here. He will die soon," answered one of the men sadly.

" And the buffalo ? "

" Dead ! " came the laconic reply.

A flood of thick blood was flowing continually from my mouth and the right side of my face. The two natives lifted me gently, to carry me back to the tent which had been erected on the bank ; but, with every movement, the blood flowed faster and the pain was excruciating.

" Quick ! " I managed to gasp out. " Bring the medicine-chest ! "

They brought it. There was only one thing to do, and that quickly. Sew, sew, sew ! Terrible necessity taught me how to ply that surgical needle and thread. With a native holding up my shaving-mirror, and another supporting me from behind, I thrust the needle through the raw flesh. A jagged, irregular hole, as large as my hand, gaped in my right cheek; and my under-lip hung down loosely, quivering. Under the horrified stare of the natives, I jabbed the curved needle again and again through my flesh. Somehow I managed to cobble up the tattered ends.

The pain was terrific. Heaven alone helped me to keep my senses and carry on with the ghastly torture of the self-inflicted surgery. My whole being was in revolt, and I was feeling a deadly sickness. To this day, I do not know how it was possible for me to have completed that operation on myself. But it got done, somehow : and more or less efficiently.

My lower jaw was fractured in two different places : near the ear, and near the lips. From this crushed mass, a long splinter of bone, with three teeth attached, hung loosely by the nerves and flesh of the gums. The whole outer flesh of my lower jaw had been scraped loose from the bone. Teeth, roots and bones showed white and shimmering through the awful cavity in my cheek. My tongue had been pierced by the point of the buffalo's horn, and half torn from its roots. I spat out, continually, large and small splinters of bone and broken teeth.

The operation completed to the best of my ability, I made the best job I could of bandaging my face. A strong neat brandy put new life into me, and furnished the necessary strength to face that other surgical operation for poor Fière.

While I had been cobbling up my tattered face, James had prepared a bed in the tent for each of us. When I reached them, he had cut away Fière's clothes with a pair of scissors and had him ready for me to do what I could for the fearful wounds. As I staggered to his side, Fière regained consciousness. Softly his white lips framed two words : " *Très mauvais !* "

A rapid survey of his mangled body showed me at once that his case was quite hopeless. I gave him a stiff injection of morphia, and then set to work to make him as comfortable as I could. I knew he had no possible chance of living for long, and my efforts were directed to easing his pain.

He had been tossed and pierced by those sharp-pointed horns no less than three times. His left breast muscle hung loose with a flap of raw flesh ; his heart and lungs, happily, had not been touched ; and, in his left side, between heart and hip, was a ghastly tear of considerable extent. I sewed up this wound at once, and then did what little I could for the others.

When I had completed my rough surgery, James washed, bandaged and put Fière to bed. I was feeling far too weak, sick at all I had seen and had had to do, and too full of pain to be capable of doing any more for my poor companion. Fière was now breathing regularly, and appeared to be sleeping. As I sat on my bed, watched and listened, I began to entertain hopes that he might just pull through the crisis and eventually recover.

Night fell, dark and dismal. It was a night filled with torturing pain, during which my mouth seemed to be filled with red-hot coals. Toward morning, a short and troubled sleep gave me a temporary measure of relief from the awful torments I had to endure. With the grey light of dawn, I awoke to fresh agonies and found everything deathly still about me.

I summoned our servants by clapping my hands together. I could not shout, or do more than whisper softly. Even that effort made me feel sick and faint from the terrible pain the slight movement occasioned.

They came and opened the door of the tent. Fortified by another strong drink of neat brandy, I arose painfully and slowly from the bed, and staggered over to Fière. The first light of a new day fell on a white and shrunken face. I knew at once that he was dead, and freed from all earthly pains. In my heart, I envied him.

So, on the very threshold of success, one was taken and the other left a shattered wreck of a man. It was cruel hard luck !

I instructed James to make arrangements to bury poor Fière's body near our camp, and then to send off a man to Kasama, in North-Eastern Rhodesia, to bring succour. This was the nearest point where any Europeans could be found. And thus, far from all medical aid and alone with my native servants, I faced the grim situation with the best fortitude I could summon to my help.

Dr. G. F. Randall, the District Surgeon, and Mr. Cookson, the District Magistrate, marched day and night for two days to my assistance. But those four to five days of waiting can best be imagined than told in cold words. They were a never-ending nightmare of excruciating bodily pain and grievous mental torture.

Randall performed further surgical operations upon me, and under the most difficult circumstances, in order that I could be moved. And then, on an improvised stretcher, I was carried back to Kasama. That journey was sheer agony to my tortured body, and rendered all the more tragic because of the death of Fière.

With the sad procession was carried the body of my late companion, and Cookson arranged for temporary burial at Charenama ; but, later, his body was taken to Kasama and buried there by the White Fathers of the Roman Catholic Mission.

For many weeks I was most carefully nursed back to health and strength at Kasama. When fit to travel, I came on up to Dar-es-Salaam for additional operations in the hospital.

That giant buffalo has turned my face into a caricature of what it was once. I can never look the same again, and must always carry these dreadful scars.

CHAPTER XVIII

PIG-STICKING AND " WART-HOGGING "

THE wart-hog of Africa is regarded by most sportsmen as a conspicuous failure. I have only had a few adventures with them, but am never likely to forget any of those experiences. Despite the contempt bestowed on this beast, he is still entitled to a place on the list of dangerous game. Personally, I would class the nimble wart-hog as more risky to tackle than, possibly, even hippo or crocodiles. There are many who will disagree, but it must remain a matter of individual experience.

Wart-hogs are always fierce, swift of action and treacherous ; always full of fight and endowed with plenty of courage ; and invariably hideous both in personal appearance and attack. They will never acknowledge defeat until dead, and, just so long as they can stand up, will fight to the very last breath in their bodies. I have known them to continue battling even when quite incapable of standing up on their feet. Pluck and agility are their long suits.

In the old sporting days of Kenya's infancy, I have often taken part in an organized pig-sticking party, with the ugly wart-hog as substitute for the pig of India. It was real good fun, and provided excellent sport and real hard riding.

There was one Indian Army Colonel, whom I met in Delhi, when first in India after the Boer War, who always insisted that the word " pig-sticking " was highly objectionable. He was a peppery old gentleman with an enlarged liver, and had spent over forty years in the service of India. He was dogmatically Early Victorian in his views, and always stoutly maintained that the sport should be called " hog-hunting " and never " pig-sticking." I understand that it was so called in his earlier days in India. The new name signified a barbaric innovation that was repulsive to him in every way, and served to illustrate the degeneracy of the modern times and the sublime

169

superiority of his golden era. As he would be now close on the century mark, I much doubt if he is alive to take me to task again on this subject.

After all, what is there in a name ? It is the sport that matters ; and pig-sticking is a real he-man sport. There are many who claim it to be the premier sport of India ; and I am inclined to agree with them. Wherever there are sporting pigs to be found—and they are generally that, fair ground over which to gallop fast, and good horses to carry you, this great sport will always find its ardent devotees.

I shall always remember one Sunday morning when pig-sticking on the Athi Plains outside Nairobi. A party of six went out after wart-hogs almost before the dawn had broken. I was riding a fast Indian country-bred mare, Judith, and she was ideal for the work—speedy, sure-footed, quick to turn, and galloped straight. Only the best mounted and good riders can hope to keep well up to a wart-hog in full flight ; and the going is always rather rough. A wart-hog brought to bay can prove an uncomfortably dangerous customer.

He is a somewhat small type of the boar family, with big and ferocious tushes ; the upper being anything up to ten or eleven inches in length, and the lower pair about six inches. He stands, when full grown, just over two feet in height, and weighs from 170 to 180 pounds. At night they generally inhabit any ant-bear holes they fancy, eject the rightful owner and enlarge the subterranean home to take their bodies in comfort. They back down into these holes, always preferring to keep their wicked tushes to the possible foe.

They are accommodating enough to come out of their refuge, or the cover in which they have hidden during the hours of darkness, in the small hours of the morning. After feeding, they return to their cover or burrows soon after daylight. Often one may disturb them during the daytime. In any case, early morn or later in the day, you may be certain of a really first-class gallop after them. Once they know you are in pursuit, they make off at a very fast pace. Only those who have enjoyed the delights of pig-sticking in India or Africa can realize how fast a boar or sow can move when hotly hustled from the rear or flank.

We had not been out on the Athi Plains very long that morning when we put up a couple of well-grown wart-hogs—a boar and a sow. We went after them hell-for-leather, and the quarry wasted no time in showing us their heels. At four hundred yards I was well up with the boar. Bending low in the saddle, I poised my spear for a thrust ; but the boar jinked and threw me off my mark. As I wheeled to follow him, another sportsman closed up on the boar's heels. Again came a sharp jink, and the quarry deftly dodged the fatal spear-point.

Now the boar was headed straight for a thick patch of cover, a hundred yards away. I held after him, spurring my willing mare to added effort. I glanced back over my shoulder for a brief instant, and saw the others at full gallop after the sow. I had the boar to myself, for the other man had gone off on a runaway horse. I chortled at my luck.

With a final burst of speed and another jink, the boar almost made the edge of the cover. I rode up alongside and thrust hard with my spear. My point took the boar in the ribs, just behind the shoulder. Mad with pain and fury, he turned and charged full at me as I tried to check Judith and return to the attack. That boar was no coward.

Before I could dodge that swift and savage charge, he had got home on my gallant little mare. Judith uttered a shrill squeal of pain, and collapsed under me. The cruel upward thrust of those large tushes had almost disembowelled her. Jumping lightly from her back, I whipped out my revolver and faced the boar as he charged full tilt again. My spear had broken off short in my hand. I was forced to shoot that wart-hog in self-defence, for it was either he or I had to go under.

I looked at my mare and saw her case was hopeless. A merciful bullet in the brain ended her torment. *That* was a rotten job to perform !

I walked back to Nairobi, carrying my saddle and bridle. My heart was sad within me, for the boar's tushes as a trophy were no compensation for the loss of Judith. Horses could be bought, at a price, but not another to equal that splendid mare.

I have hunted wart-hogs with dogs, and seen the latter tackle them with the utmost courage and cunning. I had three fox-terriers, who had devised their own plan of campaign ; and never knew them fail. They were covered with scars, but consistently brought down their quarry. I always rode close behind them to see fair play, but was seldom called upon to intervene on their behalf.

Their *modus operandi* was most interesting. Directly we put up a wart-hog, the three game little dogs were after it at once.

They knew exactly what to do, when, and how to avoid any waste of time or effort. They were experts. Their team work would be difficult to excel.

As soon as they got fairly close to the ugly beast, one of the terriers ranged alongside to the right of the boar's head, while the other two kept close up to the stern. Then one of the hindmost dogs seized a favourable moment to race in and grab hold of a hind leg in his mouth. He held on and tugged like grim death, all four feet planted on the ground and being dragged along in the wake of the beast. The boar slackened speed, and then, before he could halt and swing round for attack, in ran the other terrier and fastened his teeth into the other hind leg. At the same moment, the leading dog rushed in and fastened on to the boar's right ear. All three now held on like limpets, pulling strongly backwards.

Suddenly the boar would go down, the dogs having jerked him over on his side by united effort. Almost too quick for the eye to follow the movements, the terrier let go of the ear and grabbed hold of the boar's throat. He made no mistake about it, and had his teeth well into the wind-pipe before those cruel tushes could get in their deadly work.

At the same instant, the two dogs on the hind legs let go and ran in to bite furiously at the overturned hog's belly. The fight was pretty fierce and strenuous while it lasted ; but, before I had trotted up to the scene, it was all over. The wart-hog's throat had been torn to shreds, and the beast was partially disembowelled. A merciful bullet from my revolver ended the hog's life.

I have never seen the equal of those three little dogs. They were a mass of scars from gashes by wicked tushes ; but, no matter how severely injured, nothing could stop them returning to their sport. One by one, however, they were killed by a savage boar or sow. That was inevitable.

One evening in Nairobi, I happened to be at the Norfolk Hotel with a party of cheery sportsmen. The conversation was all connected with big game shooting, and drifted into an open debate on the various methods of hunting. The mention of wart-hogs brought forth a suggestion from me that it might prove entertaining to ride them down with revolvers. I instanced Blayney Percival's innovation, just tried out successfully, of riding down lions in this manner. My proposal was received with a frigid silence ; then someone laughed, more in disdain

Photo by Dr. L. R. Magoon

THREE RHINO HEADS

KILLED IN SELF-DEFENCE

than in mirth. John Egerton, however, acclaimed the idea as not devoid of sporting interest. I took him up at once, and he agreed to join me in a trial of the plan on the following Sunday morning. We left it at that : details to be settled later.

Not wishing to risk another favourite horse after my wart-hog sticking experience, when poor Judith was lost to me, we arranged to hire two Somali ponies from Ali Khan, the Afghan horse-dealer of Nairobi. It was further agreed that the Athi Plains should be the scene of our novel hunt, for here we could be almost certain to find hogs. We voted that the new sport should be christened " wart-hogging."

We set forth at an hour before the dawn. Our mounts were sorry looking specimens of horseflesh. For want of stable names we dubbed them " Whisky " and " Soda." They would have made an ideal pair for a hearse, judging by their speed if not their colouring.

Arrived on the scene of our hunt, we cast round for a lively wart-hog to gallop down. Half an hour passed, and we had not even glimpsed one. Then Egerton let out a yell, and pointed to our right. A family of six wart-hogs had broken cover, and were racing away through the thick grass in single file, with tails struck straight up in the air. We pulled out our revolvers from their holsters, settled ourselves in the saddles, dug spurs into the ribs of our emaciated mounts, and set off at their best speed in pursuit of the hog family. Egerton and I rode neck to neck, and it was anyone's race. The odds, however, appeared to be favourable to the wart-hogs, to my way of thinking.

Gradually we gained, and our hopes rose. When within revolver range, each selected a target and fired. But our mounts had not bargained for any firearms, and thoroughly disapproved of the noise so close to their ears. They promptly shied into each other, and almost unseated us. Both blamed the other, loudly and strongly, and slowly disentangled ourselves from the deadlock. And Ali Khan had sworn by all his gods that these ponies were not gun-shy. May he be forgiven !

Meanwhile the hogs were getting further and further from us, so we dropped the acrimonious argument and set off once more in pursuit. Slowly we began to overhaul them. When within range again, I had another shot at an old boar. I hit him full in the stern, just below that cocky tail of his : it was the only target he presented. He halted at once, wheeled about, and stood to face me. He was snarling savagely, with cruel tushes bared, and forefoot pawing the ground. His fierce, twinkling little eyes positively spat venomous hate at me. I should have felt the same way if I had been hit by a revolver bullet where he had been wounded. I drove straight at him, revolver levelled to shoot at his chest, and hoping to rake him.

When within thirty yards, I aimed deliberately. As I was about to press the trigger, my pony put his foot into a hole, came down on nose and knees, and somersaulted me clean over his head toward the boar. I landed in a sitting position, with a nasty jarring bump that rattled my teeth and winded me momentarily. I found myself facing the boar, but took little comfort in the fact when I saw those nasty big tushes bared. I still clutched my revolver, fortunately. For a second or two I sat still where I was, trying to collect my scattered wits. Then I saw the boar advancing boldly to investigate this unusual phenomenon. Instantly I awoke to the need of swift action.

I hurriedly aimed my revolver at his chest, and pressed the trigger twice in rapid succession. The first shot missed, but the second bowled him over within ten yards of me. I felt very relieved to see him drop, for I never have any confidence in the accuracy of my revolver-shooting. Close proximity to those wicked tushes did not look the least bit healthy.

Seeing the ugly little beast did not move, I scrambled to my feet and looked around for Egerton and my mount. The latter was grazing contentedly about a hundred yards from me ; the former was some distance away, galloping hard behind another boar. He was shooting at intervals, and I could see the spurts of dust all round the hunted beast. As I watched his progress, the pony suddenly jibbed and stopped dead. Egerton took a lovely toss over the sorry nag's head. I confess that I laughed immoderately, hoping that he had not witnessed my own recent discomfiture. A moment or two later, the quarry had gone into thick cover.

By the time I had recaptured my fool pony and remounted, there was no sign of any of the wart-hog family. I rode over to my companion to see if he had been hurt by his fall. Bodily he was not ; but his temper and self-respect had been badly strained. I smoothed down his ruffled feathers as best I could, and he accompanied me back to my kill. We cut out the magnificent tushes from the boar, and I strapped them to my saddle. They made a fine trophy, and I was genuinely proud of them.

" Let's on with the motley, and hie us forth to give battle to more hogs," I suggested joyously. " It's a sport which grows on one."

Egerton snorted.

" Nothin' doin'," he growled firmly. " It's a rotten fool game, and I'm through ! Let's get back to the Norfolk for an iced beer."

For some time we rode homewards in silence. On the way we suddenly put up another family of wart-hogs—pa, ma and half-grown son. I looked at Egerton enquiringly, and he nodded his head curtly. We started after the hogs.

Soon Egerton had cast off his gloom, and now rode hard after the boar. He missed badly with the first shot, but registered with his second. As he fired for the second time, " Soda " baulked badly. The sudden, twisting movement of the thin pony enforced a parting between rider and steed. Egerton landed right on top of the carcass of the old boar, which had not moved. He sat there shouting violent abuse at " Soda," simply frothing at the mouth with mingled fury and disgust. The Somali pony's pedigree was the main theme of that vitriolic oratory. I have heard horses called some hard names in times of war and peace, but——. If " Soda " had any shred of pride left in his half-starved body and soul, then his ears must have burned to a cinder on hearing that insulting harangue. But I fancy the poor beast's life had been much too hard for him to have remained sensitive.

Suddenly Egerton broke off short and leaped to his feet with a roar of dismay. The boar had jerked spasmodically under him in the final contractions of death. Then it lay still for good. It must have been an unpleasant shock for my companion; but the interruption saved " Soda " from being shot out of hand.

Having retrieved the tushes, we were once more ready for such adventure as might come our way. We walked off sedately toward Nairobi. Three miles from the outskirts of the budding township, we put up another smallish boar and gave chase at once. This time, " Whisky " showed much more inclination to share the sport with me, and we careered along in the wake of the boar at a fast clip. We were overhauling him rapidly, when I saw a large sow run for an ant-bear hole and hurriedly back down it. My young boar made for the same refuge, about turned and started to back down also. He got down about three-quarters of his length and then came out again with a rush. The sharp tushes of that old sow on his stern must have proved a most uncomfortable surprise. But he was off again before I could get in a shot. I was laughing too heartily even to attempt to fire at him.

We galloped on after him and, as we drew near once more, I started to shoot from my saddle. My first four bullets went wide : very wide indeed. I spurred " Whisky " and managed to get up alongside the boar, and sent in a fifth shot. This time my aim was better, for it got the beast near the heart and over he went. My last shot went into his head, and finished him. The third trophy of the morning was mine.

By now I had come to the conclusion that the new sport was really worth following up. As I dismounted over my kill, " Soda " ambled up alongside of " Whisky." Was this an equine hint ? I did feel most infernally parched at the throat. I looked behind and saw Egerton again seated on the bare veld. He was turning the air purple with abuse of " Soda." I mounted and trotted back to him, leading the reluctant " Soda " by the bridle. He did not seem to like my companion !

" I believe this is your mount," I suggested sweetly.

" Don't be a damned fool ; and go to hell ! " was all the thanks I received.

It appears that an ant-bear hole had dethroned the rider, just when off-guard and engaged in lighting his pipe. I must say that he had my sympathy.

The rest of our ride homewards was made in silence. It was only when we entered the town's limits that Egerton forgot his disgust with Ali Khan's steed, and burst into hearty, ringing laughter.

" Given a decent moke under you, ' wart-hogging ' is none too bad ! " he exclaimed. " Let's have another shot at it, some other Sunday. What say you ? "

" I'm game," I agreed.

But I did not have a chance to " wart-hog " again for several years. Shortly after this outing I was transferred to Kisumu. The next occasion was when I introduced Kermit Roosevelt to the sport on Kamiti Ranch. We had no success, though we rode a boar hard. He did not seem to think much of the sport. In the light of my experience, I do not think that it really appeals to me.

I must admit that pig-sticking is infinitely better than " wart-hogging." But in Kenya this sport is nothing like as good as in India. On the Athi Plains, round Nakuru and Naivasha, where I have sampled it a number of times at odd intervals, I found the going very treacherous, so that one had to pay more attention to the ground traversed at a gallop than to the quarry hunted. In pig-sticking, it is fatal to take your eyes off the hog.

The wart-hog's speed is often most surprising, and real hard galloping is necessary to come within spearing distance. He is every bit as nasty a customer as the boar in India. He will turn like a flash of lightning on you, and charge straight home.

The most interesting and amusing adventure which I have ever had with wart-hog was staged unexpectedly in Southern Rhodesia. I was photographing wild animals on Toms' Farms, near Wankie, and actually following up a fine herd of sable antelope to film them. They had just trotted over the brow of a wooded hill, and I trod a well-worn game track leading from a sheet of water in an adjacent swamp.

All at once I saw something walking daintily toward me down this path. I stood still and watched. A baby hippo? I got my movie-camera ready for action, and crept forward to closer range. The early morning sunlight had grossly deceived me, for that baby hippo proved to be a rather formidable wart-hog. Yard by yard, I crept closer and wondered what he would do ; but edged round to the right, so as to get the sun over my shoulder.

The wart-hog still advanced mincingly toward me, just as if stepping on red-hot bricks. Suddenly he halted dead in his tracks ; and I stood still also. Something must have alarmed him, though I had made no noise. There could not have been more than thirty to forty feet dividing us. Now he stood motionless, listening intently, while his shifty eyes glared first at me and then all about him. He seemed to be in two minds as to my intentions, even as I was about his. Then, most unforeseen, he lay down in the pathway ; but still those beady little eyes were fixed on me. This was all really interesting, for I had never known, or heard, of a wart-hog behaving in this way. Most generally, they charge at sight or else bolt to safety. When I had got to twenty feet from him, he rose and faced me with tushes bared and grunted menacingly. Thus far, but no further !

My camera began to register the boar's changing expressions and jumpy movements. I worked feverishly to get a good length of film ; and the results proved all and more than I had dared to expect.

That wart-hog was a perfect little gentleman ; and, there-fore, wholly untrue to type. He turned this way and that, posing really admirably for me. Then he heard the approach of my host, H. G. Robins, Colonel Tomlinson, and Jim, the Matebele headman of the ranch. He swung round to face this new menace, but on ticked the motor of my camera. Then he faced abruptly toward me, pawed the ground savagely with a forefoot, and once more bared those wicked tushes. I thought that he intended to charge home ; but he did not. Suddenly, he about turned and beat a strategic retreat. He trotted over the brow of the hill, his tail straight out behind him, and dis-appeared from view. I let him go, for I had got all I wanted from him.

I owe that wart-hog my apologies for having deprived him of his morning drink and bath ; equally my sincere thanks for having posed so perfectly for my camera.

No prince could have behaved more graciously !

CHAPTER XIX

A MASAI LION HUNT

WHEN stationed at Kyambu in 1906, both Dagoretti and N'gong were included in the large district. I often rode over there on duty, and made a point of always calling to see Ol Onana, the *Laibon* (King and Chief Medicine Man) of the warlike Masai. His chief *manyatta* (village) was situated close to Mount N'gong and within my district.

Ol Onana was a fine old man, very interesting and unusually intelligent for a native of Africa. He was a staunch friend of the British and the Government of Kenya.

The Masai are the very finest tribe in Africa, with the possible exception of the Zulu people in Natal. For many years before the construction of the Uganda Railway, they were the real overlords of the country ; at least, that part of the highlands situated around their territory. Always they had been very formidable, and the neighbouring tribes, such as the Wakikuyu, lived in constant fear of the Masai ; as also did the caravans passing to and from Uganda before railhead reached Nairobi.

These people are born soldiers, well trained and disciplined, and the aristocrats of the natives of Eastern Africa. Their military organization was second only to that created by Chaka, and carried on by Dingaan, among the Zulus. They are of Nilotic origin, and numerically have never much exceeded 25,000 people.

On one of my periodical visits to Ol Onana, he reported the theft of some of his cattle. Accompanied by a few of his men, I set out to recover them ; and, by great good fortune, accomplished my mission. He was exceedingly grateful for my help and, to show his appreciation, offered to stage a lion hunt by his warriors for my special edification. I had often heard of this amazing and thrilling spectacle, and was most anxious to witness it ; so I accepted his offer with alacrity.

179

Let me first explain that it is the ambition of every Masai warrior to kill a lion with his own spear. When this has been done, he is entitled to wear a lion's mane head-dress and becomes the recognized captain of a troop of spearsmen. You may often see these handsome, lithe young warriors proudly wearing their hard-earned trophy. It is the very highest honour to which any man in the tribe can attain and, for this reason, the trophy is worn every day. The very fact of its possession is the hall-mark of personal courage and manhood; and no man may question these qualities in any Masai who wears a lion's mane cap. It makes a most effective head-dress, not unlike the bear-skin of the Brigade of Guards.

Ol Onana was true to his word, and provided me with a really marvellous spectacle on the plains beyond Mount N'gong. On the following morning, when I rode out to the appointed place, he was there with a splendid gathering of over a hundred spearsmen. A few of them already wore the proud insignia of the lion-killer ; but the majority were *leoni* (young warriors) eager to win this coveted distinction.

All present were armed with long, narrow-bladed spears, had swords strapped to their waists, and carried heavy shields of buffalo-hide in their left hands. Those who did not wear the lion's mane cap had a fringe of black ostrich feathers framing their faces.

They looked as keen as a pack of hounds to get going after a lion which had been located near at hand by four scouts sent out on the previous afternoon. When all was ready, Ol Onana gave the signal to move off.

The warriors first drove a horn-shaped wedge down a long and narrow valley, covered with long grass and dotted with small scrub. I followed behind the line of attack, while Ol Onana walked proudly beside me. The old man's keen face was alight with excitement, his eyes fixed on his warriors; and he scarcely spoke a word.

I was rather wondering how Tobasco, the Arab stallion I was riding, would behave when we found the lion. I had only recently bought him, and he had yet to be introduced to a lion. I need not have been anxious, for he behaved perfectly.

We had not proceeded far before there came a loud and joyous shout from a warrior in the lead at the right tip of the horn. A lion broke cover about five hundred yards to the immediate front of our advance. At the same instant that he showed himself, the spearsmen broke into a jog trot after him, gradually sending out their line on either flank so as to get round the animal and wholly encircle him. They ran silently, intent on their task; while the lion trotted rapidly ahead.

Two miles or so must have been covered before the two horns of the half-circle met in advance of the lion's retreat. The warriors now all turned inwards, their spears flashing in the sunlight. A few minutes later, the lion was enclosed in a wide-flung circle of bristling spears. Silence reigned over the veld. No one spoke. The only audible sound was the sibilant swish of the grass as the warriors pushed through it. Now they were closing in upon their prey, with a deadly certainty. I could see over the heads of the spearsmen nearest to me, and clearly saw the tautly held, tawny body of the full-grown black-maned lion brought to bay. Yard by yard, the warriors narrowed their circle, ever closing in upon him with that defiant hedge of flashing spear-blades. The forward movement was sinister, relentless and unpausing.

The lion now stood his ground. He had come to an abrupt halt on finding himself completely ringed round by the spears. He twisted his grand head majestically first this way and then that, bewildered by this unforeseen and determined attack. All the time he was growling and snarling savagely, like a dog worrying a bone. Once or twice he emitted an angry roar; and the ground seemed to vibrate to that menacing challenge.

As the Masai warriors crept ever nearer, the lion began to swish his tail from side to side, all the time snarling more and more loudly and fiercely. There came, at intervals, a deep rumbling noise from his chest and throat, as if a volcano was about to erupt. Occasionally, he flung up his magnificent head and uttered a terrifying roar. The barbaric sound set my nerves tingling. That challenging note of defiance must have been clearly audible fully a mile or two distant. Tobasco shivered under me, and was a little restive; but he quickly settled down.

Now all the warriors were in their allotted posts. There seemed to be no one in actual command of the operations, but every man knew exactly what to do and when. They did not need to be told. Discipline and iron self-control were the key-notes of that relentless encircling movement aimed at the majestic brute's life. There was something terrific and awe-inspiring in that steady, sure, silent and provocative advance.

Yard by yard, foot by foot, the hedge of silvery spears closed in like a tidal wave to engulf the lion.

When first they had brought the beast to bay, the warriors must have been at least a quarter of a mile from him, even if measured from the nearest rim of that vicious circle of spear-points. Now they were within a hundred yards. I closed up to the rear ranks, determined to miss nothing of that grim duel between man and beast. And Tobasco went nearer willingly, without fear or protest. I had expected otherwise.

Suddenly, when the spears were about twenty-five to thirty yards away, the lion made four savage charges at that menacing hedge of steel. Now the warriors stood still, unflinching. They met each charge with a solid bank of levelled spear-points. Not a single man moved aside an inch ; every spear-blade was held firmly directed at the lion, and did not even quiver in the bright sunshine. Each time he charged, the lion pulled up abruptly at a short distance from that wicked hedge. He had changed his mind at the last moment, and could not bring himself to attempt a break through the ring of glittering death.

He stood erect, mane standing out fiercely and all the hair on his spine bristling, but always just out of reach of those cruel points of shining steel. For a moment or two he faced up to them, growling savagely and body held taut. Then he roared forth a mighty bellow of impotent rage and utter defiance at his tormentors. My whole body quivered to the savage note. Still the warriors neither flinched nor moved a muscle ; and I doubt if they even blinked an eyelash.

It was a most wonderfully impressive sight. They might have been a battalion of the Guards on parade, and the lion a choleric old General inspecting them and trying to find fault with those who were faultless.

Unexpectedly, the lion wheeled round swiftly and retired to the centre of the arena. Arrived there, he started to walk round the confined space, eyes watching the spearsmen morosely and a deadly hate in their expression. His mane was bristling full out like an Elizabethan ruff, tail swishing from side to side ; and he growled again and again from deep down in his chest. Now his fangs were exposed, as he opened and shut his mouth viciously like a steel-trap, mouth dripping with saliva, and walking about like a prize-fighter on his toes.

I heard and saw no signal given, but abruptly the wall of spearsmen advanced steadily once more. They came again to

THE MALE'S HEAD

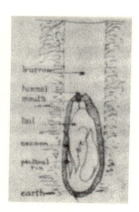

PLAN OF BURROW

THE MALE

THE FEMALE

THE LEPIDOSIREN

a halt within about ten to twelve yards from their prey; and now the spears were raised, shoulder high, threateningly at the lion. He halted suddenly in his feverish circling, and faced them with head lowered and fangs bared.

Then, like a streak of lightning, he launched himself in a desperate effort to break clear of that determined circle of men and spears. He charged full into the line of warriors, choosing a point on the far side of the ring from where I sat Tobasco and watched the fight. I thrilled to the marrow at the savage attack. The only sound was the rush of that huge body, and then a fierce roar of utter ferocity. The lion was now real mad. He knew himself completely cornered, and that he had to fight hard for his life. He was game.

It all happened so swiftly that it was impossible to see or follow exactly what occurred. I saw the shining spears raised on high to strike; saw them flash in the bright sun, and then dart forward to strike; and could see the lion standing up on his hind legs, with huge front paws clawing madly at the nearest warriors. I had a fleeting glimpse of his mouth biting furiously at them. The next instant, it was all over; and the lion had dropped back from my sight behind the wall of spears and warriors.

I trotted forward to the rearmost ranks, stood up in my stirrups and peered over their heads. The lion was on the ground, lying on his side and quite motionless. Fully a dozen long-bladed spears still quivered in the tawny hide, and two had been seized in that huge mouth and twisted almost double. The lion must have died instantly; but went down fighting hard.

The casualties among the Masai were not heavy. In view of the closeness of the contact, they were astoundingly few in number. Two men had been bitten and mauled, one rather severely; and half a dozen had received minor scratches. That was the sum total. I had expected to find many more injured, and perhaps a few even killed. I was frankly surprised.

I turned to Ol Onana. " Whose trophy is it ? " I asked. He shook his head. Who could say yet which spear had been driven home first in that mad final moment of impact with the lion ? Again I looked at the arena, and saw one of the mauled men lifting up the tail of the lion. Ol Onana saw this, too, smiled serenely at me, and then pointed to the man with the beast's tail.

There was no argument. The wounded spearsmen now

dropped the tail to the ground and strode over to Ol Onana. He saluted him gravely by holding up his uninjured arm straight above his head. His spear was still quivering in the lion's broad chest. The *Laibon* gravely inclined his head in acknowledgment of the salute. That was all. No words, no voluble arguments, no brawling and no fighting for the honour of the award of that great prize. The claim was simply lodged, accepted as correct, and the proud victor retired to the carcass to claim the lion's mane. The *Laibon* had ratified the honour won : no more was needed, except to pick up the token.

From the moment of that last desperate charge by the lion until he fell dead, only a minute or two could have elapsed. It left me speechless with thrilled admiration. I entertain the greatest possible respect for the fine and manly qualities of these Masai warriors, their splendid discipline, self-control, skill, bravery and swift action. It takes a real man to stand up to such a charge without even flinching, when armed only with a spear.

I had enjoyed a magnificent view of the entire wonderful fight. It seemed almost incredible to me that a charging lion could be killed so easily and certainly by these warriors, especially when I remembered some of my own hard fights for victory when armed with a powerful and accurate modern rifle.

I rode forward to do what I could to dress the wounds of the injured men. I had brought a small medicine-chest with me, and soon had their wounds disinfected and bandaged. Neither of the two men flinched or made a sound when I poured pure carbolic into the terrible gashes and deep bites. They stood up to this drastic treatment with a stoical indifference to pain that won my complete respect. As I worked over them, they grinned cheerfully into my face. Their heroic fortitude, and their grave unconcern at the fearful wounds, were beyond belief. From the expression on those two men's faces, you would not have thought either of them suffered any pain ; yet they must have been enduring agonies. A lion's claws or teeth can inflict terrible wounds and be most dreadfully painful.

One of the two men had been badly lacerated on the chest and shoulders : the other was cruelly torn on the back, and bitten through one shoulder. Fortunately no bones were broken. The other men's injuries were so slight, they did not even accept my offer of treatment.

While I was dressing these two men's wounds, the other

warriors were engaged in a wild dance of triumph round the carcass of the lion, waving their blood-stained spears in the air, holding their shields above their heads, and uttering blood-curdling yells in the exuberance of victory over their savage foe. They were acting like madmen.

As they danced, first one and then another drove his spear into the carcass ; and then leaped high into the air with a wild yell of savage joy. Soon the tawny hide was a mass of spear-holes, the veld swimming in blood, and the only portion of the body undamaged was the head and mane. That must not be spoiled, for the victor must have his reward.

I walked over to the scene. I had dressed the hero's wounds first of all, and he had hurried away to join in the dance of death. At first, I could not see him in the swiftly prancing circle of men ; but, presently, I singled him out in that crowd of mad warriors. He was the wildest of them all, and his shouts could be heard above those of the others. Wounds were quite forgotten though pain could not be ; only pride and lust of victory held him in their grip.

And then I lost sight of him again. I chanced to look back over my shoulder for Ol Onana, the *Laibon*, and then saw the lion-killer sitting on a boulder by himself at a little distance from his excited fellows. He was now hugging his blood-stained spear to his chest, face immobile and body still, fierce eyes watching the childish but savage antics of his comrades in arms with seeming contempt.

He was now a proved leader of men, his spear lion-blooded, and had gained the highest honour in the tribe. For the first few moments of wild triumph, these facts had been forgotten in his excitement ; but now he was alive to the need to conduct himself like a proved man and not as a child. His conceit and pride in his prowess was palpable, and rather entertained me. Secretly, I have no doubt, he longed to be back in that mad throng of dancing spearsmen, giving tongue to his savage triumph, behaving with an even greater extravagance, and displaying his honest joy. But he knew this would be undignified, so left the clownish performance to his comrades.

I saw Ol Onana stride over to this proven warrior's side, say something to him in a deep guttural voice, rest a paternal hand momentarily on the man's shoulder, and then turn on his heel. The lion-killer rose abruptly and stalked off solemnly in the *Laibon's* wake, saying nothing, looking neither to right nor left, and oblivious to the wild scene of enthusiasm around the fallen lion.

It was the signal that all was ended. Soon the trophy would be collected and borne in triumph to the *manyatta* for the rightful owner ; and the carcass of the lion would be left for the scavengers of the veld to feast upon.

That day holds a memory which can never grow dim.

CHAPTER XX

THE STUPIDITY OF THE RHINO

OF all the major game in Africa, the rhinoceros furnishes the most fruitful topic for dispute among hunters. Opinions as to this beast's dangerous characteristics are seldom in agreement. Many big game hunters of my acquaintance, all men of wide experience in Africa, place him fourth on the list of really dangerous animals ; but I know others, of equal knowledge and experience, who think he holds premier place. I have never been able to accept this latter view ; but every hunter is entitled to his own opinion on this subject.

One thing alone about the habits of the rhino is conceded universally ; and that is, he is the cause of much bad language on many occasions and can be an unmitigated nuisance.

Although not personally ranking the rhino as really a danger in normal circumstances, or as a serious menace to either human life or property, yet I am quite prepared to admit that he can be a most formidable foe. He can supply the hunter with many unpleasant moments, if so minded. His contrariness is so often exercised at the wrong moment, and he is as full of whims as a spoilt child.

The besetting sin of the rhinoceros is an insatiable curiosity. It cannot be curbed or cured. Largely on account of his extremely poor vision and this highly developed curiosity, coupled with arrant stupidity, the rhinoceros is inclined to follow the dictates of his keen sense of smell whenever danger lurks in the immediate vicinity. Given the scent, no matter how faint, of something strange and suspicious, and he will instantly advance in that direction to investigate. He does not wait to see what it may be, for he depends upon his nose rather than his eyesight. A whiff of man-tainted wind, and he feels compelled to satisfy his curiosity at once : and does so. A rhino never waits for trouble to come to him, but goes out to

meet it more than half way. He much prefers to start a fight
than to have one forced upon him.

The rhino is a blundering, brainless fathead, and always has
been ; nothing will ever teach him even a modicum of common
sense. Yet he is a real sportsman and will always give you a
good run for your money. He is utterly fearless. Challenge,
no matter how unwittingly, his presence ; and he will offer
battle at once and in a most determined fashion. Of all the
wild game in Africa, not one single other species is so
consistently set on meeting danger at once, and face to
face.

This strong trait in his character may account for the fact
that so many men insist that he is ugly, useless and highly
dangerous ; and should be exterminated ruthlessly. Granted
that rhinos and cultivated lands do not mix well, yet he is perfectly well aware of this fact and has now taken himself beyond
the reach of advancing civilization. It was not always so.

The first Traffic Manager of the Railways in Kenya, A. E.
Cruickshank, told me a most amusing story of a rhinoceros in
the early days after construction work was completed.

A few Indian railway employees started some vegetable
gardens at Kiu. One of them planted some *Bhang*, or hemp,
in addition to cabbages and the like. When mixed and smoked
with tobacco, it has much about the same effect as opium, and
Indians are very partial to the smoking of this drug. Some
of his crop had grown to maturity and was ready for harvesting,
when an old bull rhino turned up one morning and started in
to sample some of the cabbages. He passed on to the *Bhang*,
and its flavour seemed to meet with his entire approval. He
devoured the entire crop.

After this meal, the rhino became very drowsy and selected
the front door of the Indian's house as the ideal spot for a
noontime siesta. There were no windows, and only this one
door. The Indian coolie, shivering with fright within the hut,
found his only means of escape completely blocked by the
bulky form of the rhino. He was forced to remain where he
was, while hoping that the animal would soon seek pastures
new.

For several hours the rhino slept contentedly as he leaned
up against the doorway of the hut. Awakening refreshed,
however, he ambled off slowly into the bush, sampling some
more cabbages in passing. The Indian was only too delighted

to see the last of him, and wasted no vain regrets on the mangled remnants of his garden.

The Indian station-master, who was a bit of a tartar, fined the innocent victim of this rhino for dereliction of duty. That was, of course, grossly unfair. The coolie complained to the Traffic Manager, who remitted the fine on hearing the facts. The man then demanded compensation for his destroyed crops. This was refused.

The number of casualties resulting from encounters with infuriated rhinos do not warrant the assumption that he is a real menace to mankind. In all my years of wandering about Africa, I have only met three men who have been injured at all seriously by charging rhinos—Major Stigand, Benjamin Eastwood and Colonel Eric Smith. They all survived to relate their experiences, but two of them, Eastwood and Colonel Smith, lost an arm. Stigand received a nasty tear from the horn across his chest. But I have heard of a number of Africans who have been gored or killed by one of these animals.

In the light of my personal experience, I am unable to deny that the rhino is not only ready always for a first-class row, but is invariably inquisitive to an uncomfortable degree. When you can smell but not see any danger threatening, it is only natural either to advance and locate it or else make yourself scarce. The rhino prefers the former line of action, largely so that he can deal suitably with the situation. He cannot be blamed for this truculent attitude. Self-preservation is nine points of the law in civilization, and holds good just as strongly among animal life in the wild regions.

I have said that he is a crass idiot, and will never learn. That is absolutely true. The elephant is unique among beasts of great bulk in that, with its growth in size, there has also been a marked development in brain power. In order to demonstrate this fact, I will draw comparisons between the elephant and rhinoceros ; for the latter is the animal nearest to the elephant in point of size.

Both species are found in the same regions of Africa, and in bulk are more nearly equal than any other terrestrial creatures. But the elephant is the wisest, while the rhinoceros is the most stupid of all animals. Both formerly wandered freely over the plains of the Kenya Highlands ; but, in the past half-century, a marked change has taken place in the habits of these two beasts. The elephant has learned from experience far more readily than has the rhinoceros. As a general rule, therefore, it will be found that the former no longer lives in the open country, whereas the rhinoceros continues to roam the plains and risk being completely exterminated.

An elephant will cross the open spaces at night time only, usually, for he is perfectly well aware that danger lurks there during the sunlit hours of the day. No elephant, in regions where they are hunted regularly, would be so foolish as habitually to spend his days on the open plains. But that is exactly what the fool rhinoceros does. The former animal is wisdom personified ; the latter no more than a brainless, chump-headed dunce.

Moreover, the sight of both beasts is very indifferent. In consequence, the elephant has quickly learned to take refuge in those areas where sound and scent count for far more as protective measures than good eyesight. Both animals depend almost entirely upon ears and noses for warning against, and the location of, danger threatening them ; and both sadly need a visit to a first-class oculist. In many respects the elephant surpasses the rhinoceros in powers of vision ; but neither of them can boast of even moderately good eyesight. It is well for all hunters that neither of these animals wears spectacles, though it might prove an amusing sight. Their powers of scent and hearing, however, are so highly developed as to compensate for their defective vision.

The black rhinoceros formerly inhabited Africa from the Cape to Abyssinia and Somaliland. By retreating to the cover of the dense thorny forests or uninhabited areas of southern Africa, this species has, so far, escaped entire extinction at the hands of ruthless butchers. A few exist in the game reserves of South Africa, and of late years steadily have been increasing in numbers. Isolated specimens still can be found in the bush-lands of the north-eastern portion of the Transvaal and in the two Rhodesias ; and a fairly large number are known to inhabit the forests in the southern area of Portuguese East Africa. But they are only seen in anything approaching large numbers in Central and Eastern Africa, and even further northwards.

The few surviving specimens in South Africa are now strictly protected. They are breeding there, and thus will prevent any possibility of extinction, as will happen probably to the few remaining survivors of the " White " species in Zululand and in the Nile regions.

The last black rhino shot in the Cape Province, according to Hall, was an old bull killed not far from Port Elizabeth in 1853. In the Orange River Colony, the last one recorded as shot was in 1842 at Rhenoster Kop, on the south side of the Vaal River. This spot later earned fame in the Boer War, and will be linked in history with the name of the elusive Boer General, Christian De Wet.

It is rather an interesting fact that the " White " rhinoceros subsists almost entirely on grass, while the black species lives off the leaves of trees and shrubs.

The rhino feeds during the evening, night and early morning ; but, occasionally, may be seen on the move on cloudy or rainy days. Like most animals in the wild state, these ungainly beasts are never found at any great distance from water, to which they resort to drink during the evening and also at dawn. After the early morning drink the rhino wallows in the mud, which subsequently cakes all over his body and helps to smother the ticks which attach themselves to the softer or thinner portions of his skin.

By habit, the rhino sleeps during the hot hours of the African day ; and, if a hunter or safari suddenly awakens him, he resents this in no undecided manner. A peeved rhino can be very liverish indeed ! Nobody likes to be disturbed suddenly in the midst of a pleasant siesta ; and there is no reason why a rhino should like it any more than a human being. How distressingly obnoxious an awakened rhino can be, I will explain later.

Both species are quite easy to stalk if their bird sentinels do not happen to be on duty. The experienced hunter, before attempting to get within easy range for a fatal shot, first examines his intended quarry very carefully with a pair of field-glasses. Should he detect any of these birds on the beast, he knows that he must approach with the utmost caution. After a long and tedious stalk, the hunter is frequently detected by the birds, and at once the alarm is raised by them. Thus, more often than not, a trophy is lost.

Should these birds be perched on the back of the rhino, the hunter stalks the animal rapidly. So long as he keeps on the proper side of the wind and takes reasonable care not to expose himself, he will almost certainly get within easy shooting distance.

When disturbed, the black species moves off with the head

well elevated ; and if a cow is accompanied by her calf, the latter follows the parent instead of preceding it. This is in marked contrast to the habit of the " white " rhino mother and her calf.

The black rhino differs also from the meek and inoffensive " white " species in the matter of temper. The former is morose, irritable and always uncertain in attitude. When wounded, frequently he charges down upon his persecutor ; but if the hunter is able to get out of the way of the charging beast, usually but not always, the rhino passes straight on and does not turn to seek out the attacker. He has often been known to charge without the slightest provocation through a safari, a team of oxen or donkeys in a wagon, or even a camp. While doing so he lunges right and left viciously with the cruel horn, and can inflict serious casualties in a very short space of time.

When warned of danger by the bird sentinels, the rhino charges off more or less blindly. As likely as not, he proceeds straight for the hunter, who imagines that he has been seen and the charge is a deliberate one. But such is not always the case by any manner of means.

During my residence in Kenya, and even before that time, it was quite common for a rhino to charge a railway train when crossing the plains between Nairobi and Tsavo. In 1906, when a passenger on the mail-train from Mombasa, an intrepid old bull rhino did so, but came off a mighty poor second in the encounter. He must have suffered from a sore head for weeks afterwards. It is to be hoped that it taught him a salutary lesson ; but it is expecting too much of a rhino to look for any show of real intelligence.

On the Athi and Kapiti Plains there used to be quite a large number of rhino ; and often I have seen them quite close to the railway track when passing through this area on a train. When the rails were being laid down through this region, a rhino charged a locomotive drawing a few trucks from railhead camp to Simba.

Sam Pike, a veteran engine-driver, told me of his adventure with a wealth of picturesque detail. It was a highly entertaining story. They left Simba to load up with material for the gangs engaged on construction work, and Pike had allowed a number of Wakamba hunters to have a free ride in the empty trucks. He had taken his shot-gun with him in the cab of the engine,

KIRO   A   BELGIAN   POST   ON   THE   NILE

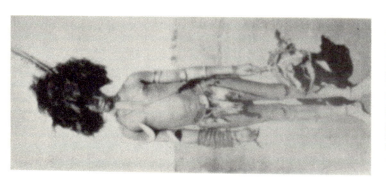

A   KAVIRONDO   FISHERMAN

in the hope of getting some guinea fowl. At a point about a couple of miles or so from Simba, an old bull rhino attempted to cross the track ahead of the train. Pike saw it, and put on a burst of speed. He just managed to cut off the animal's advance, and blocked its passage across the railway.

Enraged by this baulking of its desires, the rhino charged full tilt at the engine and tried to drive its horn into the side of the tender. Naturally, it made no impression. Pike fired both barrels of his shot-gun into the rhino at point-blank range. The only effect was still further to anger the big beast. It now raced alongside the train, and tried repeatedly to charge the engine off the track. Fearful that the animal might get mixed up with the wheels and bring the train to grief, Pike put on more steam and gradually drew ahead.

When the rhino came abreast of the Wakamba hunters, they seized upon this rare opportunity with delight. They started to pump arrows into the beast as fast as they could shoot, but it still raced beside the train and struggled to overtake the engine. It seemed to be obsessed by a grim determination to wreck the locomotive, which each additional arrow imbedded in its hide served only to intensify.

From Simba camp, the railway engineer, R. O. Preston, watched this unique race between train and rhino. He was keenly interested, and not a little amused. By the time that the rhino got close to Simba camp, it had a mass of arrows sticking into its thick hide. According to both Preston and Pike, it resembled a gigantic, bounding porcupine. Scarcely a square inch of its great bulk was free from an imbedded arrow, for the Wakamba had not wasted a second in using the beast as their unconventional target.

At the outskirts of the camp, the unusual race ended abruptly, for Preston gave the beast a pretty hot reception with his magazine-rifle. All in all, what with the arrows and now the bullets, the rhino had had enough. Pike won that race by a short head. The rhino turned about and galloped off into the bush, looking exactly like an immense pin-cushion. That was the last they ever saw of the beast.

What might really be interesting would be to know how that old rhino explained his condition to his wife when he met her again after his day out. I am thinking it would take some explaining !

Preston told me of another amusing experience he had when

at the construction camp at Mtoto Andei. Early one morning he was awakened by a camp-guard and informed that the hospital tent—fortunately unoccupied at the time—had been dragged off into the bush and the night watchman discovered almost dead from fright close to the wreckage. He hastened to the spot to investigate, and found the Indian watchman just recovering consciousness.

The man told him that a rhino had come up while he was sitting beside the camp-fire. He had no other weapon than a long bush-knife, and struck at the beast with this. The enraged rhino thereupon rushed straight forward and tossed him into the air. He stated that he did not know what happened after that, for he fainted from sheer fright.

Preston came to the conclusion that the rhino, after first tossing the Indian, had charged full into the tent, got his horn entangled in the ropes and canvas, and carried off the tent on his head into the bush. The wreckage was found a little distance away.

The watchman was fortunate enough to escape with no worse injuries than a broken collar-bone, a severe bruising and shaking. He had been very badly frightened, however, and insisted on being repatriated to India forthwith, or somewhat sooner. No doubt, on arrival in his native village in India, he posed as the immortal hero of a deadly combat with a rhino in the African night, in which he completely worsted and killed the savage beast. We can rest assured that the story lost nothing in his version of this strange affair.

When the railway had been built as far as Sultan Hamoud, rhinos were unpleasantly plentiful in that neighbourhood. In actual fact, they became a regular nuisance in disturbing the work of laying down the rails and preparing the track ahead. At odd moments during the day, they made a habit of turning up to see how the work was progressing and to stare at the Indian coolies from a rather uncomfortably close range. No man in the world can concentrate on the work in hand, let alone in laying down a railroad track through virgin land, if he is being closely watched by a rhino from a distance of a few hundred yards. Such brutes make a distinctly unpleasant " gallery " for those chiefly concerned !

When selecting a site for a camp, it is never wise to pitch your tent on an old rhino path. I did so on one occasion, but am never likely to repeat such an act of folly. I was on safari with John Egerton, and we had camped for the night in typical rhino country. The bush was cut up in every direction by old rhino paths; and, not suspecting any trouble, we had our tents pitched in the centre of the broadest one. We had marched far and for many hours that day, and the sun had been terrifically hot. We felt disinclined, therefore, to ask our native porters to clear the ground for our camp site. They had been carrying sixty-pound loads, and were probably as tired as we were; and a little consideration for your human beasts of burden is just as essential as for your animal transport.

In the middle of the night a rhino walked down that path, collided with our tent and wrecked it completely, and then passed on over it on his or her way. I never did know its sex. It does not matter, in any case.

Neither of us was hurt, but both were very irate at being so rudely awakened and at the damage done to the tent. I struggled out from under the wreckage, grabbing my rifle as I did so. There chanced to be a full moon, and I could see the black stern of the brute lumbering off into the bush. Beyond sending a bullet after the beast to hasten its departure, I could not take action. Angry as I was at the rhino's senseless destruction, I had no inclination to hurt it. We might have fared far worse than we did!

Like the elephant and buffalo, the rhino is a one-coloured beast; and its colouration pattern is that which is most visible in either green or yellow bush country. But I have often failed to perceive one, even for some time after Hamisi had done so and pointed it out to me. In each case, the rhino was standing quite motionless about fifty to eighty yards from us, either in scanty bush or else in open grassy plains among ant-hills.

I have observed that they usually stand immobile when first disturbed, waiting to see if they can locate the danger. It is possible, of course, that they are really trying to evade being seen by remaining perfectly still; but I am inclined to think this is not so, and primarily they are searching for hint of the danger threatening them. Nobody can really say for certain, for the mind of a rhino is indeed difficult to fathom. I have often wondered if it has a mind at all, except to cause the maximum amount of trouble to those who cross its path.

Once, near Nairobi, I was out hunting lions with Hamisi. The latter suddenly called my attention to a grey mass on the plains, and whispered: "*Kifaru, Bwana!*" On creeping near to it with great caution, I saw that it was a big rhino and fast asleep. He was lying down on the ground, with his legs doubled up under him. It was not until we had approached to within fifty yards or so of the beast that he awakened suddenly. He twisted his head to and fro, but did not appear either to have seen, heard or scented us. All at once, he rose to his feet and stood facing us, contemplating the advisability of charging. I did not want to harm him, merely to observe what he would do. I stood ready to fire in case of need, and waited. Several minutes went by, and he still seemed undecided. Then he walked slowly forward to us, and broke into a trot. This meant real business, and I could not afford to be inquisitive any longer. I aimed deliberately, and killed him with the first bullet.

Very often a rhino, wounded in the vitals, will perform a curious death waltz. In the case of a mortally wounded beast, this is generally a sure sign of death being very imminent; but is not always so. It is much safer to take no chances, and shoot again to kill.

As the animal falls down dead, you may often hear it utter a curious screaming whistle, not unlike the escape of steam from a small engine. I have heard this several times; but not on every occasion.

CHAPTER XXI

A RHINO'S " CONTEMPT OF COURT "

IN the latter part of 1904 I was sent down to Makindu to prosecute in a most unsavoury criminal case, in which the four Indian accused were to be tried by Ranald Donald, a noted Indian shikari and then Town Magistrate of Nairobi. There were many witnesses for the prosecution and the trial detained us at Makindu for three or four days. It is on the railway between Mombasa and Nairobi, on the Tsavo Plains, and was a noted area for big game and bird shooting. Lion, rhino and even buffalo were constantly found hereabouts.

Each morning, before the Court sat, Donald and I went out for a couple of hours' bird-shooting. We enjoyed wonderful sport and had large bags—greater and lesser bustard, spur fowl, guinea fowl, sand grouse, and both quail and snipe figured in our list each day. On our return to Makindu, we consigned the birds by the first train to Nairobi for distribution among our friends.

On our last morning, a fool rhino butted into the picture and completely spoiled our outing. I would not have minded that so much, but could not forgive his greater sins. We were armed with nothing more deadly than shot-guns, as we had no desire to hunt big game ; and, furthermore, had not anticipated any danger. Our gun-bearers had not accompanied us, but Donald's two sporting little fox-terriers completed our party.

I had just brought down a brace of sand grouse, when a much disturbed rhino bull charged full tilt at me from an adjacent path in the bush. Neither of us had the slightest suspicion that one of these beasts was anywhere close at hand. He caught us quite unprepared for action.

There was only one thing to do in the circumstances, and that quickly. I ran for the nearest tree and shinned up it as fast as possible, unmindful of the cruel thorns. Even these were preferable to a rhino's horn in my body. Unfortunately, I dropped my valuable shot-gun in my haste to get out of the way of that rhino. I only just managed it. Once safely up in the tree, I had time to look round for Donald. He also had climbed up into a nearby tree, and I saw that he had his gun with him. He called across to me that he had only one cartridge left in the breech, and had dropped his ammunition-bag when getting into the tree.

" Better save it to tickle up this fool rhino, in case we're marooned here too long," I shouted back.

" A lot of use small bird-shot would be," he laughed.

We had abandoned our morning's bag of birds, and now the rhino advanced warily to sniff at the heap. Very quickly he had made mincemeat of them. Then he turned his attention to my shot-gun, and tossed it into the air with his horn. When it landed on the ground, he stamped savagely upon it. I groaned aloud, for that weapon was a Daniel Frazer, which had cost me sixty guineas in Edinburgh and was my most prized possession. Time and time again the brute repeated this little act of pleasantry ; and, by the time he had finished amusing himself with it, my shot-gun was not worth sixpence. I could have wept !

I wondered what had happened to the two fox-terriers, for there was no sign of them. Later, we discovered that they had considered discretion the better part of valour, and had made a bee-line for the Dak Bungalow at Makindu. Wise little dogs !

The rhino now came forward to sniff round the base of my tree. We both climbed higher. Unfortunately, we were in long-thorned Acacia trees and our perches were confoundedly uncomfortable. For some days afterwards I was engaged in picking out these toothpick thorns from my body, and so was Donald.

Another hour dragged by, and still we were held prisoners. I was fast growing cramped in my legs and arms, and the thorns were beastly painful. If it is true that we are all descended from the ape family, I have no desire to revert to type if this was a sample. As for my temper, it was very severely frayed ; and with good reason. The absurdity of our predicament did not appeal to the streak of humour in my system. All I wanted was to be revenged on our cantankerous foe, and then return to Makindu : neither was possible. And we were both long overdue in Court,

I called out to Donald and suggested that it was about time for him to tickle up the rhino's posterior with his sole remaining cartridge. I wanted my breakfast, and to complete that criminal trial. Donald was not having any, and firmly declined to carry out my suggestion.

The rhino appeared to have come to an anchor for the rest of the day ; another hour dragged by slowly, and he seemed to be asleep. By this time both of us had our fill of being imprisoned in tree-tops. We were thirsty and hungry, bored and angry, full of sharp thorns and cramped, and wanted to be rid of that pestilential rhino. Once again I proposed that my companion in misfortune should fire at the rump of the beast, and see if this would have the effect of making him move on his way. This time, Donald agreed to expend his last cartridge in a desperate throw for release.

The rhino was probably more startled by the sudden report of the gun than hurt by the pellets, for the hide is so tough that the latter could not have done more than glance off it. The remedy, however, was instantly effective. The ugly brute woke up and snorted angrily ; and then, to our immense relief, rushed off into the bush.

We gave him a good fifteen minutes to make himself scarce before climbing down from our thorny perches. Having retrieved our wrecked property, we hastened back to Makindu for break-fast-lunch combined. On the way, we kept a watchful eye for our late tormentor or any of his ilk, but saw no more rhino on that weary tramp.

Immediately we had eaten and the trial was completed, we decided to go back after that most annoying rhino. We both wanted revenge for the indignities inflicted upon us ; and, furthermore, were convinced that the brute would be recognized with ease. We had been given ample time to take in every single characteristic of that rhino's personal appearance. After two hours' tracking, we located him in the bed of a small nullah. He went down to Donald's first shot.

Neither of us had the slightest compunction in killing him, and knew his sentence of death was wholly deserved. He had been guilty of gross " Contempt of Court."

If I am not likely to forget the rhinos of Makindu, there were two other men still less likely to do so ; that is to say, if their story is genuine.

This unrehearsed comedy occurred in the early days of

railway construction, and the details were related to me by Dr. Stewart in Nairobi. I have his word for its truth, and he always enjoyed a reputation for being the soul of veracity. Some time afterwards, I also heard the tale from a railway engineer and was assured that Larkin, the other actor in the hilarious scene, had sworn to the facts.

It was Stewart's first encounter with a rhino. The narrative of his experiences would have ruined his reputation for truthfulness had it not been for Larkin's staunch corroboration of every single detail. True or not, it is a curious and amusing adventure, and, as such, deserves being recorded. I do so, as nearly as possible, in the words of Dr. Stewart.

The doctor and Larkin, a South African railway engineer, had gone out shooting from the railhead camp on the Makindu River. After trudging for a couple of hours or so through the bush without seeing any game to shoot, Larkin decided to climb up into a tree for a better view of the surrounding countryside.

With the assistance of Stewart, he grasped a low hanging branch and swung himself upwards. Presently, he spotted a large greyishblack object coming straight in their direction through the scrub. In order to see it better, he climbed out along a branch. It snapped suddenly under his weight, and deposited him unceremoniously in a thick and thorny bush. Now Stewart climbed up into the tree, while Larkin struggled to free himself from his uncomfortable nest in the thorn-bush. At that moment, a large rhino passed quite close to the two men and seemingly without knowing of their presence.

Badly scratched and his khaki clothing torn to shreds, Larkin finally extricated himself from the bush. Keen as mustard now, he picked up his rifle and set off on the trail of the vanishing rhino. Stewart jumped down from the tree and followed him.

The rhino was making for the railhead camp. Stewart, noting this fact, suggested that they should keep the animal going in that direction and not attempt to kill the beast until quite close to the outskirts of the camp. He argued that this would simplify the labour of bringing in their trophy. Larkin agreed. All went well at first, for the rhino kept straight on in the desired direction, while the two sportsmen followed quietly in the rear. Both were blissfully unmindful of the danger if the beast faced about and reversed the route of its constitutional.

About half a mile from camp, the rhino left the dense bush

A BULL HIPPO YAWNING

and emerged on to a grassy plain ; and now made off in the opposite direction. This was too much for the hunters. Stewart fired at the broad stern of the beast, the only target offering, in the hope of thereby turning it once more toward the camp. The rhino seemed to be completely staggered by this sudden violent assault in the rear portion of its anatomy, and stood still. No doubt it was wondering who had taken such an unfair advantage and kicked it so hard. The beast stood without movement for some considerable time, chewing the cud of reflection.

Larkin was nonplussed by this unaccountable behaviour. The two men began to shout their loudest in the hope that the rhino would move on again, and toward the camp. As their combined vocal efforts had not the least effect, they began to bombard it with big stones ; but this also proved fruitless. Larkin now broke off a stout sapling, and approached cautiously to their quarry. He belaboured the rhino's rump with all his strength, but without moving it. As all these drastic measures proved ineffective, the two sportsmen decided to kill the beast where it stood.

Just as they were about to shoot, the rhino made up its mind to move onwards. It went off slowly, and away from the camp. This contrariness annoyed Larkin, and he ran after the beast, grabbed hold of its small tail, and strove to swing round the huge beast in the desired direction. The rhino positively declined to answer to its helm, and from a slow walk now broke into a sharp trot. Larkin hung on firmly to the tail, and still fought to swing the beast's body so that the head pointed toward the camp. Stewart trotted along behind this unique procession, carrying both rifles on his shoulders and wondering what would be the ultimate conclusion of their strange adventure.

They had not progressed far in this manner when the rhino appeared to throw off its stupor and realize that all was not normal at the rear. It halted abruptly, and wheeled round to investigate this unaccountable drag on its tail. In so doing, it swung Larkin completely off his feet ; but he hung on to the tail like a leech. At the same instant, the rhino got a whiff of the doctor's wind.

That was when the real trouble started !

Stewart hurriedly sought cover behind a convenient bush, and was only just in time to get his rifle ready when the beast charged home at him. There was no mistaking the rhino's intentions, he assured me. Larkin, in acute anxiety for his own safety, yelled out to the doctor not to fire as the bullet might hit him instead of the animal.

Fortunately, the big brute came to a halt just beside the bush behind which the doctor was hidden. It appeared to be listening intently. Then, after a few minutes of immobility, it got another strong whiff of Stewart's wind and started to chase him round the bush. The hunt continued for some considerable time, the rhino enjoying the game of " here we go round the mulberry bush " far more than either Stewart or Larkin. The doctor led, closely pursued by the rhino, while Larkin brought up the rear of the procession. He was still firmly clinging to the rhino's tail. Round and round they sped, without a word being spoken by either man. The angry rhino was snorting at intervals, while both men gasped for breath ; and it looked like being the animal's race. Finally, completely winded and exhausted, Stewart made a desperate dive into the thorny bush.

The rhino, with Larkin still attached grimly to its rudder, rushed on past the bush. It had not seen the doctor's sudden manœuvre to shake off that relentless stern pursuit. Larkin stated afterwards that he was just about all in and could scarcely keep his feet on the ground, but he dare not let go of the tail, for he felt more or less safe as long as he clung to the stern of the beast.

Suddenly losing the doctor's scent, the huge beast came to an abrupt halt. This was the chance Stewart had been hoping to get. Picking himself out of the bush, he took steady aim and sent a bullet into the neck of the rhino. The animal let out a whistling sound as of the escape of steam, crumbled and went down on its side. It did not move again.

Running up to his kill, Stewart found Larkin in a state bordering on collapse, but still automatically clinging to the beast's tail and with a stare of desperation in his eyes. The doctor assured him that all was well now, and the rhino dead. But Larkin declared vehemently that he was at the safest end of the brute, and intended to remain there.

It was some time before Stewart could persuade his companion to relinquish that tenacious grip on the defunct animal's tail.

Practically all my own meetings with rhinos have not been of my seeking. I seldom have had any particular wish to slay them and, in most instances, merely acted in self-defence or to protect my property. Too often for my liking I have been the object of an unprovoked charge or wanton attack. My experience has been that they are more wilfully vindictive than actually dangerous. If the hunter keeps his wits about him, the odds are largely in his favour. The rhino's great weight—about three tons—is detrimental to any fast speed, while its defective eyesight is a severe handicap.

If the wind is blowing toward you when charged, the odds are that you can safely stand your ground and get in an effective death-shot. But a rhino is never an easy animal to kill, for its hide is like the armoured sides of a battle-cruiser. The neck is the most vulnerable spot at which to aim, for then you are almost certain to break the spinal vertebræ.

To my way of thinking, the most curious thing about a rhino is that you generally bump into one when least expecting to do so. You may often hunt its known habitat for days on end and never even get a glimpse of one; and yet one fine day, when thinking of anything but such a beast, you walk right into a rhino. For example, once when actually searching for a very fine bull which had been reported to be haunting the Stony Athi River, I devoted seven days out of a fortnight's leave to hunting for it. I never even got a sight of the beast.

On a number of other occasions, I have encountered a rhino on the open plains or in bush country when not desiring either to hunt or kill a specimen. In the majority of cases, they insisted on giving battle and generally made themselves such an unmitigated nuisance, that I had to put a stop to their nonsense. If only they had left me alone, I should not have interfered with them or taken their lives. Only their arrant stupidity and vindictive nature sealed their death-warrants.

I can quote a number of illustrations of this spirit of aggressiveness on the part of rhino, but the following instance will serve.

I was returning to Nairobi from Fort Hall, and was near El Donyo Sabuk, when I was attacked by a rhino when not even hunting but engaged solely on my lawful occasions. When least expected, a bull appeared from behind a clump of mimosa trees and advanced menacingly towards my safari. He was too far away to have seen us, but probably either had caught a whiff of man-tainted wind or had heard my porters' lusty chanting. This old and cantankerous bull appeared to strongly resent our presence in his private preserves, and straightway gave vent to his displeasure.

If I had been given any choice in the matter, I should most certainly have side-stepped any argument with that beast, even one with an exceptionally fine and long frontal horn as had this specimen. It was not to be. He was simply spoiling for a fight, and shouting aloud for trouble. He got both.

His ponderous and determined advance at a walk soon changed into a fast trot; and then he raised his head, held his tail erect, and charged full gallop at my safari. Rather than have any of my porters injured, I tried to head him off by firing a shot close to his head. I might just as well have saved that cartridge. Instead of turning him, the whine of the bullet past his ears seemed to make him even more furious; and he increased his speed. My Wakikuyu porters had halted to watch the rhino, seemingly in two minds whether to stand fast or bolt to cover.

Head well down now, he was obviously bent on real mischief. I fired again, and hit him at the base of that long and thin frontal horn, but the shot neither turned nor stopped the brute. He held on his way, straight for the centre of the safari. This proved too much for the nerves of the Wakikuyu. They dropped their loads to the ground and incontinently sought refuge in some nearby trees. Hamisi shouldered up to me, the spare rifle thrust forward ready for the lightning exchange of weapons, and stood ready to fight it out with that infuriated beast. Trust Hamisi not to run from danger !

The rhino was on top of us far too rapidly for a chance to hit him in a vital spot. That opportunity had been missed owing to my reluctance to injure the brute. He reached my abandoned loads, braked down on his wild gallop, and halted to investigate this strange litter on the veld. I fired a glancing shot at his rump, in the hope of making him desist and seek pastures new. The idea of my personal effects being converted into playthings for a fool rhino made no appeal at all, but I did not want to kill him. It was his room I desired, not his company.

The slight flesh wound seemed to make him all the more determined to wreck everything in sight. He proceeded to do so in a most thorough and methodical fashion. Every time that I advanced to drive him away from my property, he turned round and drove me away. Often I had to run hard and seek cover behind a convenient tree, while Hamisi ran for another. Promptly, the rhino halted mid-way and returned to my loads, which he seemed to prefer as toys. Judging by the howls and shrieks of glee from my porters in the surrounding " gallery " of trees, the undignified retreat of Hamisi and myself afforded them the most intense amusement.

All my well-intentioned efforts to frighten away the beast having failed signally, and now being exceedingly weary of his unwelcome attentions, I fired from behind the cover of my tree and brought him down. Another bullet at close range ended his vicious life. It served that persistently pugnacious beast right ! And he had provided me with one of the best rhino trophies that ever fell to my rifle.

It was some time before I could re-assemble my grinning porters, gather up the scattered remains of my baggage, and resume my march to Nairobi. The damage this idiot rhino had committed was considerable. My valise was badly torn, the ridgepole of my tent broken in three pieces, and—unkindest thrust of all—my only bottle of whisky had been shattered and the contents spilled out on the thirsty veld. I could have sat down and howled, for there was no chance of replacing it until a week later.

And I do so enjoy my daily " sun-downer " !

During the Sotik Punitive Expedition in 1905, I was out on patrol with a brother officer. He had only recently arrived in Kenya to join the King's African Rifles, and as yet had no experience of big game shooting. We were marching ahead of our men, each carrying a sporting rifle. Without any warning whatsoever, a big bull rhino charged viciously over the top of a ridge and headed straight for us. We had neither seen nor heard him until he breasted the ridge, some thirty yards away. The instant my sights came on I let rip, and down he came on his knees and stomach. We stood still, waiting for him to rise again ; but he was dead.

My companion was hugely elated, even though it was not his trophy. The rhino had fallen in such a position that it made a most realistic picture of a beast actually charging over the summit of the ridge. He begged me to take a photograph of him as he took a close-up of a charging rhino. I complied, and the resulting negative was a lifelike record of what he had hoped to get.

No doubt, he sent that snapshot to his best girl in England, with a graphic account of how he had faced a charging rhino, armed only with his camera, and taken a snapshot of it before the beast was killed by a companion. The photograph would have deceived most people.

Perhaps I do him a grave injustice, but it was a most tempting chance to pose as an intrepid photographer of wild animals of the dangerous type.

And human nature is ever frail !

CHAPTER XXII.

" WHITE " AND BLACK RHINOS.

BURCHELL'S " white " rhinoceros is really misnamed in so far as colour is concerned.

They are not white at all. They differ from the black or common variety of the species in that they are square-lipped, in temperament and in the nature of their food. How the name " white " rhinoceros came to be applied to this rare species is uncertain, for it is of a dark slate-grey colour and, by no stretch of the imagination, is it white. Selous told me that, when standing in the open with the sun shining full on their backs, in the early morning they do appear to be white when viewed from a distance. I later found this to be so, when observing these creatures in the Lado Enclave of the Belgian Congo (now Mongalla Province of the Sudan).

Quite possibly, seeing them thus upon the grassy veld, the old Boer hunters bestowed upon them the name of *witte rhenoster*, and it stuck. On the other hand, the name may have arisen from the animal's habit of wallowing in whitish clay, which is so commonly found on the bottoms of pools and water-holes in Africa. On emerging from its mud-bath, the sun and air rapidly dried the clay on the hide, which then showed up white when viewed from any great distance.

" Square-lipped " rhinoceros would have been a much more appropriate name for this species, and more correctly have described it. The upper lip of this beast is square and not of a proboscis-like nature as in the black variety.

At one time they were common on the grassy country of the open plains in South Africa, between the Orange and Zambezi rivers, but have never been recorded south of the former river. At the present time, the only surviving specimens in the Union of South Africa are a very small number in the game reserves of Zululand, and in the coast lands of Portuguese East Africa a few may still be found. It was formerly thought that the

Zambezi was the most northernly limit of the " white " rhino, but they have been found and shot, however, in the north-east section of the Congo, in the southern portions of the Sudan to the west of the Nile, and in a few other isolated parts of Equatorial Africa. In no case are they ever found very far from a river or water-hole.

Before the advent of the European colonists to South Africa, it is known that the " white " rhino was quite commonly found beyond the Orange River. The earliest writings of hunters and travellers teem with accounts of the slaughter of considerable numbers of these animals. During the course of one single day's trek with an ox-wagon, it was common for the trekkers to see anything from fifty to a hundred of this now very rare species.

Between the years 1840 and 1850, these prehistoric-looking animals were recorded as abundant in suitable localities in the Limpopo River and Lake Ngami regions of southern Africa. Search as you may, none will now be found outside the game reserves in Zululand and in those other scattered areas already mentioned.

If we may judge by the writings of the majority of European hunters at the beginning and in the middle of the past century, game animals were slaughtered for the sheer lust of killing. For example, two hunters, whose names are often quoted in natural history works, mention having killed ninety rhinos during one short trip ; and the majority of the victims were of the now almost extinct square-lipped species. Another hunter recorded having killed sixty of them in one single season. This is not sport, but sheer butchery. It is indefensible.

Even in the remote districts where the European hunter had not then penetrated, this senseless slaughter was carried on by natives who had somehow obtained possession of arms and ammunition.

The last known specimen to be killed in southern Africa of this " white " rhinoceros, other than those preserved in Zululand, was shot in Mashonaland, Southern Rhodesia, toward the close of the last century. They are now completely extinct in the Rhodesias, and almost so elsewhere.

The " white " rhinoceros is always an inhabitant of the open grassy plains and wide valleys, and feeds chiefly, if not entirely, on grass. They associate in pairs or small family groups, generally speaking ; but sometimes travel solitary. Though not

TWO HIPPO IN THE MIRUI RIVER

ONE COMES UP TO INVESTIGATE

now grouped in numbers, formerly they must have congregated in very large bodies in restricted areas, if we can trust the old records to be accurate.

With the sole exception of the elephant, the "white" rhinoceros is the largest of all the land animals. An adult bull often stands from six feet to six feet nine inches at the shoulder, measures nearly fourteen feet from the tip of the nose to the root of the tail, and has a circumference of fully twelve feet. There are two horns, the frontal, or nose one, being more slender usually, longer and less acutely curved, than in that of the black variety of this species. Sometimes the frontal horn is straight, and even inclined forward. This horn often grows to a length of about four and a half feet. The posterior horn is generally shorter than the frontal one.

Unlike the black variety, the "white" rhino has a very prominent hump over the withers, and an even larger one on the neck. The huge misshapen head differs in all respects from that of the more common variety.

Realizing how extremely rare and how near to complete extinction is this variety, though I saw more than a couple of dozen during my hunting trips in the Congo near the Nile, I refused to shoot a single specimen. Often I side-tracked them purposely, rather than be drawn into any argument likely to force me to shoot in self-defence. I am most tremendously glad now of that spirit of forbearance. The trophies, as it has transpired, would have been an encumbrance to me and not an asset, and I should have killed, therefore, without legitimate reason.

Instead of hunting and shooting them, I found ample reward in observing their habits in a natural environment.

Several times, during the hot hours of the day, I have stumbled upon a small group of these rare beasts asleep, and gave them a wide berth. I have also seen them feeding in the early, cool hours of the morning. At times, I met them in parties of three or four, but mostly they were solitary or a pair.

On one day, I came across a bull, cow and calf feeding in an open glade. They must have heard my approach before I saw them. While they stood hesitating what course to pursue, to bolt or charge, three others suddenly dashed out of the cover and raced away. My small family followed their example. I let them go. I had sworn to myself not to shoot one unless it was quite imperative—the animal's life or mine. I kept my vow, despite the strong temptation to break it. The bull had offered a very generous target, and was a wonderful trophy. I am glad that I refrained from shooting him.

These animals progress at a rapid trot, with the head carried low and the long anterior horn almost parallel with the ground. Although, at a trot, it can outdistance any man on foot, yet it is easily overtaken, so Selous assured me, when ridden down on horseback. That is one reason why they became such easy victims of the old-time hunters in southern Africa. Kermit Roosevelt, when hunting them on foot in the Congo, below Rejaf, actually kept up with them when they made off at a fast trot, and got his trophy. I know of no other man who can say the same.

The family group, just mentioned, provided me with an interesting lesson in the maternal instincts of the cow of this variety. When they bolted off, the mother ran in behind her wee calf and guided it on the course to take by the tip of her horn, which she gently pressed on the small scrap's rump as occasion dictated. In this way she was able to keep it in full view and, at the same time, protect it from a rear attack. As I have already stated, the calf of the black variety follows the mother when escaping from danger.

The " white " rhino is timid and generally quite inoffensive, but when wounded and brought to bay, it has been known to charge the hunter.

The old Boer hunters of South Africa, as well as the natives, killed these beasts for the sake of their horns and hides. The former were sold as curios, and made into walking-sticks, whips, knife-handles, combs and so forth; while the latter were converted into sjamboks and wagon-whips.

Selous said that the eyesight of this species was as poor as that of the black variety, and he was often able to walk up openly to within thirty or forty yards of them in the veld without, apparently, attracting their attention. Their sense of smell, however, is very acute, while their hearing seems to be rather indifferent.

An elephant poacher in the Congo, who had shot several of this rare species, told me that, when real hard pressed, the " white " rhino breaks into a lumbering gallop. When a hind leg is broken it is unable to run, but with a broken shoulder it can travel for a considerable distance at a gallop. He also told me that he was once forced to kill a most savage cow, accompanied by a very small calf. When the mother was dead, the calf refused to leave her body and stubbornly resisted all efforts to drive it away. The little orphan charged boldly, directly my friend tried to approach, and it was only with the combined efforts of himself and a number of natives that the wee beast was captured. It lived for only two days in captivity.

Other hunters have told me of almost identical experiences with calves of the black variety.

The view seems to be generally prevalent that the black rhino is also being exterminated rapidly; but there is ample evidence to the contrary. What is much more likely is that he is retiring before the closer settlement of his former stamping grounds. Though they can never be said to have been endowed by Nature with any marked degree of intelligence, they have the sense to realize that, if remaining near the rim of civilization, their ultimate destruction is inevitable. Consequently, they leave their old-time haunts on the open grassy plains, and hide further away in the forest glades or in sparsely uninhabited regions. As long as they keep well away from human settlements and behave themselves properly, there is no reason at all why they should not be protected from the senseless butchery to which they have been subjected in the past.

There is plenty of room for the rhino in the unsettled and undeveloped areas, and it is to be hoped that he will not become wholly extinct. He is no beauty, and useless to man's needs, but he still has his rightful place in the clever scheme of Nature's own devising.

Personally, I have no particular liking for the rhinoceros, the more especially when I remember how they have wantonly broken up my safaris and damaged my property; but I am not so utterly vindictive as to wish to see the rhino family quite exterminated. I confess to a strong liking for seeing wild fauna of all varieties in their natural surroundings, and have always been a staunch supporter of all sane policies of game preservation. Just so long as they keep themselves clear of men and their works, I can find no excuse for butchering them ruthlessly. Of late years, they have displayed an intelligent desire to keep beyond the rim of advancing settlement. Fool he may be, but, at least, he shows that much common sense.

One of the most amazing adventures with a rhino was that experienced by the " Buffalo " Jones cowboy expedition. I met Means, one of the cowboys, shortly after his return to America, and he told me about it.

There were seven Europeans in the party and five trained cow-ponies, to say nothing of a small pack of dogs and hundreds of native porters. Besides " Buffalo " Jones, there were two more cowboys, Means and Loveless ; a photographer, my old friend Cherry Kearton ; an American journalist, Guy Scull ; and two professional hunters, Ulyate and his son.

Guy Scull was a fellow-guest at Sagamore Hill, Colonel Theodore Roosevelt's home at Oyster Bay, and told us that the three cowboys were first-class experts at their work, being quick, fearless and superb horsemen. They had to possess all those qualities for the job in hand. Their adventure remains unique in the annals of big game hunting.

The lassoing of the rhino must have been crammed full of thrills, even in comparison with their many other exciting experiences. They put up a bull in a valley of the Sotik country and Jones dashed in at the beast, being closely followed by Means and Loveless. The rhino went off at full speed down the valley, with the three cowboys in hot pursuit. Means told me that they galloped over two miles before the rhino halted, about turned and prepared to give battle.

After a brief consultation, Jones rode forward to make the big beast charge. The rhino watched him with its little pig-eyes flashing with anger. Without any warning, it suddenly charged full at Jones. It was very quick off the mark. The cowboy leader of the expedition swung his pony out of the way and galloped off, closely followed by the determined and aggressive rhino. Means now took a hand in the game, and succeeded in throwing his rope round the rhino's head. The noose settled down on its neck, and he was able to check the mad rush temporarily ; but, a few minutes later, the rope broke under the severe strain, just like a thin piece of twine.

For over an hour the three cowboys chased and baited that rhino on the veld, each taking it in turns to be pursued by the beast in order to give the others a chance to lasso it. At last, one of them caught the rhino's hind leg, and this time the rope held. The huge animal dragged man and horse after it. Time and time again it charged first one and then another of the daring horsemen, but always failed to get home. The rope round the hind leg still held, while Loveless stuck manfully to the other end.

Means now dashed in and drew the beast in a headlong charge after him, whereat ensued a prolonged and terrific battle for victory. Scull told us that men and horses behaved splendidly, but the rhino was too much for them. Repeatedly they roped it, but the beast either towed them or else soon broke the rope. For five hours the final issue was always in doubt. Then the rhino showed palpable signs of being exhausted, and Jones decided to make the animal surrender.

He planned to get it roped to a tree. Loveless was sent off to get the brute on the run again, while Means roped it. His throw caught the beast by a hind leg. Yard by yard the huge beast was dragged and driven nearer to the selected tree. It was liberally bedecked with dangling rope-ends, but this one held. Finally, they got one end of the rope securely tied round a stout tree trunk, and the beast was captive.

The seemingly impossible had been made a fact. For the first time in history, a wild rhino stood roped to a tree in the middle of the Sotik plains. It was really an astounding performance, and deserves to be emblazoned in the annals of great adventures.

Not one of the party had any desire to kill any animal, and the only beast not released after being successfully roped was a lioness, as recorded earlier. Having achieved their object, they wanted nothing further from the vanquished except to set the rhino free to go on its way. But the gallant, stubborn captive was still too full of fight. Nobody could get near to unloose the rope from the hind leg. Every time they tried to do so, it promptly charged.

When it was dark, their fruitless efforts were abandoned. They left the rhino in command of the field of battle, still glowering savagely, snorting and making short rushes at them. If it could have got near, it would have killed them.

Means said that the beast was the real hero of that severe duel, and all had the greatest possible respect for the gallant fight it had made. Its courage was outstanding.

On the following morning, they all returned to the spot to make another attempt to release the beast, but the rhino had broken the rope and departed. They did not see it again.

After the cowboys had gone back to camp, the rhino probably soon recovered wind and strength. For a time, possibly, it stood still, harnessed to the tree and sunk in " prehistoric thought," as Kermit Roosevelt so picturesquely described a rhino's pensive attitude on the plains. Then a quick jerk at the rope, and it was once more free to roam its customary haunts, but took with it many scars of that unique trial of strength, in the shape of a great number of dangling rope-ends.

Not long after my arrival in Kenya, I went off on a hunting expedition with a friend through the Uasin Guishu Plateau. I was forced, much against my will, to kill three rhinos in a group—father, mother and three-quarter grown son.

For some unknown reason, they persisted in disputing my safari's line of march. Probably they picked up our wind from a distance, for they approached us suddenly over a rise. We had not even known they were there. For several minutes they stood and watched us thoughtfully as we trailed past their grandstand, and we were under the impression that they intended to leave us severely alone, even as I proposed to give them a wide berth. This was not snobbishness on my part, simply that I did not want rhino trophies, good as the bull's horns were. I have wished often since then that they had acted more wisely. I hated to kill the family.

But their inborn curiosity got the better of them, and induced all three to investigate us more closely. They began to walk towards us in a rather threatening manner. I held my rifle ready for action, though loth to take the initiative. All I wanted was to proceed on my safari without let or hindrance.

When they had got uncomfortably close and still showed no inclination to sheer off, I asked my companion to shoot into the ground in front of the beasts. I hoped this would serve to turn them away from the safari. Often this plan has the desired effect ; but, in this instance, it did not answer. The three of them at once charged full at my porters. I have no very great objection to the unwelcome attention of a solitary animal, but three rhino charging in a row is a most unpleasant crowd. I fired across their bows, but this only seemed to speed up their rush. They were as obstinate as mules, and obviously bent on breaking up my safari. This was more than I would brook, and so was forced to take defensive measures.

I killed the grand old bull with my first shot, and hoped this might force his wife and son to beat a hasty retreat from the danger zone. This was expecting too great a measure of intelligence from any member of the rhino family. The cow and her big son charged home on my porters, who promptly dropped their loads and fled to cover. My companion fired at the cow, and hit somewhere but did not stop her charge.   Then his rifle jammed.   The rest of that fight fell on my shoulders, with Hamisi standing stolidly at my elbow.

Seeing that the pair really intended serious business, I killed the cow just as she tossed my roll of bedding skywards. Her fool son, meanwhile, got home on a chop-box filled with Fortnum and Mason's choicest delicacies.   He wrecked this and three others of tinned provisions, a case of whisky that I had been commissioned to carry to the District Commissioner, and my tent.   He was old enough to have known better, the overgrown lout.   But the mischief was done before I was able to get a good shot at a vital spot.   At last, he ambled up close to his dead mother in search of more toys, and I put a bullet into his heart. Damn his eyes !

I had used every devise to scare them off us before shooting to kill.   Their nonsensical display of ill-manners had to be checked and punished severely.   They had been their own worst enemies.   Had they not shown themselves over the brow of that ridge, I should never have known of their presence in our vicinity.   Then they could have continued to roam the bush to their heart's content.

Stupid, stupid rhino !

CHAPTER XXIII

AFRICAN FISH AND FISHERMEN

WITHIN comparatively recent years, the Victoria Lake has been the subject of important scientific investigation in regard to the fisheries. Mr. Michael Graham, a well-known British naturalist, conducted an exhaustive enquiry on behalf of the Colonies whose territories border on its shores, and later published a report on the best means for the preservation of the indigenous species of fish in those waters, as well as for their sound commercial exploitation. His report furnished a fascinating chapter to our book of knowledge.

While much has been written concerning the big game of Central Africa, practically nothing has been recorded in regard to the fish and methods of native fishermen. Nearly all the tribes of Africa are fond of a fish diet ; especially those residing near large fresh-water lakes. The African is ingenious in his fishing. For the most part, they use either nets or traps ; but some spear fish in rivers or the shallow waters of the lakes.

The various types of native fishing are interesting as depicting the difference between primitive man's ideas of angling and those of civilized races. The African's are not according to Izaak Walton. However, it must be remembered that the native of Africa fishes for a living, while we are largely actuated by instincts of pure sport.

While serving in Kenya, I was stationed on the shores of the Victoria Lake from 1904 to 1905, and again from 1907 to 1908. Thus I had a very fair opportunity of studying the various methods adopted by different tribes in catching fish in lake or river. Often I was amazed by the novelty of their traps, and the dexterity displayed. Those happy years also gave me a chance to investigate, in an amateurish way, the different species of fish inhabiting the Victoria Lake and the many large rivers flowing into it.

The Wakavirondo, who live round the Kenya shores of the

lake, are gluttons for a fish diet ; and are never content unless there is a plentiful supply in their larders. As a general rule, these naked people employ three distinct methods in fishing— rod, net or trap.

The latter consists of converging walls of stones carried down into the beds of the tributary rivers of the lake, at an angle of some sixty degrees. The space between the stone walls is filled with fish baskets made out of fibrous substances and very neatly woven. The fish coming down stream find their only exit blocked, and thus are trapped in the baskets when trying to swim through the barricade.

Whenever travelling through this territory, or resident in Kisumu, my table always was well supplied with fresh fish ; and very delicious eating they proved. Care had to be taken when making purchases, of course, for the Wakavirondo prefer to eat their fish in a highly advanced state of decomposition. In fact, one may often meet these people carrying bundles of sun-dried fish, which give warning of approach from a distance of a hundred or more yards.

In order to provide this delicacy for the gourmets of the tribe, the women hang up the fish caught in nets or traps, and dry them in the tropical sun until a hard-baked, smelly mass. This is pounded on stones until it resembles flour, and then either they eat it raw or flavour other food with it. It is much the same as " Bombay Duck," which is so much in favour among the curry-eaters of the East.

For many hours I have watched the native fishermen at their labours on the Victoria Lake. It was interesting to see how diligent and successful they proved ; the more so, as in all other labour they are consistently lazy. Their methods were very primitive, it is true ; but effective.

Often they use seines made out of papyrus stems, which are weighted at one end with sinkers while floats are fastened to the other. The seines hang down vertically in the water and are arranged in the lake in a half-circle. On being slowly dragged inshore, large catches are always enclosed. I have seen many pounds of fish caught in this manner during the course of a single hour. Indeed, it is not uncommon to see as many as three hundred or more fish, varying in weight from one to three pounds, caught in just one cast of such a primitive net.

The seines are always arranged in the water by a native, who works from a raft made of dried papyrus reeds or ambatch.

All the time he is poling this round the outer edge of the net, he warbles a weird African melody. He stands erect as nude as the day he was born, for these people, both men and women, scorn clothing. They prefer to be garbed in a smile and the atmosphere. It is a carefree life, that of the native fisherman on the Victoria Lake.

At the Ripon Falls, near Jinja, I have seen the natives spearing the larger fish as the terrific flow carried them over the Falls into the Victoria Nile. They were experts in the handling of the long-shafted spear, and rarely ever missed their aim.

On the banks of the Victoria Nile, just below the Falls, I have spent many a delightful hour or so at morning and evening when fishing for the *Bagrus Docmac*, which is specially prized by the Basoga tribe in Uganda. One of the sights at the Ripon Falls is to watch the larger fish jump out of the swift river, clear the low-lying banks of the Falls, and land with a splash in the lake beyond. The jump is astounding, but very few fail in the attempt. In the pools, both above and below the Falls, the keen angler may often land fine fish running up to forty pounds in weight, and affording first-class sport. They are a cousin of the Mahseer of India.

I have also enjoyed real good angling with the huge and ugly " mud fish " of the Victoria Lake. To the zoologist this queer fish is known as the Lepidosiren (*Protopterus Æthiopicus*) ; or, in plain English, the lung-fish. The Baganda people call it the *Mamba*, and prize it very highly for food.

Africa enjoys a reputation for the possession of many oddities in the way of people, flora, fauna and insects ; but few are so curious and interesting as the Lepidosiren. In so far as I am aware, only one living specimen of this quaint fish has been brought out of Africa. It was captured some years ago by C. W. Woodhouse, one of the Assistant Game Wardens of Kenya, and presented to the Zoological Society of London. It proved one of the most interesting gifts ever made to the Society, and was valued highly.

Woodhouse dug it out of a swamp, which had been drained previously over a period of seven months ; and there was some two feet of dry and dusty soil over the mud in which the fish had buried itself. The specimen was brought to London by keeping it in a large tin of thick, black mud, from which the water had been allowed to drain. It was conveyed thus to the

Reptile House in the Society's Gardens at Regent's Park, and there the mud was partly scraped away and partly washed off with warm water. All at once the fish gave a wriggle and emitted a loud, gasping bark ; and, equally unexpectedly, made a vicious snap at Woodhouse's fingers.

This particular specimen of the Lepidosiren was between two and three feet in length ; pale grey in colour ; shaped like an eel ; and had long, tapering, cylindrical fins. While out of the water it was noticed that the fish breathed air like an amphibian. Its diet consisted of frogs, worms, insects and crustaceans. It is a most voracious feeder, and is also known to exhibit cannibalistic tendencies in its own habitat, for it will bite and eat its own species. Although the native fishermen delight in capturing and eating the Lepidosiren, yet they fear its bite on account of the scissor-like teeth, which cause terrible wounds. The fish is a ferocious savage.

The Lepidosiren is really a remarkable fish, possessing a long and cylindrical body like an eel, and has been known to attain a length of fully six feet. It is peculiar in many different ways, but the more especially for the fact that it has lungs as well as gills. In the dry season of the year, the marshes and swamps, in which it is usually to be found, naturally become dry ; but this does not worry this fish at all. In order to meet this change of conditions, the Lepidosiren works its way into the mud to a depth of about eighteen inches, coiling up at the bottom of its burrow. The latter is a kind of cocoon or capsule of hardened mucus secreted by the glands of the skin.

Sequestered in this cocoon, the fish breathes entirely by aid of its lungs for half of the year ; and, in this condition, the earth in which the fish is imbedded may be dug up and transported anywhere without fear of the fish dying, always provided care is exercised to keep the cocoon at an even temperature. If this precaution is not observed, the fish does not live for any length of time, for it is very susceptible to varying degrees of temperature.

When its cocoon is placed in water, the fish awakens from its long slumber and immediately resumes the double process of breathing through lungs and gills. In its ordinary surroundings, the Lepidosiren will remain in the cocoon until the rainy season floods the swamps and marshes in which it has hibernated during the dry period of the year.

It is of interest to note that specimens of this fresh-water fish are also found in some parts of South America, but very little is known about it and few specimens ever have been brought out of their natural surroundings. The Lepidosiren is far more a fish of the continent of Africa than it is of South America.

All of the specimens of this quaint fish that I have seen around the Victoria Lake have had large filamentous fins ; and, of these, the pectoral was longer than the pelvic pair. I noted, on a few occasions, that one of these fins was bifid.

During the course of one of my journeys round the shores of the lake, I came across an interesting specimen of this queer fish and carefully observed its habits. When first found, the fish was about to burrow in the mud at the approach of the dry season. My attention was directed to it by one of my Waka-virondo porters. Instantly, I halted to watch it at work and made some rough sketches.

The Lepidosiren burrowed deep into the mud and, after making its cocoon, left a mouth to the flask-like cavity. This was later closed by a kind of lid, perforated at the top by a small aperture. The margins of this opening were then drawn inwards so as to form a funnel for insertion between the lips of the fish. By this means it could obtain air during the period of hibernation.

I was told by an ancient, but unusually intelligent and observant Kavirondo Chief that the male fish always made the nest for the female ; and was fully alive to its parental responsibilities. Not only does it build a home for its mate, but guards the spawn larvæ. The actual nest is about one foot deep and irregular in shape, and always built in the weeds of a swamp.

From close enquiries which I made, it would seem that this curious fish is widely spread over tropical Africa; at least, wherever swamps are to be found. Some specimens have been found in the Gambia River on the West Coast. In fact, I am told that the natives of Gambia search diligently for it in the encrusted state and are particularly fond of eating it. They can keep the prize for a long period in the clod of earth which envelopes it, and no cold storage is necessary. The Lepidosiren preserves itself until required for consumption.

I have watched some native fishermen spearing this fish. They walk about in the reeds in the shallow parts of rivers or in the swamps, and employ spears specially designed for this

A GUNBOAT IN SUDD BELT ON THE NILE

purpose. They often capture large specimens. It is most fascinating to see them at work, and to hear their loud shouts of triumph when a large fish is speared. Later, it is taken back to the village and dried on frames of green wood, under which fires have been kindled. They turn the fish over and over until well smoked and perfectly dry. I have never heard of the natives curing them by any other means or by any salting process ; but the flesh treated in this manner is most delicious. One could not possibly desire anything more pleasing to the palate.

The Victoria Lake has an area of about the size of Scotland, and an indented coast of about 3000 miles. Scattered along the shores are over three thousand native fishermen, who employ methods not unlike those used in some European countries. For example, the Unyala tribesmen use a type of landing-net in which is to be found a true " sheet-bend." They told me that they had used them long before any white man came to their country. There is also a plaited fish-trap used in the rivers flowing into the lake, which is almost identical with one employed in poaching for salmon in the waters of the British Isles.

The lake offers a very rich field for investigating not only the fish found therein, but also the methods of catching them. In comparatively recent years some revolutionary changes were accidentally effected by an old Scandinavian fisherman, A. Aarup, whom I knew well at Naivasha some twenty odd years ago. He was a most cantankerous old man, but a first-class sailor and fisherman. During 1910, Aarup discovered on the Victoria Lake a native fishing industry that had existed probably for thousands of years. His accidental interest in the lake fisheries changed the whole course of an age-old industry in these regions.

After many experiments, Aarup introduced a five-inch flax gill-net, which is now in general use among the natives. He arranged to import a large supply of them from Ireland ; and they proved almost immediately successful. His nets were always filled with the prime fish of the lake, the carp-like *Ngege*. Many others now joined in, and shared this fabulously rich harvest. To-day, natives can be found everywhere on and around the lake using the net that old Aarup introduced to them. The going was too good to last for long, however. Both hippo and crocodiles caused considerable damage to the nets ;

and, to-day, I understand there is only one European still engaged in the fishing industry on the Victoria Lake.

Aarup, when a very old man and almost blind, lost his way during a terrific storm at night on a coffee plantation near Nairobi. He died from exposure.

A problem has always existed as to what eventually is going to happen. Whether the industry will continue to decline ; whether the growing scarcity of fish could be attributed to some natural cause, such as a rainfall cycle ; whether the lake is teeming with some other kind of fish which can be utilized to relieve the strain on the *Ngege* ; or whether, by economic exploitation, the yield can be increased while the supply is conserved.

The trend of past investigations into this acute problem has elicited the fact that crocodiles are a serious menace in both lakes and rivers. They are known to take fish from the nets, but there is no conclusive evidence procurable that they catch them while swimming freely in the waters. Other enemies of the fish are the otter and numerous birds—cormorants, darter, kingfisher and other fish-killing birds like them. But these mostly feed on small fish, which abound in both rivers and lakes ; and, therefore, may actually be performing a real service in keeping down the numbers.

The problem still awaits definite solution.

While in Uganda, I found that fishing was one of the staple industries and employed thousands of natives on shore and islands in the lake. Fish, both from the lake and the tributary rivers, form one of their chief articles of diet ; and particularly among the poorer classes of Muganda. The wealthy members of this race of Africans, who are passionately fond of fish to eat, employ professional fishermen to keep their tables well supplied. The really poor natives buy their fish in dried form at the market-places.

For all deep-water fishing, the Muganda employ drag nets, which are fully a hundred feet long. They are made from the stems of papyrus reeds, tied close together. Along the top are fastened many small basket traps with wooden floats attached ; and these are so fixed that, when the net is let down, they are under the water. On the lower edge of the net, plantain leaves are tied ; and, at intervals, weights are attached to maintain their position and keep them submerged.

In shallow water, it is their general custom to fish with a

line. The one most commonly in use is at least twenty feet in length and has large hooks attached, which hang down at intervals from shorter lengths of line and are baited with very small fish. No rod is ever used, but the fisherman lets down the line with floats attached to it. The lines are made from fibrous material obtained from aloe plants growing near the lake. The hooks have no barbs, but are simply sharpened ; while an eye fastens them to the line.

When making a net, the fisherman adheres strictly to the custom of neither eating meat nor salt ; and this rule is rigidly observed until the first catch is made. The superstitions of the African are many, but none is so closely heeded as those peculiar to the fisherfolk.

The Wakerewe tribe on the islands in the lake do most of their fishing by means of weir baskets, or else by hook and line ; and this practice appears to prevail among all the various peoples of the lake islands. For some years it was strongly suspected that fish carried the dreaded scourge of sleeping sickness and, in consequence, the Government of Uganda removed the fishermen from shore and island villages. All fishing in the northern portions of the lake was also forbidden. The fish have now been proved innocent, and the ban is lifted.

The most curious feature of the other large fresh-water lake in Kenya, Naivasha, is that there were no fish at all. And this, even though many rivers flowed into it. Black bass have since been introduced successfully. Colonel Roosevelt shot an otter in these waters. To the best of my belief, this was the first otter ever obtained in Lake Naivasha, though others had been seen. Undoubtedly, it was the otter which was responsible for the fable that a huge sea-serpent frequently had been seen swimming on the surface of this lake. I am firmly convinced that this alleged sea-serpent was no more than a number of otters travelling in single file on the surface.

A few days after Colonel Roosevelt had killed his specimen, I went out in Aarup's sailing boat and saw four otters swimming in this fashion. Viewed from a distance, they certainly gave the impression of a big python.

On examination of the contents of the stomach of the otter killed by Colonel Roosevelt, and also the crops of pelicans and other fish-eating birds shot at the lake, we could discover no trace whatsoever of any fish diet. We made certain that their food consisted solely of worms and small frogs. The fact that

Lake Naivasha is of volcanic origin might account for this strange absence of fish in the waters. Yet, it is curious that they did not come down the rivers into it; and, also, that the black bass, introduced in recent years, have thrived.

On the Nile, when near Kiro, I have found many species of fish, all of which were edible. One of these was a long eel-like specimen with eyes covered over by skin, while the dorsal fin runs down to join the diminutive tail. The snout was long and tabular, and the flesh lies in long and delicate flakes somewhat like that of a snake.

Another quaint species had the head and forepart of the body encased in an adamantine shield, and was armed with dangerous looking spikes on the back and pectoral fins. Its tail was shaped like a shark's, which it closely resembled in general appearance though the mouth was not underneath the head as in the case of the shark.

A third species, very common all over this upper part of the Nile, and justly prized for the richness of its flesh, was covered with enormous circular scales. Its general form approximated to that of the mullet.

The fourth curious fish, which I found at Gondokoro on the Nile, was an electric eel. I placed it in an iron bucket filled with water, and received a severe electric shock both on touching the fish and the water in which it was placed. Kermit Roosevelt and I had great fun with this, for our native porters had never seen one before.

The commonest type of fish found thereabouts, however, is the gorgeous tiger-fish, which is surely one of the most beautiful fish in the world. They are found in great numbers near the Victoria Falls and on the Zambezi River also, and are fierce fighters. There is no mistaking them for any other species, for the brilliant colouring and sharp interlocking teeth clearly identify the tiger-fish. They have an adipose fin similar to that of the salmonidæ, and also an extra set of bones. The mouth is very hard, and impervious to anything except the sharpest hook.

They provide excellent sport and demand careful angling. In the early part of the season, towards the end of June, the fish are mostly found at the mouths of tributary rivers and where water from adjoining swamps drains into the falling river. Later on, when the river falls to its lower levels, they will be found in pools either just above or below rapids.

The best results can be obtained by spinning with a spoon or large metal Devon.   Casting from a canoe or the rocks gives the best sport ; and they can also be caught by trolling from a canoe.   The fish strike with great power for their size and leap from the water at the end of their first rushes.   These are always fierce and frequent, and vary in direction.

I have caught good tiger-fish on the Nile and Zambezi which weighed as much as six pounds as a general rule, but a few up to ten pounds in weight.   Higher up the Zambezi above the Victoria Falls, they have been caught up to fifteen pounds ; but I have been told that the fish between six and ten pounds give the best fight.

That is only what I have heard.   I have had no experience with a tiger-fish above ten pounds ; and they gave me all the fight any keen fisherman could desire.

CHAPTER XXIV

HARMLESS HIPPOPOTAMI

I HAVE not the slightest hesitation in saying that the hippopotamus is definitely the most uninteresting of all the large animals found in the wild state in Africa.

Generally speaking, there is a complete absence of any real element of sport in killing them ; unless it is that, despite their great bulk, they offer such a difficult target to the man behind the rifle. I can say, with a perfectly clear conscience, that never once have I killed a hippo except for a very good reason. Certainly I have never done so for the sheer lust of killing or even for trophies.

Though open to conviction to the contrary, I believe there are only four legitimate excuses for killing hippo. Firstly, when they have become really vicious and attack human beings in a wholly unprovoked manner ; secondly, when seriously damaging standing crops, and can be proved to be doing so ; thirdly, when specimens are required for scientific purposes ; and, lastly, to furnish fat and food for your native followers.

For some years, hippopotami were protected everywhere in East Africa ; but it had to be recognized that crops and hippo could not thrive side by side in the same district, and the hippo had to give way to the urgent needs of mankind.

This animal is a voracious feeder and can soon make short work of any growing crops that tickle his palate. When a three-ton hippo has been through a native *shamba*, there remains very little of the crops growing thereon. An acre or two of cultivated land can be made to look like a shambles in the course of one single night by a destructive hippo. What he has not been able to eat has every appearance of having been flattened out by a heavy steam-roller. Then he is sentenced to death.

When stationed at Kisumu, on the Victoria Lake, I was often urged by the Wakavirondo villagers to rid them of pestilential hippo. They swore by all their known and unknown gods that the animals were seriously damaging their crops and also attacking their fishing-canoes. Careful investigation on the spot, however, proved these allegations groundless. It was the fat and flesh of the beasts they really desired, not to be rid of public nuisances. This is their favourite food ; while the fat is used to anoint their bodies profusely and as pomade for the hair. Every man to his own unguent !

Much to their disgust, I declined to be the official fat-provider and hair-oil dispenser for the entire neighbourhood by the killing of an innocent hippo.

I have always made it a strict rule never to shoot a hippo without just cause. It would be well if others, who like to call and think themselves sportsmen, would abide by this same humane line of conduct. I have heard some men boast of having fired off a large number of rounds of ammunition, and yet never waited to collect their possible victims. That was wanton butchery of the worst possible type : not sport. Nothing could possibly justify such acts. Instead of boasting of their diabolical lust for killing, they should have bowed their heads in shame.

Taken all in all, hippo are perfectly harmless ; but they are known to attack human beings, and sometimes in the most fierce and unwarranted manner. In the big lakes, where they are more disturbed than elsewhere, they are far more vicious than in the rivers. In the latter, they are seldom hunted or harassed by men and their deadly weapons. I have watched schools of hippo playing in the rivers of Africa for several hours at a stretch ; and also been savagely attacked in a small craft when on the lakes. I have found them in amiable mood and been allowed to take close-up photos of them ; and have also found them possessed by a devil of vindictiveness. You have to take them as you find them ; some are good, and some are bad. Mostly they are quite reasonable.

The acquatic and nocturnal habits of the hippo very largely protect them from man's attack. It is generally accepted as a fact that they only walk ashore in the hours of darkness in order to feed ; but such is not always the case. Whatever else he may be, the hippo cannot be accused of being rigidly hidebound by rules.

When on inspection duty at Karungu, near Shirati on the Victoria Lake, I went out duck shooting at a nearby swamp. The District Commissioner, F. K. Webster, told me that it was

an ideal spot to get a good bag of water-fowl of many varieties.
He was quite right. I had most excellent sport.

The swampy area was badly cut up in every direction by
wide hippo runs, and I could hear them grunting and squealing
in the lake near at hand. Every now and again, one would
rise to the surface, blow joyously and splash about in frolicsome
play. It all sounded most peaceful and ideal. But I was
killing birds : . not hippo. The latter did not appear to mind
my shooting in the least. The constant discharge of my gun
certainly did not interrupt their aquatic sports in the lake.
Having got all the water-fowl necessary for Webster's and my
own needs, together with a dozen brace of snipe, I started back
to the Boma. It was still quite light, and wanted an hour to
sundown.

Ahead of me I saw three hippo quietly feeding on dry land.
They allowed me to creep up near enough to watch them closely,
and continued feeding. There were two cows and a half-grown
bull calf. Presently, they were joined by three males and two
females. The new arrivals livened up matters considerably.
They were feeling frisky and insisted on an evening gambol on
the turf. For a time they played childish games rather resembling " Nuts in May " and " Kiss in the Ring," accompanied
by much squealing and mock fighting. They soon tired of these
nursery games, and settled down to eat their supper.

I used up the dozen films I had with me, often photographing
them from no greater distance than twenty yards. For a full
hour I walked about close to them, taking no precautions to
conceal my presence. They made no attempt to attack, and
simply ignored me. I might just as well not have been there
for all they cared ; and they were sublimely indifferent to all
I did and where I moved. Obviously, they had seldom been
molested. Later, when discussing this experience with Webster,
he admitted that neither he nor anyone else, to his knowledge,
had ever fired a shot at them.

Hippo have their favourite haunts and are loth to leave
them. At night they can be very noisy creatures indeed ; for
this is the time when they are most active and generally come
out of the water to feed. Their vocal utterances beggar description. They start off with a deep grunt which steadily
increases in volume ; and then abruptly change their tune into
a succession of snarls of varying depth and intensity. The
extraordinary voice of the hippo, without doubt, is one of the

A PUFF-ADDER

OSTRICH CHICKS HATCHING OUT

weirdest of all the many strange noises heard in the stillness of the African night.

One night in 1908, when returning to Kisumu from a visit to G. A. Stafford Northcote, District Commissioner at Kisii, I made camp on the banks of the Mirui River. It is a wide tributary of the Victoria Lake and empties itself in that sheet of water at Kendu Bay. My tents were pitched near the mouth of the river, and I knew this particular spot to abound with both hippo and crocodiles. My night's rest, which I needed badly after a forced march under a blazing sun and with the thermo-meter standing at 120 degrees Fahrenheit in the shade, was utterly ruined by the impromptu serenading to which I was subjected by two cheerful hippo in the river below my camp.

I do not know whether their cantata was intended to be an aria buffa or pastorale ; but I do know that it was a dreadful crescendo of discords and far from soothing to my nerves. The syncopation of their duet was not good, and sounded to my ears exactly like an exceedingly blunt and rusty saw being operated upon a log of very green wood. It set all my teeth on edge.

By the time they had become bored with running up and down their vocal scales, I was real mad with them. But I did not want to shoot, not even to frighten them away from my vicinity. That was very self-sacrificing. Those unsolicited waits, however, could not be punished justly with a bullet. It was their home, and I was an intruder : the uninvited guest. After an hour or two of this ghastly noise, they grew tired of their choir practice. I had long ago !

It was a great relief when they came ashore to partake of their supper, and thus enabled me to resume my interrupted slumber. I was soothed to sleep by their deep-chested grunts of relish as they fed.

Hippo used to bother us rather badly at Kisumu in the early days. I was much chaffed about one experience I had with four of them during the midnight hours.

With infinite trouble, labour and expense, I had made the first flower garden in Kisumu. It was in front of my bungalow, overlooking Usoga Bay. The lava-rocks had to be excavated, earth brought from a good distance outside the town, and seeds, shrubs and rose-trees imported from England. The garden was coming on nicely, and I was real proud of my achievement.

One night, shortly after midnight, I was awakened by strange noises in front of my house. I rose from my bed and stepped out on to the veranda to investigate the cause of the commotion. In the bright moonlight I could see four hippo rolling on and trampling down my carefully nursed flower-beds. One brute was eating my treasured rose-trees ; and appeared to be enjoying the meal. This was more than human nature could stand : I saw red. I ran back into the house for my rifle, and let drive at the nearest beast.

I hit him somewhere. I heard the dull thud of the bullet strike home ; and he snorted in surprise, and grunted savagely. I fired again. This scared them effectually, and the bulky trespassers rushed pell-mell across my wrecked garden, out into the roadway, and headed down the hillside to the lake.

Procuring a lantern, I went out to inspect the damage. I moaned in anguish, for my garden was completely ruined. The rose-trees stood naked of buds and leaves ; every flower-bed was flattened out and deeply pitted with immense feet-marks ; and my shrubs had been eaten down almost to the roots.

My treasured garden was a thing of the past : a wilderness of utter desolation. No longer could I truthfully croon in my morning's bath : " Can't remember any garden hasn't got a single flower." There was no garden : not even a vestige of anything even resembling a flower. It was tough !

A short time after this devastating episode, I had another adventure with a hippo at Kisumu. It was a beast which seemed to favour a midnight stroll through the budding township. It was a strange taste, for the scattered railway terminus offered no attractions, scenic or otherwise. The place was as dull as ditch water ; and with not a blade of green grass to be seen.

I had dined with some friends from Uganda, homeward-bound on leave, and left them at the Dak Bungalow at midnight with a promise to see them off by train early next morning. I started to walk up the hill to my own residence. I was perfectly sober, though what follows may impress some with a contrary belief. I must insist that this would malign me. Only two glasses of light lager beer had passed my lips that day : one before, and one at dinner.

There was a full moon casting an ethereal light over the countryside, and I could see distinctly around me for a radius of about a hundred yards. Not anticipating any trouble, I walked unarmed. Stepping out briskly, for the air blew chill from off the gaunt Nandi Escarpment, I made my way up the roadway to the top of the hill overlooking the Victoria Lake.

All at once I saw a bulky object waddling down the centre of the highway toward me. I halted and stared ahead, wondering what it could be. Presently, I made out the unmistakable shape of a solitary hippo. I decided that he or she had the right of way; and having no desire to offer the beast any nocturnal salutations, I stepped off into the bare veld. When about twenty-five yards from the road, I halted and faced about to see what was occurring. The ungainly beast continued its progress down the road toward the lake, quite unmindful of my presence. When it had passed, I hurried back to the roadway and resumed my journey homewards. Far be it from me to interfere with any hippo's rambles in the moonlight.

When I related this adventure at the Nyanza Club, at noon on the following day, my brother officials chaffed me unmercifully and insisted that I had dined too generously. Again I insist that I *was* perfectly sober!

The same wanderer was reported on a number of different occasions thereafter. It delighted in cruising about the hill, which was the residential section of Kisumu, and was also seen walking around the houses and gardens thereon. The beast was even encountered lumbering up the main street of the Indian Bazaar on two different nights, much to the surprise and fright of the Punjabi policeman on that beat.

About two months later, Blayney Percival, the Game Warden of Kenya, sat up and waited for a hippo which had done a lot of damage to the growing crops of the natives. He saw a beast near the lake's edge, and shot it dead. In the morning, when he examined his kill, he found that the old bull had been blind. There can be little doubt that this was the same meandering animal, for the real marauder was killed on the following night; and when in the very act of devouring the standing crops.

Hippo have a playful habit of diving under a canoe or bumping it from underneath. Such incidents are seldom in the nature of hostile attacks, but more a spirit of fun and mischief.

A terrible tragedy occurred at the Victoria Falls some years ago from just such a cause. Four tourists, two men and their wives, went out in a native dug-out canoe on the Zambezi River just above the Devil's Cataract. A school of hippo was playing about in the river, and the tourists went too close to watch the frolicsome gambols. One of the hippo, after a deep dive, came up right under the canoe and upset the frail craft. All the occupants were spilled out into the water.

The native boatmen swam ashore, and one man and the wife of the other were also rescued. The swift current carried the other two Europeans down the river and washed them over the Falls. Their bodies were not found until three days later. They had been swept over a sheer drop of over four hundred feet into the Main Gorge, washed through that into the fiery cauldron of the Boiling Pot, and thence down the other Gorges into the Silent Pool. When found in the latter spot, not a single bone was broken and neither body was the least bit disfigured. This was really remarkable, and seems incredible after viewing the rough course followed by the bodies. Yet the fact is well known, and on official record.

The two survivors of this tragedy were married about two years later.

I have often been asked how long it takes for a dead hippo to rise to the surface after being shot and sinking to the bottom of river or lake. It depends on a variety of circumstances. If the animal has fed recently and the water is fairly warm, the body will generate gases rapidly and float to the surface in a very short space of time; but should the stomach be empty or the water cold, it will take a long time for the carcass to appear. On more than one occasion, I have seen hippos' bodies rise within an hour or two after being killed; whereas, others have taken as long as two days to come to the surface.

Because of this great uncertainty, it is next to impossible to feel positive that the hippo at which you have fired, and which has sunk from view, is dead in actual fact. Time alone can set your mind at rest on that point. Often the sportsman has neither time nor patience to await a definite decision of the problem. But the natives in the vicinity possess both, and prize the fat of the hippo as much as we covet gold or precious stones. They will benefit if your aim has been true. The target, however, is never an easy one on which to register; and you can seldom be sure that you have killed. Nature must first do its work, and then you will know.

The result is that hippo have been constantly slaughtered by novices quite unnecessarily. Quite genuinely enough, they have harboured the opinion that they had missed their target, and so have shot at the next head to appear above the water. When that also sank and did not float to the surface quickly, they wrote it down as another bad shot. So the senseless butchery proceeds, but quite unintentionally. Some hours later, or after several days, the local natives enjoy a disgusting gorge on three or more beasts that were killed outright by the novice. The bodies had now risen. The sportsman, however, had gone on his way without any conception of the wholesale slaughter for which he was responsible.

Lake Naivasha has always been a notorious haunt for large numbers of hippo. While the guests of Commander Fredrick Attenborough, R.N., at Saigai-Sai Farm, the Roosevelts obtained most of their hippo trophies in these waters. On one occasion, Colonel Roosevelt was attacked by a school of fifteen or more beasts, while out hunting them in a small row-boat. He killed the two specimens required to complete his collection for the Smithsonian Institute in Washington, and then contented himself by shooting into the water to frighten away the rest. Some few hours later, to his dismay and regret, five bodies floated up to the surface. He was only aware of having killed the two animals, after deliberate aim at them.

Our cheery host at Saigai-Sai had only recently retired from the Royal Navy, and had been in command of the submarine flotilla that made the historic thousand-mile journey under the North Sea in the pioneer days of submarines. He was now farming in partnership with his brother, and kept a steam-launch on the lake to remind him of his naval days.

Saigai-Sai derived its name from the nearby crater-lake. This queer sheet of water had an area of about two hundred yards, and was about 150 feet below the surrounding hills. Its surface stood at about the same level as that of Lake Naivasha ; but, unlike the latter, the waters were very alkaline. All round the edge were many mummified trees. The Masai told me that cows which drink this water invariably lose their calves ; and so named the lake Saigai-Sai—literally translated, " Hot Stomachs." Curiously enough, sheep suffer no harm from drinking here ; but I saw a number of dead pelicans and flamingoes floating on the placid surface of the little lake. What was one creature's drink, however, was another's poison !

There are deep fissures to be seen between this little lake and Naivasha ; and there are other craters on the far side of Hippo Bay, a spot just below Attenborough's homestead. But there is no water in these deep gorges, only rank vegetation and huge larva-rocks.

It was Saigai-Sai which gave Rider Haggard his inspiration for the story of Alan Quatermain. He was staying in East

Africa as the guest of Sir Frederick J. Jackson, and the latter told him of the Masai legend to the effect that an underground river connected Saigai-Sai with the Victoria Lake. It is only a legend, for no such river has ever been found. Some distance away, in the Great Rift Valley, the Kedong River mysteriously disappears underground. Its further course can easily be traced by the brighter green of the vegetation on either bank of its hidden waters. The whole area is volcanic ; and Saigai-Sai once formed part of Lake Naivasha, undoubtedly.

The Masai legend is interesting. They say that, many years ago, Lake Naivasha was much larger than it is to-day. Then came a white man, who was anxious to cross the water to hunt for elephants in the Sotik country. He built himself a small boat to cross the lake. The Masai elders tried to persuade him from the attempt, insisting that he would surely disturb the dormant evil spirits and bring down great trouble on the entire country. Their arguments failed to deter the white man.

One morning, they saw his frail craft push out from the shore and the sail hoisted, and soon it was skimming across the still surface. The Masai relate how, when the boat was about halfway across, the wrath of the evil spirits was aroused. Suddenly, to the accompaniment of vivid flashes of lightning and the heavy roll of thunder, the sky became dark and day was turned into night. A great mass of flame shot heavenwards from the centre of the lake. When the terrific storm had abated and its fury was spent, the great lake had dwindled to its present size ; and Crescent Island was seen for the first time. The Masai insist that the white hunter travelled along an underground river to the Victoria Lake, and never again returned to their country.

This legend, doubtlessly, originates from the last known volcanic eruption at Naivasha. It did actually form Crescent Island and a few other smaller ones near it.

Sir Frederick Jackson was the original of the character of " Captain Good, R.N.," in Rider Haggard's thrilling story of adventure. He told the author how he had been caught one day by the Masai with one side of his face shaved and the other still lathered with soap. He was dressed only in a shirt and socks. As he always wore a monocle, the picture was complete. The Masai believed the glass to be an evil eye, and feared it greatly.

Crescent Island is responsible for an amusing file of correspondence in the Land Department of Kenya. Early in 1904, Barton-Wright, then Land Officer at Nairobi, received a letter from an old gentleman living in the North of England. He wrote that the doctors had advised him to take his wife to live in Africa on account of lung trouble, and both favoured Kenya as a future home. They were much afraid of wild animals, however, but had been given to understand that there were some islands in Lake Naivasha. He enquired if he might either buy or lease one of them from the Government.

The Land Officer replied to the effect that he could buy or lease Crescent Island. The purchase price would be a penny an acre ; or it could be leased for ninety-nine years at a rental of a halfpenny per acre a year.

In due course came another letter, this time asking if there were any wild animals on the island ; if there was a low and high tide in the lake ; and if wild beasts could cross over from the mainland.

Barton-Wright replied that there was no appreciable difference in the tides, and it was a moot point if there was any tide at all ; no wild animals were known to exist on the island ; and, with the exception of the hippo, none could possibly cross over from the mainland. He added that there were, of course, a large number of hippo in the lake ; but these were, more or less, harmless.

The would-be settler then wrote to ask if it would be possible for the Government to exterminate all the hippo in the lake. If so, he would be prepared to purchase Crescent Island outright at the price named.

To this astounding suggestion Barton-Wright replied that he regretted the Government could not possibly entertain such an outrageous proposal.

The correspondence ended with that courteous official rebuke. Kenya lost a settler.

I have a friendly feeling for these ugly mammoths of the water. They are quite harmless in all ordinary circumstances. If found to be otherwise, it is largely due to a spirit of sheer vice in an individual or else to schools of the beasts having been unduly harassed by human beings.

Leave them alone, and mostly they will leave you alone.

CHAPTER XXV

LAKE, RIVER AND SWAMP PESTS

I HAD often been told that pythons lived and swam about in the water, and were equally at home there as on dry land. I never believed it. But now I have good reason to know it is true. In view of the peculiar circumstances in which this personal proof was obtained, it seems necessary to insist emphatically that I had been most abstemious.

Captain Hutton, the commander of the S.S. *Sybil*, of the Railway Marine Service, invited me to dine on board when his ship was alongside of the pier at Kisumu. The others present were Grey, the Chief Officer, and an Auditor from Entebbe in Uganda.

The depth of water alongside the quay is not more than six feet, and the Usoga Bay is fringed with papyrus reeds where hippos and crocodiles are supreme. Grey had been out sailing that afternoon, and the gangway was still lowered on the lake-side of the vessel.

Dinner over, we settled down to a quiet game of Bridge. The only sounds were the lusty chanting of the Muganda sailors in the fore end of the ship, and the monotonous, irritating buzz of swarms of vicious mosquitoes and lake-insects. At the end of the first game, Hutton remarked casually that he had heard rumours of a sea-serpent having been seen in the bay. All present laughed scornfully, for we knew the natives probably had mistaken a drifting log of wood for a serpent. It was my deal, and I was about to call No Trumps on a first-class hand, when we suddenly heard the watchman on deck call out in a horror-stricken voice: " *Nyoka! Nyoka, Bwana; nyoka mkubwa!* "

A large snake! We stared at each other, startled; and then threw down our cards on the table and jumped to our feet. With one accord we raced up the companion-way to the deck, and found the Baganda watchman cowering back from the gangway, while pointing a shaking finger at it. There, stretched at full length, was a huge python slowly moving upwards on to the deck.

" The sea-serpent, right enough," laughed Grey, as he ran down to his cabin to get his shot-gun. We stood spellbound, awaiting his return.

Taking steady aim, he fired both barrels into the great reptile. For a minute or two the python thrashed about madly and then slipped over into the lake with a heavy splash. We ran to the rail and stared over the side into the moonlit waters. The ripples on the calm surface, clearly seen, bore testimony to the writhing in progress in their depths.

" Swing out a boat ! " roared Hutton ; and the Muganda sailors ran to obey his command.

We were soon seated in a ship's boat, armed with a boat-hook and lanterns, and being lowered on to the water. Grey reloaded his weapon, and waited for the python to show up again. Slowly we drifted over the spot where the reptile had sunk, while one of the native sailors felt along the bottom with a boat-hook.

" *Hapa, Bwana !* " shouted the man abruptly. Grey put his gun to his shoulder, while we held lanterns over the side so that he could see his target clearly. Slowly the sailor raised his catch to the surface. The body of the python came into sight, savagely thrashing the water, staining it with crimson foam, and struggling to free itself. So heavy was the burden that the native cried out for help ; and Hutton and I caught hold of the reptile's tail while Grey covered it with his shot-gun. The Auditor tried to slip a noose of rope over the head, but failed.

So great were its struggles that the body broke loose and sank again. After a short period of search, once more the boat-hook found and brought it to the surface. This time the reptile seemed to be dead, but the muscles still contracted and the huge body writhed. We passed a rope round it, and had the prize hauled on deck. All were well pleased with the unexpected adventure. For a long time the immense body thrashed about on the deck ; but, finally, was still. When we measured it carefully from nose to tip of the tail, the python registered just under sixteen feet.

The sailors danced in wild triumph round it, whooping and jumping with joy. This reptile had been greatly feared by all the fishermen of Kisumu.

It is generally an irascible old hippo who turns crusty and attacks everyone and everything in sight. The sex does not appear to make any difference. There is nothing strange in that, for even human beings, when grown old, are most uncertain of temper and suffer from enlarged spleens. Such a choleric old hippo can be particularly nasty, if so minded, and give you a most unpleasant time. ,

I retain a vivid recollection of one such meeting. I was then attacked, admittedly with justification, in a wholly unexpected manner. When proceeding on inspection duties to Karungu and Kisii, I hired the steam-launch *Ruwenzori* for the journey across the Kavirondo Gulf between Kisumu and Homa Bay. This was an ancient and small vessel, owned by my old friend, P. H. Clarke, of Kisumu ; and we were loaded down to the water's edge with my porters, baggage and native servants. The *Ruwenzori* had known many adventures, and was long past its prime. Once it had been sunk by a charging hippo ; and had also been capsized by another brute. I anticipated no such excitements on this journey across the placid waters of the Gulf.

It was a terribly hot day, and the voyage was exceedingly tedious. The *Ruwenzori's* engine was incapable of more than three or four knots, even when driven with a full head of steam ; but she was saving me two days' of hot marching across the scorched Kavirondo Plains.

Midway out in the Gulf, as I sat in the bow, I saw a lone hippo's head floating on the surface of the water. I estimated the range at about seven to eight hundred yards. More out of sheer boredom than desire either to hurt or kill, I took a long shot in its direction. Purposely, I aimed slightly to the right of the square nose. The bullet struck the water close to the huge head, and immediately the beast sank from sight. I was rather pleased with the accuracy of my range-finding.

I watched closely, but saw no signs of the beast reappearing to serve as my unconventional target. I assured myself that it was just badly scared, and had made off into the open waters of the Gulf. Dismissing the animal from my mind, I picked up a book and started to read.

However, I had done a great deal more than merely frighten that hippo. I was soon to know this.

A short while afterwards, the small launch received a terrific bump on the starboard quarter. It careened over dangerously to port, and porters and baggage slid across the narrow deck.

The natives yelled in panic, while I leaped to my feet and grabbed my rifle. It was well that I did so, for suddenly the ugly and large head of a big hippo, followed rapidly by shoulders and forefeet, appeared over the starboard rail of the diminutive launch. It was actually trying to clamber on board in its fury at being used as my target. I had stirred up a hornets' nest, for it wanted to get to grips with us and make mincemeat of all on board—the launch included.

Three tons of lively hippo added to an overloaded small launch is not to be encouraged. We already voyaged at a point below the Plimsoll line : no Board of Trade Inspector would have passed us as seaworthy. I fired, directly my sights came on, straight into that yawning cavern of a mouth. It was an easy target, and the hippo slipped back into the lake and sank from view. I hoped it was dead.

The launch gradually assumed an even keel. For a moment or two, however, this seemed a very doubtful possibility. Every second, I fully expected to feel it turning turtle ; and shouted to Sefu and Hamisi to drive the porters back on to the starboard rail. They did so with enthusiastic energy. I stood ready to repel boarders, but had no further occasion to use my rifle. I do not know whether I killed that hippo or not, but am reasonably sure that I did. In any case, it was impossible to wait and see. Duty called. I might not have heard the stern mandate had it not been for the fact that the neighbourhood was far too unhealthy for any dawdling on our way.

When we had steamed to a safe distance from the scene, I examined the side of the lanch. There was a large dent in the steel plates where the hippo's head had struck ; and the starboard rail was broken and twisted out of shape. How we had escaped being sunk or capsized is little short of a miracle.

There must have been something about the old *Ruwenzori* which was particularly objectionable to hippo, and made them take a violent dislike to it on sight. I can sympathise, for I loathed it also. The craft was a tortoise in speed, highly odoriferous, none too clean, and far from safe.

On my return journey through Homa Bay, we were about midway down its waters when a very vicious cow hippo made a most hostile demonstration against us. It was unpleasant, for the attack was unlooked for and without just cause. I managed to turn her charge with a couple of bullets into the head, and she then made straight for a canoe in which two Wakavirondo were

fishing peacefully.   She overturned the canoe and spilt the
innocent fishermen into the water.   It was all over in the
twinkling of an eyelash.   My two bullets must have had some
effect, however, for she sank from sight after this last act of
wilful mischief.

We steamed over to the capsized canoe and rescued the
surprised natives.   They were more angry than hurt.   One of
them told me that this particular hippo was a notorious *badmash*
(bad character), and always had been a grave menace to the local
fishermen.   He said that she had upset and wrecked many of their
canoes at different times, and always without the slightest
provocation.   I gathered she suffered from a bee in her bonnet ;
and, like Carrie Nation, had a passion for smashing things.

I agreed to land these two men near their village, if they
would take me out in a canoe to hunt down that destructive
and savage old female.   It was obviously my duty.   They
readily agreed to this plan, and seemed eager to assist me in
encompassing her death.   I spent over three hours paddling
gently about the smooth waters of the bay, while the *Ruwenzori*
performed the useful rôle of live-bait.   Although we all kept a
sharp look out for her, particularly so the native passengers on
the launch, she did not rise to give battle.   Then we saw her
dead body, floating feet upmost on the surface.   We towed the
carcass ashore.

On examination, I found both my bullets had been fatal, but
placed slightly too far back.   This had enabled her to wreak
vengeance on the innocent fishermen before she died of her
wounds.

On another occasion, when camped beside the Mirui River,
I was begged by the villagers to kill two hippo who persistently
ruined their crops.   There was ample evidence of the truth of
the charges made against these two brutes, and I passed sentence
of death.   The following morning, I saw the pair in company in
the river, swimming about with heads close together on the
surface of the water.   They were on the opposite side of the
river, so I fired a shot close to them in the hope of making
them attack.   Both sank immediately and shortly afterwards
bobbed up again close to the bank where I stood waiting.   They
were very close, and appeared to be hesitating what to do.
The water was so shallow that they were actually standing on
the bottom and only half submerged.   I took two photographs
of these criminals first, for the Rogues' Gallery ; and the results

ANT-BEAR IN RHODESIA

A SUPERCILIOUS GIRAFFE

Photo by Fred A. Parrish

were excellent. Then I killed them. The natives were very delighted, both at being rid of these pests and at the windfall of food and fat.

While the public executioner went on his way, the local inhabitants gorged themselves on the slain.

On one of my shooting trips, when on leave, I stumbled accidentally upon a marvellous scene in a big swamp, with a lagoon in the centre and fully six hundred yards in width. Close on a hundred hippo were lying about the banks and in the water itself. As, in most parts of the lagoon, the water was not deep enough to fully cover their huge bodies, they resembled so many large seals basking in the brilliant sunshine with evident relish.

Fascinated by this unique spectacle, I stood and watched them for some time. They climbed in and out of the lagoon, strolled about on the land, rolled and wallowed in the water, splashed and blew heartily, made love and fought with each other in mock fury. My presence was utterly ignored.

Not only were the hippo there in great numbers, but the banks of every mud-hole and channel in the swamp were lined by thick yellowish green masses of crocodiles. Their immense scaly bodies glistened in the sun as they slept on the banks. I do not know how many were congregated there, but fancy well over a hundred. I have never seen so many crocodiles massed in so small an area, not even in the Sudd belt of the Nile in the Sudan.

Presently, I sent Hamisi to the far end of the lagoon, with orders to drive the hippo past me. He took half a dozen porters with him, and soon all were yelling lustily and bombarding the beasts with stones. Immediately the thick mat of crocodiles awakened and slid swiftly into the lagoon with a heavy splash. The water's surface boiled. I was tempted to shoot, but there were too many targets to make a choice. I held my fire, being determined to await a more favourable opportunity for attack.

At the first instant of alarm, the hippo had also taken fright. They rushed *en masse* for the narrow channel of the waterway leading out of the lagoon. Down this they swarmed in a solid mob, kicking and splashing the water many feet into the air, throwing back their heads, roaring and thundering noisily, and crashing along in a panic-stricken jumble of immense bodies. It was not so much a retreat as a riot.

I stood on the bank, not more than twenty to twenty-five feet away, and watched their terrified passage. I deplored the fact that my camera was packed away in a suitcase—it generally is when most wanted—for that scene would have made a most astounding photograph.

Then they had gone. Silence settled down over the lagoon, and the waters returned to their placid state but just licking the shores in murmurous movement. I waited for the crocodiles to recover from their fright and show up again, for I never neglect an opportunity to slay these cruel, repulsive and loathe-some brutes.

Thousands of wild fowl, which had been nesting in the hippo holes, now returned to their homes. They kept up a ceaseless shrill chatter for some time, nervous about settling down on their nests ; and then peace reigned once more over this remark-able spot. In the distance, I could hear the dog-like bark of baboons ; and monkeys swung themselves from branch to branch in nearby trees, screaming blasphemous abuse at each other. Herds of many varieties of wild game were grazing all round the edge of the swamp, now fully recovered from their momentary alarm. The whole picture furnished a most interest-ing page out of the book of Nature ; one surely worth travelling many thousands of miles to see. I would not have missed it for anything.

An hour or so passed slowly before the crocodiles got over their fright and began to show themselves. I held my fire, and waited until they had crawled out on to the banks once again. Then I started shooting as rapidly as I could get my sights on to a good target. Fortunately, I was carrying a magazine rifle and got in some quick work. It is not easy to hit a crocodile so as to kill it outright. The only really vital spot is the eye, and then death is practically instantaneous.

In the short space of time available, I managed to kill four of the ugly brutes. The remainder slithered back into the lagoon, and sank from view. No doubt some wounded ones went with them ; but I had no feelings of mercy. I rejoiced that four of these vicious beasts, at least, would no longer prey on living creatures. As for the wounded, I had no regrets. I hoped they would die later. Crocodiles are the enemies of all life, and should always be slaughtered without any compunction.

A crocodile will take as much lead as you may have time to pump into him ; and even then escape you, unless you happen to hit him in the neck, brain or heart. Not one is easy to get. There is nothing certain about slaying a crocodile : the only thing you can be reasonably sure of is that he is an inveterate killer of all creatures within reach.

It is never, under any conceivable circumstances, safe to take any liberties with one of these foul brutes. Even if you have shot one, in a seemingly vital spot, and he does not move, you must still act with the utmost caution and keep out of reach of that wickedly powerful tail. It is always wisest to give him still another bullet or two so as to make positive that he is killed. No matter how dead he may appear to be, if only rendered temporarily senseless, as so often happens, you will be sure to lose him. Suddenly there comes a gentle wriggle of the thick tail, and he slides swiftly and silently into deep water.

Then the lust to kill the brute is overpowering, but seldom satisfied.

At Jinja, near the Ripon Falls, hippo and crocodiles always have been, and still are, very plentiful. Both do a great deal of damage. The fairways and greens of the local golf club are continually suffering from the unwelcome attentions of hippo ; and natives are always being carried off by crocodiles.

Active warfare has been declared on these hippo, and they have had a pretty thin time ; but they show no signs of evacuating their customary haunts or of diminishing in numbers. They are still being shot, trapped and speared ; but appear to be holding their own against all comers. When I was at Jinja, at the end of 1929, I saw several small schools of hippo in the Napoleon Gulf and also just above the Ripon Falls. Two were killed in the few days I spent there ; and two others had been killed before my arrival and were actually being cut up by the natives.

The fairways and greens of the golf course were pitted nightly by their heavy feet, and not even native watchmen could keep them off. They still tell the story of a game of golf played on this course by His Royal Highness the Prince of Wales, during his first visit to Kenya. His ball came to rest on the edge of a green in a deep impression made by a hippo's foot. The question arose as to what could be done legitimately. Might the ball be lifted out into play, without the player incurring a penalty ? It was an interesting problem, not covered by any rules, and there was much argument. It was finally agreed, I was told, that no penalty could be imposed ; and the ball was lifted and played.

Above the Ripon Falls, and in the Victoria Nile below them

many crocodiles may always be seen. They are a constant
threat to all life.

Hippo and crocodiles appear to remain on terms of friendly
intimacy, for they are nearly always to be seen basking together
on a sandbank or mud-flat. They share the same haunts
habitually. A case in point is Jinja. There appears to be a
permanent armistice between these beasts, for a crocodile will
never attack a live hippo. It is a curious friendship, and does
not say much for the hippo's discrimination in the choice of a
playmate.

The crocodile is a really formidable beast, and a potent
menace to all life. Nobody should ever hesitate to kill one.
It is either a murderer many times over or a potential slayer of
all living things. I shot and killed one in the Nzoia River, near
Mumias, which was a twelve-footer. It had a most catholic
taste in food. On opening up the stomach, we found the following list of things : sticks, stones, a woman's foot, a man's
hand, some native beads, an assortment of bangles and anklets,
the hoof of a waterbuck, the claws of a cheetah, the shin bone
of a reed buck or other antelope, the shell-plates of a large river
turtle, the horns of a goat, the foot of a calf, and a variety of
other strange objects impossible to identify. There could be no
doubt about it being a man-killer. I was glad to have been
its executioner.

Crocodiles take toll indifferently from among their fellow-
denizens of the rivers and lakes, always excepting the homely
hippo ; and also from all creatures, human and animal, that
come to drink thereat. All is grist that comes to that capacious
mouth and greedy stomach : nothing is too big, nothing too
small.

One afternoon, when at Kisumu in 1907, I was walking along
the shore of the lake toward Mumias. I saw a couple of Wakavirondo boys driving a herd of cattle to the water's edge to
drink. While I stood and admired the sleek cattle, a crocodile
appeared suddenly and grabbed hold of a wretched heifer by
the nose. The poor beast let out a terrified bellow, and struggled
violently to escape from the vice-like jaws of the reptile. Running to its assistance, I saw the crocodile gradually winning that
ghastly tug-of-war and dragging the heifer forcibly into the lake.
When close enough, I sent a bullet into the brute's neck. It
let go at once, and sank like a stone. We did not see it again,
and I hope it was killed. The poor wounded heifer, no doubt,

recovered in the fullness of time from its terrible mauling. The native stock are hardy animals.

Through the Sudd belt of the Nile, between Gondokoro and Khartoum, I have seen hundreds upon hundreds of crocodiles asleep on the banks, on papyrus islands or sandy spits. I have sat, hour after hour, on the deck of a paddle-steamer and shot at them as we steamed by. I have no shame in making this confession, for the hand of all men should be raised constantly against these killers. They should be shot on sight, just as you would a mad dog ; and rightly are classed as vermin.

It is never really safe to bathe in an African lake or river. Often, however, the temptation is too great to resist, the more especially after a long and hot day's march over the sunbaked plains. But it is taking a big risk.

In the middle of 1908, I was returning to Kisumu from duty at Mumias, and had marched since before the dawn. I camped at noon on the flat banks of the wide Yala River. After tea, I walked down to the river and stood staring at the cool waters with hungry eyes. I could not withstand that strong appeal for a swim. As I stripped, I called out to Hamisi to come and stand guard over me with a rifle.

Then I plunged into the river, and swam right out into the middle of the stream. I kept a sharp look out all around me, but saw no suspicious movements ; and, for a few minutes, I played a game with Fate and thoroughly enjoyed myself. Then, like a giant refreshed, I started to swim swiftly back to the bank. I was within fifteen yards or so of it, when I was startled by hearing Hamisi's voice shouting at me frantically. He was pointing behind me, but could not hear what he said. I halted, trod water and turned to look. I saw a hippo's head on the surface near the opposite bank, but nothing else. Then I caught Hamisi's words of warning : " *Mamba ngwena, Bwana !* "

A crocodile ! I waited for no more, but swam with all my strength for the bank. Fear drove me on, and I fought and splashed through the water at a great pace. I did not dare to look behind. I never swam so fast in my life before or since. I can recommend any swimmer who desires to win a race to try having a hungry crocodile in pursuit !

I reached the bank safely and joined Hamisi, having won by a bare couple of lengths. I saw the wicked head of that huge crocodile only a few yards from the spot where I had emerged from the water. His devilish eyes were fixed on me.

Snatching my rifle from Hamisi's hand, I shot twice at those taunting eyeballs. My bullets hit the water just beyond his head. He sank immediately and there was scarcely a ripple on the water where he had been.

I was determined to slay that brute, if I had to wait there all night to do it. No crocodile ever hatched out of an egg was going to play such a grim joke on me and get away with it unpunished. I dressed hurriedly, while Hamisi's sharp eyes scanned the water for the brute's reappearance. We discussed the best plan to adopt ; and he suggested a tethered goat at the spot, while we both concealed ourselves and waited for the beast to attack the live-bait. I agreed ; and sent him off to a nearby village to buy a goat. He returned after a short interval, tugging the live-bait behind him. The goat was protesting plaintively at being separated from the flock, but would have been even more woeful if aware of the rôle it was destined to play in this drama.

An hour dragged by while we waited. Suddenly we saw a few slight ripples, and our sights came on to the spot. A moment later the brute's head floated up into full view. It had a good look round. This was its last view of anything on earth, for both rifles spoke together. The brute sank at once.

Our first act was to release the sorrowful goat. It did not waste any time, but ran back to the village. We could hear its joyful bleatings for some time after its departure.

The dead crocodile floated to the surface at dawn. It was the biggest brute I have ever slain ; and must have weighed close on two tons, measured just over thirteen feet in length, and had a girth of a little under six feet at the shoulders.

Examination of the stomach contents produced mute evidence that he had been a persistent man-killer.

CHAPTER XXVI

A MIXED BAG

LIKE many other parts of Africa, Kenya has always given a twist of humour to its wealth of pioneer stories. Tragedy and laughter have walked side by side, fortunately for the sanity of many people. During the earliest days of that Colony, there was ample cause to laugh at some of the incidents of which others were the victims; and even some of those which happened personally.

Just after the railway was opened as far as the Kikuyu Escarpment, elephants became a great nuisance. One of the railway construction engineers told me that they could always hear them trumpeting close to railhead camp at night, but seldom saw much of them. They appeared to haunt the vicinity of the Lari Swamp.

One day, however, a train was due from Nairobi, and the engine was derailed not far from the camp as the result of this herd having crossed the track. They had trampled down the earthwork so badly that there was no support for the rails.

When the engine reached this weak spot, the track collapsed and the locomotive was overturned. Fortunately, the driver had noticed that something was wrong ahead and had promptly slackened speed. Otherwise a most serious accident must have occurred. As it was, the delay in getting up material and supplies was a great inconvenience to all at railhead.

One can picture the face of the harassed Traffic Manager in Nairobi when he received the accident report by telegram: " Engine up-material train derailed mile below camp at railhead. Cause, elephants."

It was quite a common occurrence for telegraphic communication to be cut off through giraffes breaking the wires with their long necks when crossing the railway track; and I have already instanced the passion of rhinos for charging locomotives or trains. Railway journeys through Kenya, in

247

those piping times, were never dull or devoid of thrilling incidents.

Near Kifaru Bridge, just beyond Makindu, another material-train met with a peculiar accident. R. O. Preston, the construction engineer at railhead camp, one day received a report that the engine of this train had been derailed near the bridge. The message concluded with the cryptic remark : '" Cause, guinea fowl." This was a new one on him, and he was consumed with curiosity to find out how a guinea fowl could possibly derail a heavy locomotive. An elephant or rhino, yes; but a guinea fowl ! Hastily he trolleyed off to the scene of the accident.

The driver explained that, when approaching the bridge, he saw a large cloud of dust and a mass of guinea fowl enjoying a dust-bath in the soft soil of the embankment. He paid no particular attention, and proceeded without reducing speed. When the engine reached the spot where the birds had been, it lurched over on its side and left the rails.

When Preston made a close investigation, he found that some wooden sleepers at the approach to the bridge had been completely undermined, evidently by the guinea fowl grubbing for the white ants attacking these sleepers. The accident report had been correct. Thereafter, iron sleepers were substituted for all wooden ones.

The " Buffalo " Jones expedition to lasso wild animals had a curious adventure in roping a giraffe. Means, one of the three cowboys, told me about the episode with great glee.

They had roped a big bull giraffe without any great difficulty and brought it to a standstill on the veld. The animal stood quite still, staring down at them reproachfully and wondering what would be the next indignity inflicted upon it. Loveless, one of the cowboys, offered to bet Means that he could not throw a rope over such a tall beast's head. Means promptly took up the bet, and won easily with his first throw of the lasso.

Then came the problem of how to liberate the giraffe, as they now had no further need of its services. All the efforts of the cowboys to shake the rope off the giraffe's neck proved futile. The neck was too long. They scratched their heads, and considered a variety of solutions to their difficulty. Many were tried, and proved abortive. They then decided to throw the animal on the ground and take off the two ropes. This was done quickly and neatly, without damage to the beast. The ropes

A DEJECTED ELAND FOLLOWS THE GIRAFFE

recovered, they encouraged the giraffe to rise and take itself off ; but it would not get up, despite all their persuasion. They spent quite a long time trying to make the animal accept its freedom, but it would not budge. They tried to lift it on to its feet, but found it too heavy. It just lay flat on the ground and presently expired.

Means said the giraffe died of a broken heart at the gross indignity placed upon it. He may be right. This animal is very timid by nature, and may suffer from a weak heart. The shock would have done the rest.

" We were real sorry to see that poor beast just die on us," declared Means. " We had no wish to hurt it, and only roped the giraffe to say it had been done. It was too bad ! "

J. Alden Loring, one of the naturalists with the Roosevelt Expedition, had rather an unpleasant adventure with a cock ostrich at a settler's farm ; but the incident caused us all intense merriment. They were camped on the Kapiti Plains, and Loring went out early one morning to inspect some traps he had set on the previous evening. He was wearing a very vivid green shirt, and walked over the ostrich farm. A cock bird took a great fancy to his garment, and started at a fast run for Loring, who took to his heels. With the bird in hot pursuit, Loring sought refuge in an ostrich kraal and was followed inside by the bird. Thrice round the fenced paddock both raced, Loring only just holding his own. With a final desperate burst of speed, he bolted through the open gate of the paddock, which a native slammed shut after him. He only just managed to evade the unfriendly attentions of that cock ostrich. These birds can be very dangerous in attack, kicking forward very viciously. Their sharp claws will easily disembowel a victim.

Ever afterwards Loring was much chaffed if he dared to don his green shirt. Kermit Roosevelt always insisted that the bird mistook it for a bundle of luscious lucerne.

On my ranch in Southern Rhodesia, I found there were a few wild ostriches, cocks and hens, and would not allow them to be harassed. They could often be seen wandering freely about my lands, and soon grew accustomed to the protection they were afforded. One day, when riding through a distant portion of my land, I discovered their nest. The cock bird was sitting on the eggs, while the hen was nowhere in sight. I was keenly interested, and posted a native on guard to see that nobody went near the nest. One morning, this Mashona came running to my house to say that the chicks were actually hatching out.

I galloped over to the nest with my camera, and found the big birds had departed. A few of the chicks already had hatched out and were wobbling about like drunken sailors ; others were in the actual process of forcing their way through the shells to gaze upon this sad world. The colouration of the chicks was perfectly matched with the bushes surrounding the nest, but I secured a most unique photograph from close range. The chicks show up fairly well ; and, if you look close at the picture, those breaking out of their shells can also be seen. I prize this negative greatly.

On this ranch I was much bothered by really big snakes. The deadly Black Mamba was often found and killed ; and I have also destroyed three or four large banded cobras, as well as a number of other varieties. My cat, Mickey Mouse, had a playful habit of assisting in their destruction round the homestead and was a wonderful shikari where rock-snakes were concerned. One night, when we were sitting beside the fire and reading after dinner, she walked into the room and jumped up on my wife's lap. Just as quickly she jumped down again, but left a half-dead rock-snake on her lap. Mickey Mouse was responsible for considerable excitement for several minutes ! In fact, she was not a bit popular for several days.

On the way down to dip the cattle one Saturday morning, I walked right into a large puff-adder. Fortunately, I saw it first. I happened to have my camera with me, and got a good photograph before killing this very dangerous specimen. It was the biggest puff-adder I have ever seen, and most beautifully marked. After the Black Mamba, this is the most dangerous snake in Africa.

In all the years I have lived in various parts of Africa, I have only once seen an ant-bear, or *aardvark*, in its natural state and surroundings. Their burrows are plentiful, but these curious animals are strictly nocturnal in habit.

I was engaged in issuing tools to my native farm-hands on my ranch in Southern Rhodesia, just after daybreak. A sudden shout from one of the Mashonas attracted my attention, and I saw a large male ant-bear hurrying past us in long bounds just like a kangaroo. Obviously he had been out courting or had been far afield in the night's hunting, and was now hastening home to his burrow. We raced after him, and a Mashona threw a heavy stick at close range. The aim was true and hit the animal on the head, knocking it down stunned. Before I could intervene, unfortunately, the Mashonas had slain it.

Because of its nocturnal habits, it is a very rare event to see one roaming about the veld. Nearly every ant-heap has a widely gaping mouth on the southern aspect, this point being selected by the ant-bear either because it is next to the habitation of the queen-ant or because the structure is not baked so hard by the sun on the south side. They make these burrows their home. Sometimes, hunting-dogs oust them from these subterranean dwellings, and run them to death.

This particular specimen was a fully-developed male, measuring six feet in length from the tip of the snout to that of the tail. The body was long, low and sparsely covered with black hair, while the snout was an exaggerated snub, rather giving an impression of a bulbous nose acquired by persistent heavy drinking. The ears and tongue were enormously long, the former being rather bat-like in shape ; and the legs and tail were short but very strong. The forelegs were shorter than the hind ones, as is the case with the kangaroo. The claws were long and sharp, being well adapted to digging for its main food supply, namely, ants and grubs. The tail was very thick at the base but tapered off to a thin point.

In general appearance and movements, it reminded me of a kangaroo more than any other creature. It travelled at a fast pace over the veld, and in long jumpy runs. The head and ears also were not unlike those of the Australian mascot.

My Mashonas prized this kill greatly, and assured me that the flesh had a very delicate flavour. I took their word for it, having no wish to sample the dish. The competition for the tail and the skin was keen, the former being the real tit-bit, and the latter making durable sandals.

The Government in Kenya, at one time, seriously considered the project of rounding-up large numbers of zebra and taming them for domestic purposes. It was also proposed to " Burbank," by inter-breeding with donkeys and horses. A number of us were invited to play the part of cowboys at a rodeo in the first big drive, which was staged at Naivasha under the direction of Dr. Robert J. Stordy, the Principal Veterinary Officer. A big herd of zebra was successfully driven into large and strongly built kraals, already prepared for their reception. During the night, however, they grew panic-stricken and fought viciously with each other. In the morning, the kraals were a shambles. Dead and dying, seriously injured, and badly bitten or kicked zebra were heaped up in the kraals. The remainder had broken down the strong walls and made good their escape. We had to shoot a lot of the poor beasts to end their pain. The scheme was forthwith abandoned.

On Lord Delamere's ranch at Njoro, two eland and a couple of zebra quietly joined the cattle and Masai donkeys. They all four became perfectly tame, and could not be separated from the domestic herds. Every night they followed the cattle and donkeys into their kraals ; and, at daylight, went out with them to graze. I have often seen them mixed up with the cattle, and was able to approach quite close to photograph them. They did not appear to mind in the least.

One transport-rider in Nairobi, Mr. Morrow, had captured a zebra stallion and trained it. It was quite a common sight, in those days, to see this beautiful creature trotting along with the mules and harnessed with them to a wagon.

During the course of a most interesting day, during 1929, taking " still " and motion-pictures of wild game on Toms' Farms in Southern Rhodesia, I followed up a herd of beautiful sable antelope. There must have been at least sixty of them when first I saw these creatures ; and some had wonderful heads. There was one old bull with the best sweep of horns I had ever seen on any sable antelope. He was truly magnificent—a king among sables !

They allowed me to approach quite close. One of the young bucks stood up on his hind legs and nibbled at the lower branches of a tree, making a very attractive picture ; but he was too distant to photograph. A few others light-heartedly gambolled in the sheer joy of living. Then, on a sudden unaccountable whim, they bolted at top speed. I could have cried in mortification, for I was just in position to film them.

Troops of monkeys and baboons were scattered about in the adjacent trees, but beat a hasty retreat at my approach. The baboons were particularly resentful, and noisily barked their displeasure at having their morning's siesta interrupted. I do not know what they said, but it sounded pretty rough stuff. They were far too churlish to pose for their pictures. As they scattered, a family raced across the veld in front of me and made for some trees on the far side of the valley. The female carried a wee baby on her back, with its arms tightly clasped round her neck. It looked exactly like a diminutive jockey riding home a winner.

I soon found the elusive herd of sable again, for they had not gone far away ; and filmed them from rather too great a distance. The results were poor, partly due to heat-haze. One old sable bull was lying down in the grass, asleep. I nearly trod on him. He leaped to his feet and dashed straight at me in his sudden panic, knocking over both myself and my camera. Luckily, no damage was done. There were now close on a hundred in the herd, and many had really magnificent horns. The graceful curve backwards of their long, sharply pointed horns is unequalled. I would, however, rather face their stern than their heads if they were bent on mischief.

On our way back to my host's homestead for lunch, a big bull giraffe stalked, with ungainly stride and most laughable deliberation, across the roadway ahead of our car. He halted in the middle of the track to take stock of us, and stared down scornfully from his lofty field of vision. Being looked down at from such giddy altitudes makes one feel real puny. I had been inclined to laugh at his absurd gait ; and now the laugh seemed to be on me.

I climbed out of the car hurriedly, and got to work with my cameras. The giraffe posed admirably, but soon got bored with the sitting. He strode off disdainfully into the bush, unhurried and contemptuous. As he went forward on his stroll, an eland followed across the road and brought up the tail of his procession. It looked horribly despondent, and its head was held earthwards in dejection. Neither seemed to care a brass button for us, even though the engine of our car was still throbbing loudly. Again I felt snubbed !

I followed the giraffe through the bush, and once or twice he turned round to stare disdainfully. Once he halted for some minutes, while making up his mind whch way to go. He headed for a group of zebra, standing under the shade of Acacia trees. They made a very pretty picture. The protective colouration of both animals was perfectly exhibited against the background of trees.

Then the tall animal got bored with watching me, and stalked off on his lonesome. He was quickly lost to view.

I wanted no more of him, so let him go.

CHAPTER XXVII

WILD ANIMALS AS PETS

WHILE in Kenya I captured a number of baby wild animals, and mostly was able to rear them successfully. A few, however, proved untamable; and I had to admit defeat and give them their freedom. At some stations I had quite a good-sized private menagerie of various species; and, always having been fond of any animal, obtained a lot of amusement out of my strange pets.

While at Kyambu, I had a baby duiker, which thrived in my care and grew to maturity. It was wonderfully tame, and used to wander about the Boma at will. This pet always followed me about like a dog, and made free use of my house and office. Often it would settle down comfortably at my feet, and have a quiet nap while I was working in my office; and it was never absent from my table at meal-times. Greedy little beast, was Susan!

I also had four guinea-fowl chicks, which became quite tame and made the Boma at Kyambu a home from home. One day, to my sorrow, they were missing. I firmly believed that they had reverted to the wild state. In a manner of speaking, they had; but only for a brief period—a happy domestic event. Some weeks later, they returned to the Boma and resumed official residence. They brought with them a family of chicks reared in the forests.

When I was transferred to Nairobi, I left these birds at Kyambu. They had become an institution there. The four had become forty or more birds, and were steadily increasing. Every breeding season, they departed to the forests on their family affairs, laid and hatched out their eggs, and returned to the Boma with their new families in due course. It looked like a case of perpetual motion.

I have tried unsuccessfully to rear Colobus monkeys in captivity. I had two at Kyambu at different times, but they

254

soon languished and died. While other varieties of the monkey tribe throve in my care, the beautiful Colobus species always died early. It was a source of great regret, for I hated to see the pitiful expression in their wizened little old-man faces. I soon abandoned all efforts to keep them as pets, as it was obviously futile and, therefore, cruel. They were always quite tame and affectionate, but slowly pined away and died.

Then there was my old friend, Marmaduke, the chameleon. I found him one day in my kitchen garden down by the river, and carried him up to my house. Flies were very troublesome, and I thought he would make a useful member of my household. I guessed right, for he did. Marmaduke was the most expert shikari ever born, and I used to sit for hours watching him stalk and snap up a fly on my walls or ceilings. He could do it easily in any position, even upside down.

I learned a whole lot about stalking from Marmaduke.

He made himself quite at home, and spent most of his waking hours in the pursuit of the fly and small insect pests in my house. He was a positive asset. It was great fun to sit and watch him carefully stalk a fly, shoot out his long tongue like a streak of lightning, and roll back the fly into his capacious mouth. His accuracy of aim was marvellous, and I never remember seeing him miss a kill. His expression, as he captured an insect, was priceless. He always looked as if he was winking at me and rubbing his well-filled tummy with enjoyment.

Then I conceived the idea of taking a photograph of him actually capturing a fly. At first, I experienced no luck at all. Hamisi, who entered whole-heartedly into the spirit of my task with evident amusement, spent his spare time in capturing bait for Marmaduke, so that I might take a snapshot of my pet at work ; Sefu and my other native servants joined in the fun, and soon Marmaduke was being waited on hand and foot like royalty. He grew visibly stouter and stouter, day by day ; and became more and more lazy. Instead of hunting for himself, he expected the victim to be placed ready for his long tongue to collect.

Roll after roll of films proved failures. My shutter was always just too soon or just too late to record the perfectly timed picture of the kill. That confounded long tongue of Marmaduke's worked much too swiftly for my eye to follow.

Next, Hamisi erected a special stump of a tree for Marmaduke to pose on ; and put up another at just the right distance

for the flies to settle on.   This latter was smeared with treacle
as bait for the insects.   More weeks sped by without my getting
just the picture for which I hungered.   Then, one day, I got it.
This was with my one hundred and fiftieth negative, but exposed
at just the correct fraction of a second.

That was a costly business, both in time and money.   It
demanded an infinite degree of patience and optimims, but also
afforded a lot of fun.   You could not be serious with Marmaduke
about, for he was a jolly old rascal.   I consider the resulting
photograph was well worth the time, labour and cost entailed.

Poor Marmaduke !   He was fast asleep one day when my
sandy-coloured cat, Matthew-Mark-Luke-and-John (or Matthew
for short), found him on my writing-table.   That was the end
of my chameleon.   Matthew always was a savage, and later
reverted to type.   He deserted me in Nairobi and kept a large
harem in a disused ant-bear hole near my house ; and   only
visited me for occasional meals.   Soon a new breed of wild
sandy-coloured cats spread through Nairobi, the illegitimate
offspring of Matthew.   I abandoned him to his immoral ways
when transferred to Kisumu.

At Naivasha, I had a most interesting collection of pets—
two cheetah cubs, a rock jackal, and a serval cat.   They were
all quite tame and lived, more or less, in harmony ; with the
sole exception of the serval cat.   The latter was always vicious
and untamable, and, eventually, I released her.   She raced
off into the bush without as much as a " thank you " for my
months of hospitality.   Ungrateful, ill-mannered beast !

The cheetah cubs were great fun and did nicely, until attacked
by distemper.   I managed to nurse them through this severe
illness, but they never fully recovered.   A few weeks later, they
had a relapse and died.

The rock jackal had no vices and few virtues.   He was so
very dull and uninteresting that I gave him his liberty.   Even
then I had to chase him away, and three or four times he
returned to the fold.   Finally, he disappeared for good.   Whatever his faults, he showed more appreciation of kindness than
the serval cat.

Mrs. W. F. S. Edwards, the wife of the Inspector General of
Police, had the jollies little pet in Nairobi—a genet cat.   It was
a charming little beast, and blessed with a most affectionate
disposition.   Except for its tail, which was ringed, it was not
unlike a squirrel in general appearance ;   but its coat was

THE GIRAFFE JOINS THE ZEBRA

spotted like a serval cat's. The principal diet of the genet cat was either raw hen's eggs, nuts or fresh fruit. His slogan in life was : " Eat more Fruit " ; and he lived up to it. Yet I never knew him turn up his nose at anything edible. Greed was his chief vice.

When travelling between Kericho and Muhoroni, I found a very wee zebra foal. It was obviously lost. By its starved appearance I am inclined to think that it had been parted from its mother for a day or two. I carried the poor little soul into Muhoroni, and fed it on milk. It lapped this down greedily, and I had strong hopes of saving its life.

The Dak Bungalow was full when I arrived, which was most unusual. I had to share a room with a very corpulent stranger, who was the loudest and most persistent snorer I have ever encountered. He kept me awake for the best part of the night. Towards midnight, I put my hand down beside the bed to see if the baby zebra was quite all right. The body was stone cold, and so I knew it was dead. I lay awake cursing my room-mate for lifting off the roof with his snores and thus spoiling my sleep. At last I was driven frantic, and picked up the body of the wee foal and heaved it at the noisy sleeper.

The body landed plumb on his fat stomach with a heavy thud. He awoke with a start, and let out a string of fierce oaths. I retorted that he had ruined my sleep by his loud and persistent snoring. I was fed up. For some minutes, we both sat up in bed and upbraided each other angrily. Then he threw the foal's body at my head, and I ducked.

After a period of mutual vituperation, we settled down once more to sleep. It was useless in so far as I was concerned, for the fat man started snoring at once with increased vigour. I heaved the zebra's body at him again and registered on my target. He was more than angry this time, and threatened to beat me up. He was a big man, too ! But he contented himself by heaving the small corpse at my head, and again missed. Three times during that miserable night did the battle break out again. I got no sleep at all.

As might be expected, the morning found us not on speaking terms. I never knew that man's name. We travelled together in the same compartment on the train to Kisumu ; but a deadly hate journeyed with us. I had buried the baby zebra at Muhoroni ; but the hatchet had not been buried between us. It was really all very silly !

When I visited my brother, Jack, in Sumatra some years ago, he had two most rare and interesting pets. One was a Binturung ; the other, a Siamang monkey.

The official name of the bear-cat is *Binturung*, genus *Arctictis*, but to his friends this pet was just plain Peter. A very distinguished person was Peter, for he was the sole representative of his genus. Although closely allied to the palm-civet tribe, yet it is so very different from the members of that group in certain respects as to demand special notice in all zoological works of reference. It is covered with long and coarse fur, black in colour but marked with grey on the head and fore-limbs.

He was caught by Malays when a mere infant, in the dense jungle forest of Sumatra. My brother bought him from them as a pet. Peter became so tame in his care that he lost all the instinctive desire to live in the wilds. He became as docile and affectionate as a domestic cat, and settled down in the household as an honoured member of the family.

Peter's genus has a rather wide distribution over the regions ranging from Assam through Arakan, Tennasserim, Siam, the Malay Peninsula, Sumatra and Java. They live for the most part on small animals, birds, fish, fruit, insects and earthworms. Owing to their purely nocturnal habits and retiring disposition, bear-cats are seldom seen and very rarely captured.

The Binturung is chiefly distinguished from all other species of the civet family by the long tufts of hair surmounting the ears, and by the prehensile nature of the long and bushy tail. The latter is of great assistance in climbing trees. The length of the head and body varies from twenty-eight to thirty-three inches—in Peter's case it was thirty-two inches—and his tail measured twenty-six inches. The tail is nearly as long as the head and body, and very thick at the root from which it tapers gradually.

A fascinating and most unique pet was Peter.

Gollywog, the Siamang, was also captured by Malays in the Sumatran forests and when quite young. They caught it close to Lebong Donok, and sold the little chap for a small price to my brother. He was one of the very few Siamang monkeys in captivity, and there was none in the European zoological gardens at that time. This was due to the fact that the Siamang will not survive the change in temperature, being extremely delicate.

He was a quaint little fellow, long armed, small bodied, and as inquisitive and mischievous as a puppy. He was accustomed to walk hand in hand with my brother to his office in the gold mine at Redjang Lebong, near Benkoelen, and then would fill in the time of waiting for the return journey by an intimate enquiry into the workings of the mine. My brother had a cabled offer of £500 for Gollywog, but refused this as he knew his pet would not survive the journey to Hamburg.

Gollywog died from a severe chill caught on a rainy day when still with the owner in Sumatra.

Leslie Tarlton's brother, Henry, captured a baby rhino near Nairobi and took it to his house in Parklands suburb. He cabled to Carl Hagenbeck in Hamburg, offering his captive for sale. An offer of £300 on board at Mombasa or £500 delivered alive in Hamburg was promptly cabled back. Henry Tarlton accepted the former, as he did not believe in taking chances. It was some weeks before the order for shipment arrived by mail, and meanwhile the baby rhino had become a great pet of the family; but it was a costly one.

He was a greedy little fellow, and blessed with an abnormal appetite. Tarlton told me, with deep dismay, that his pet was ruinous to keep; and the Bank Manager was getting quite stuffy about his heavy withdrawals to meet the colossal food bills.

" He eats three packets of Quaker Oats and six tins of Nestlé's condensed milk at every meal," groaned Tarlton, mournfully. " And the little beggar wants three such meals every day ! "

At last, he received the order for shipment, and, much to his relief, placed the rhino calf on the train for Mombasa. He told me afterwards that it was a toss up who was the more relieved to see it go, the Bank Manager or himself During the prolonged period of waiting the rhino baby had just about eaten up all the profits !

I cannot recommend rhino calves for pets, except to those who are millionaires.

When I was resident in Southern Rhodesia, a few years ago, a goods-train from Livingstone ran into a herd of elephants near Dett. The animals left a small calf behind them, and it ran up and down the track shrilly calling for its mother. The train was stopped, and the crew captured the little chap after a severe struggle. They bundled the captive into the guard's van, and took it with them to Bulawayo. En route, they christened him Malindi.

Negotiations were set on foot to dispose of the jolly little fellow to the highest bidder. All of the train-crew looked for handsome rewards and a profitable ownership of Malindi. I told them of Tarlton's experience with his rhino calf, and their faces dropped. Negotiations for sale were hanging fire. The guard hurried off to send an urgent wire to the highest bidders to accept their offer.

Before the sale was completed, however, Malindi died. During his short stay in Bulawayo he had become perfectly tame and most popular. I have always suspected that the poor little chap died of gluttony or indigestion, for he was a greedy beast and all visitors fed him with anything they chanced to bring with them.

Judging by the varied assortment of foodstuff consumed by Malindi, it would require more than the digestion of a baby elephant to survive the ordeal.

CHAPTER XXVIII

MY FIRST ELEPHANT: AND OTHERS

ON landing at Mombasa early in 1904, I was obsessed with the same kind of ambition as had gripped me at Bombay on my first arrival in India. Then I hungered to kill a tiger : now I wanted an elephant. Shortly after reaching Nairobi, I went out alone to hunt elephants in the Nyeri district, and camped on a spur of the Aberdare Range. Below me was a deep valley through which ran a brawling brook of clear water. I had seen many old and a few quite recent elephant tracks hereabouts, and was encouraged to hope that luck might favour me.

Early next morning my Wandorobo hunters brought me word that a big solitary elephant, with exceptionally large and heavy tusks, was roaming about the vicinity. For three days I searched industriously for him, but never saw more than his spoor and recent droppings. I almost despaired of finding the brute, but Hamisi, my gun-bearer, was an optimist and urged me to persevere. I had chosen him from among many applicants at Mombasa, largely because he had such excellent records to show from hunters of proved experience. His testimonials were exceedingly good ; and, in the six years during which he loyally served me, I found every word in them to be fully justified.

Soon after daybreak on the fourth morning, I saw a large dark object moving about in the valley below my tent. I trained my glasses on it, and caught the flash of a pair of gigantic tusks. Next I made out the bulky form of a big elephant headed straight for my camp. In my excitement, I did not wait for Hamisi ; but grabbed my rifle, shouted to Sefu bin Mohamed to find my gun-bearer and send him after me with my heavier rifle, and hurried off to give battle.

At first, I thought the elephant intended to walk straight through my encampment ; but he paused abruptly, and then turned off to the right and proceeded up the valley. He must have caught a whiff of man-tainted wind, and was disinclined to look for trouble.

I followed in his wake, unmindful of the fact that Hamisi had not yet overtaken me. I was far too excited at the prospect of getting my first elephant to think of anything else.

Then I saw him come to a halt in a thick patch of bush. The big bull was standing with ears widely distended, trunk stretch-out in my direction, and his wicked little eyes positively scin-tillating with devilment. Although I could see the whole of his head, yet the rest of his great body was hidden completely from view by the large bush behind which he stood.

For some minutes I remained motionless, looking fixedly at him. I was conscious of a surge of intense excitement not unmixed with fear. My body was quivering, nerves jumping and heart pumping fast. He was the first elephant I had seen in the wild state ; and the trophy was a real good one. I made a rough guess at the weight of those gleaming bars of ivory, and estimated them to be a good eighty or more pounds each.

Here, at last, was the reward of those three days of arduous tracking ; but I stood alone, for Hamisi still had not come. I wanted that pair of tusks ; but now hesitated to shoot in case of only wounding instead of killing outright. I was confronted with that relentless, unchanging law of the jungles—kill : or be killed. I knew fear. Which would it be ?

Now I could see his trunk waving gently from side to side. Throwing caution to the winds, I advanced noiselessly until within thirty yards of him. Again I halted, hesitating to take the decisive step. It all sounds very ridiculous now ; but I was a novice, and felt such a puny atom beside that mammoth beast.

As I stood immobile and stared at his head in doubt born of fear, he showed evident signs of suspicion and rest-lessness. Now his trunk was searching for my wind. Had he seen or heard me ? A cold shiver ran up and down my spine for I knew that, if I was to make certain of killing, I must get even closer. But what if he charged before I could get a decent aim ?

Gradually my nerves steadied ; and my fears and doubts evaporated like the morning mists before the sun. I crept forward slowly and soundlessly, eyes watchful and rifle held to my shoulder for instant use. At twenty yards, I halted again to

take deliberate aim for the brain shot. I had been advised in
Nairobi, and had read it in the books of the famous elephant
hunters, that this was the most vital spot in the vast target.

Gently I pressed the trigger, holding my breath as I did so.
As my shot rang out, the elephant plunged forward unexpectedly
and the bullet hit him almost at the root of the tail. It must
have proved a most unpleasant surprise ! The great beast let
out a shrill scream of pain and shock. He cut a most ludicrous
figure with his spine curved out and tail tucked in. I was
reminded of a pariah dog trying to get out of reach of a vicious
kick. Instead of watching his reactions to my bullet, I should
have let him have another.

Before I had time to realize my error and fire the second
barrel, he made off straight through the bush in the valley,
trampling down everything in his mad rush and making a
terrific din. A fairly stout sapling got between his front legs,
bent almost double and snapped with a report like the crack
of a heavy whip. I followed in his wake at a steady trot, for
he had left a broad trail. Ahead of me, I could hear the constant
noise of breaking branches and his angry snortings. Once or
twice he trumpeted shrilly.

Suddenly there came a deep silence, and I knew that he must
have halted once again. I worked round the spot in order to
obtain a good view and a fair chance for a head shot ; but must
have misjudged his exact position. All at once, I found myself
facing him at a most unpleasantly close range instead of being,
as I had supposed, on his flank.

He saw me immediately, and charged like a runaway locomotive. It was impossible to dodge that mad rush in the thick
undergrowth, much as I wanted to do. The nature of the
terrain, however, presented no difficulties to that outraged
elephant. He smashed down everything in his path like so much
chaff. Ardently as I longed to be anywhere else but in his road,
I was forced to stand my ground. I knew that I had to kill,
or be killed. Under such circumstances, the jungle ordains that
only the fittest shall survive a duel to the death.

Sheer desperation gave me the necessary nerve to hold my
fire until the elephant was almost upon me. As the huge body
towered over me, with trunk thrust out to grab hold of my
body, blocking out the whole of my horizon, I fired point-blank
between the eyes in the hope of either turning or blinding him.
I emptied the second barrel into his broad chest. Both bullets

sped true to their mark, for they could not fail to do otherwise at so close a range ; but failed to stop or turn him.

I threw myself backwards into a bush to avoid that infuriated charge ; and, as I fell, heard the report of another rifle from just behind me. Picking myself out of the thorny bush and reloading as fast as I could, I looked over my shoulder for Hamisi. He was not visible.

The elephant had fallen on to his knees just in line with me. I saw him stagger to his feet several times, but he seemed unable to stand erect. Each time that he fell forward, the big tusks were buried in the ground. Squeezing myself between the trees and his body, I passed round behind the colossal stern. As I did so, he stepped backwards and I only just escaped being trodden under foot. Getting round to the opposite flank, I was able to fire between his ear and eye as he fell forward once more on knees and tusks. At the moment that I pressed the trigger, he raised his head a trifle. My bullet struck too low to be instantly fatal, and he quickly regained his feet.

As the huge beast stood erect, I realized that his recent actions were due neither to wounds nor weakness. To my horror, I saw Hamisi rolled up in the brute's trunk. The elephant held him round the waist, and was now swinging him from side to side. Before I had time to shoot again, he flung the unfortunate gun-bearer through the air with a powerful swing of the trunk. Hamisi's flight was stopped by the trunk of a tree, fully thirty yards distant ; and I heard the sickening thud as his body hit it.

And then, while I stood paralysed with horror, the severely wounded brute staggered off into the bush. He disappeared from view.

I ran swiftly to where Hamisi had fallen, expecting to find him crushed to a pulp and dead. To my amazement and intense relief, he raised himself on an elbow and greeted me with a sickly grin. His clothing was torn to shreds and blood-soaked. As I hurriedly examined him to ascertain the full extent of the injuries, he explained that he had just caught up with me when I had fired twice into the charging bull. It was his shot which I had heard on throwing myself backwards out of the path of that galloping mountain of flesh. Before he could get out of the way, the elephant had seized hold by the trunk and held him captive. Hamisi was thrown heavily to the ground, and the old tusker tried to crush the life out of him with a wicked

TAME ELAND ON LORD DELAMERE'S RANCH, NJORO

battering by that massive head ; but the length of the tusks rendered this impossible. My gun-bearer found himself safe as long as he managed to keep his body between those bars of ivory.

Once, he had managed to crawl away from the spot for a short distance, but the old elephant promptly hauled him back by grabbing hold of his ankle with the trunk. The brute was actually making a further attempt to crush Hamisi when I had fired into the head. The blood on Hamisi's clothing was not his own, but that of the wounded beast.

Making him as comfortable as I could, I ran back to the camp to get help. Soon we had carried the gun-bearer back to my tent and placed him tenderly on the bed. A careful examination now disclosed that his chief injuries were five broken ribs ; but he also suffered from many bruises, abrasions and severe shock. It might have proved infinitely worse.

Once I had done all I could for Hamisi, I set off again to find and kill that wounded bull. Two of my Wandorobo hunters volunteered to accompany me ; and this time I felt devoid of fear, perfectly calm and collected, and consumed with a spirit of revenge.

About two miles from the scene of my encounter with this solitary bull, we found the dead body of my foe. I had got my first elephant.

I am never likely to forget that thrilling adventure ; nor did I fail to profit by the experience gained. If I had only known, I should have acted as the old Boer hunters of South Africa and fired at a knee to cripple the beast. On two occasions, I have found this most effective ; and quite the best way to stop an elephant's charge at close quarters. On my arrival at Nyeri with Hamisi, to get medical aid for him, I met an old Dutchman from the Eastern Transvaal. He gave me this solid tip, and I owe that old bearded Boer a debt of gratitude for that kindly advice.

A few weeks later I had an opportunity to put his idea into practice. Early in the morning I ran unexpectedly into a cranky old bull in the bamboo forests below Mount Kenya. He was an ancient and solitary beast, and I had no idea there were elephants anywhere in my immediate vicinity. I was quite unprepared for such an antagonist. He charged on sight. Whether he got my wind or heard me first, I cannot say ; but I am sure he saw me. His charge was both swift and vicious. It all occurred so rapidly that I was unable to consider cause and effect, and had to act immediately in self-defence.

It was rather unfair of this brute to vent his spleen upon me in particular, for I was only tracking a splendid buffalo and had no intention of hunting elephants. There was no chance of taking the brain shot, and so I risked one into the centre of his chest. It brought him to his knees, but he was up again immediately and held straight for me. Now I fired at his right knee, and broke it. That brought him up short with a nasty jerk. He stood on his three sound legs, with the broken one swinging above the ground ; ears extended to their fullest stretch ; trunk straight out in an endeavour to seize hold of me ; mouth wide open, and screaming with pain and fury ; and the small eyes flashing with deadly hate. He was an awe-inspiring sight.

Hastily slipping another cartridge into my rifle, I decided to wait and see what he would do. It was vastly interesting, yet I would have felt happier if my trusty Hamisi had been beside me ; but he had gone down to Nairobi into hospital to have those five broken ribs properly cared for.

The forest was ringing and echoing with the brute's angry screams and trumpeting, but he made no attempt to advance.

Fortunately, I had my camera with me and bethought myself that here was an unique opportunity to secure a really splendid picture of an elephant. Covered by my temporary gun-bearer —a rather poor fish—I slowly walked up to the beast. Just keeping out of his reach, I focussed my camera. Immediately I had my photograph, I took my heavy rifle from the native and put a bullet into the beast's brain. He went down instantly, and did not move again.

That rogue elephant was asking for trouble : and got it.

On examination, I found that he had been wounded on a number of previous occasions, which fact would account for him being so pugnacious. Rogue elephants are always nasty customers to bump into ; and this one had been no exception. There could be no mistake about him being very old. One of his tusks had been broken off close to the head, and weighed only thirty pounds ; but the complete one turned the scale at just one hundred and sixty-six pounds. It measured eleven feet on the outer curve. As a trophy it was exceptional ; but such is the base ingratitude of man, that I found myself regretting one tusk had been broken off short. I sold the pair in

Nairobi for £100. If I had known more about ivory, I might have got an even better price.

When I came to develop my negative a few days later, I found myself the owner of a wonderful close-up of an elephant seemingly charging straight at me.   While the plate was still wet, and before I had even taken off a print, I proudly showed it to a friend.   While holding it up to the light, he turned to exclaim on its perfection and accidentally dropped the negative on the cement floor of the room. It was smashed to atoms ; and I could have wept. As it was, never was there such a blasphemous silence ! I had invited him to dine, but now chased him away with virulent abuse. He lost his dinner, and I lost a friend. No man could ever forget all I had said to him.

I suppose it was all very childish of me, but I felt that blow more acutely every moment. I have never been able to forgive him for that gross carelessness.

It is not widely known that the bull elephants in Africa are rarely the fighters of a herd. The largest and oldest bulls are generally to be found solitary or in small parties by themselves. My best elephants have always been killed when on their lonesome, though I have also got a few quite fair-sized tuskers out of a large herd.

Carl Akeley made a close and comprehensive study of the African elephant in its natural environment. He always insisted that there was very little danger from a bull elephant, whereas such was not the case with cows. We often discussed this point at great length, both in Africa and in America, but he would not budge from his views. I do not think many really experienced elephant hunters will entirely agree with Akeley. In the light of my own observations, I cannot accept his dictum as beyond dispute. Not for anything would I insist he is wrong. Merely that it does not coincide with my personal knowledge of this species of animal. No two men ever have the same experience in hunting ; and while in generalities agreement may be found, in particularities a wide difference may exist.

You must judge bull elephants just as you find them. There really is no room for theorizing : only for cold facts and actual experience.

Admittedly, he is a very contrary fellow, and a creature of varying moods. Sometimes he is quite good and sweet-tempered ; but more often he is bad, very bad indeed. His changing moods and uncertain temperament may be accounted for easily enough.

Mostly he is cantankerous when suffering from a sluggish liver, toothache, growing pains, or a senile grouch against the world at large. I have known some bulls to be most intolerably peevish and ill-tempered ; while others have been most un-accountably good-natured and kindly disposed to human beings. Some of my elephant hunting friends have assured me that this also has been their experience.

Most killers of elephants will agree that the cows are nearly always more vicious than the bulls, but will not go so far as to insist that they are more dangerous. Cows are of very uncertain temper, and never are blessed with a really amiable disposition. Particularly in the mating season, or when pro-tecting their calves or bulls from danger, they can be very highly dangerous. But I should never single them out as more so than bulls.

In the actual breeding season I have seen cows with their calves, accompanied by immature bulls, travelling in herds at some distance behind the older bulls. The latter are more usually to be found in small groups or else quite solitary at some distance ahead of the main herd, being guarded from an attack from the rear by the cows and young bulls. When mating is in progress, it is wisest not to attempt to hunt big bulls. That is rather asking for trouble ; and you are likely not to be dis-appointed. At other times, especially in the case of large herds, you may find the big bulls mingling freely with the remainder of the herd. There appears to be no fixed rule in regard to this. When actually mating, the courting couple always go off by themselves.

A few years ago, when in Southern Rhodesia, I photographed a small mixed herd of elephants for over two hours at very close range. There were about twenty to thirty of them—cows, calves and immature bulls. Not one of the latter animals had tusks of much over thirty pounds in weight ; and many must have weighed even less than that. On the following day, I encountered this herd near the same spot ; but this time there was a grand old bull leading them through the scrub and bush. It was just about the beginning of the breeding season, and a big cow was sticking close to the patriarch and driving off all other females who evinced a desire to flirt with her selected husband. She knew what she wanted and was not going to be baulked by any upstart young hussies.

I had given up hunting elephants with a rifle many years

A SERVAL CAT

TWO CHEETAH CUBS AND A ROCK-JACKAL

previously, and had no desire to do more than photograph the herd. I watched them pass on their way.

I have often read, and heard it stated, that the cows and calves are found together invariably. But I have seen the bulls with the calves, when there were no cows within sight. On the other hand, I have also seen cows and calves together, and the bulls a short distance away. What may be true to-day, is quite likely to be reversed on the morrow. Always the unexpected is happening.

The cows are the guards and fighters of a herd, if trouble threatens, but often they depute the job of being nursemaid to the bulls. On Toms' Farms, near Wankie in Southern Rhodesia, I saw a herd at really close range and, for some time, watched the young bulls playing with the calves while the mothers stood on guard at the outer fringe of the herd. It was a most fascinating scene. The bulls appeared to be thoroughly entering into the spirit of this romp with the youngsters. It was most amusing to see a calf butt a bull in the stern with its head, and then bolt while the bull pursued. Others were engaged in mock trials of strength, the calf lustily trying to push the big uncle backwards, while the latter gave way step by step as if being really defeated. Yet I have often heard, and seen it stated, that elephant calves do not play or frolic.

This little peep at the family circle of the African elephant was most absorbingly interesting, and confirmed me in my long formed view that the young bulls are really the nursemaids in elephant herds.

African elephants have many signals among themselves. For instance, I have known a cow get my wind and obviously signal to the rest of the herd to be instantly alert and ready either to attack or bolt. Immediately, every beast stopped feeding and listened with the tip of its trunk held to the ground. They remained as silent and still as the grave, while I moved off slowly and cautiously from the danger zone until the wind was blowing from the herd into my face.

Directly the suspicious cow was satisfied that the danger had passed, she must have signalled the " all clear " sign to the herd. At once they began to move onwards, feeding as they walked.

I have seen this happen on more than one occasion, and am of the opinion that they communicate by vocal expression. Some of the noises obviously originate in the throat, while others are made through the trunk. Often a low rumbling noise, rather like muffled drums, can be heard, and seems to come from their stomachs or deep down in their chests. It may, of course, be merely a nasal note. This is invariably the alarm signal. I have already told how I heard the shikar elephants making this sound when I was out tiger-hunting in India for the first time, and the jungle-cat was being driven up close to us.

Cows often rally round a wounded bull and help him away from the attacker. On two or three different occasions, cows have robbed me deliberately of a legitimate trophy.

One day I shot a big bull in the Karamoja country. He was with a large herd of immature bulls, cows and calves, and I had been unable to get really close enough to make sure of killing. I had only succeeded in wounding severely. At once, four of the cows went to his assistance, while the others formed a guard round them. It was quite impossible to get at the wounded beast to finish him off, much as I wanted to do so. I knew enough by this time to take no undue liberties with a herd of elephants when angry or disturbed. I possessed my soul in patience, and bided my time. Meanwhile, I took careful note of all that took place. It was all most interesting.

The four cows divided forces, two taking up a position on either flank of their wounded mate. Then, half-supporting and half-pushing, they more or less carried him from the field of action into the bush. It was patent to me that the bull was " very sick," but the four cows managed to keep him on his feet and moving along.

I followed up that bull and his four loyal nurses for three most strenuous days, but never got a remote chance to finish him. Meanwhile, the rest of the herd had gone on their way in a different direction. The four cows never left their sorely wounded mate for a single moment. It was really astounding how fast and how far they travelled with him, for I knew that bull was mortally hurt.

Towards dusk on the third day, I came up with them again. I was just in time to see the old tusker go down, and die. For quite an hour the cows stood over his body, every now and again uniting in an effort to lift him on to his feet; but they found it beyond their strength. Finally, they must have sensed that he was dead. They departed from the spot slowly, halting every few yards to look back at the prostrate body of the giant.

At last the jungle swallowed them, and I saw them no more.

My followers quickly got to work and cut out the bull's tusks, which weighed seventy and sixty-six pounds apiece. This task accomplished, we retraced our steps to the camp. I had given Sefu orders to make camp beside a river, some five miles back on the trail. We reached it at midnight. I was hungry, thirsty and footsore; but had got my tusks. Better even than that, I had been given a most touching glimpse of Nature's kindly heart.

That was one of the most interesting experiences which I ever had in hunting elephants. I had been much intrigued by the manner in which the four cows had stood by their wounded mate and half-carried him away from me.

It is by no means a rare occurrence. Abel Chapman told me in Nairobi that he had one or two similar experiences, and was robbed of one exceptional old tusker owing to some cows helping it away. Though he had followed them for several days, he had not been able to catch up with them and finish off the wounded bull.

When this happens, it is particularly annoying. Not only do you lose a prized trophy, but you are filled with deep regret for the pain you have inflicted and cannot end.

CHAPTER XXIX

THAT " ELEPHANT CEMETERY " MYTH !

THE widely accepted belief that elephants go to one special spot to die has no foundation in fact. Nobody has ever been able to produce authentic evidence that such is the case; and, it is practically certain, never will.

The fable of the " elephant cemetery " is most picturesque, but is founded only on supposition. The Boers of South Africa were firmly convinced that sick elephants always made their way to some secret and inaccessible place to die. But you will never find any European or native hunter who can say truthfully that they have found an actual " elephant cemetery." Such a legend dies hard, chiefly because it sounds so romantic. While very interesting, it is born solely of the imagination.

Vultures and scavenging animals would soon attract the attention of natives to such a spot, if any existed in reality; and so very little of the continent of Africa to-day is unexplored, that even one such death-chamber for wild elephants could not have escaped notice for very long.

I have often asked natives of widely distributed tribes if they have ever found any large collection of elephant skulls and bones in any one particular area. The reply has been nearly always an emphatic denial; but a few have told me, doubtfully, that they had. They were patently lying to curry favour, being under the impression that I desired to hear an affirmative reply and would reward them suitably for it. They guessed wrong !

If anyone had genuinely known of the whereabouts of such an unique spot, the tusks would have been recovered quickly ; and a most careful watch would have been kept over the " elephant cemetery." The natives of Africa regard elephant meat, fresh or putrefying as the case may be, in the light of a great luxury ; and are not indifferent to the value of the ivory as a commercial proposition. Such a heaven-sent larder would never have been abandoned to hyenas, jackals, vultures and such like carrion creatures, any more than such a source of wealth would have been ignored.

One or two old-time hunters have told me that they have found the corpse of a very old animal, and sometimes one of an animal dead from someone else's bullet ; and one man declared that he had found the remains of a number of elephants in one small area. All these instances merely prove simple facts, and not that there exists a recognized " elephant cemetery " or more than one.

An old animal, grown very feeble and aware that death is near at hand, naturally would seek out some sheltered spot in which to end the balance of its days, and this would be close to water and easy food ; but, as a matter of self-preservation, the selected sanctuary would be far removed from danger of molestation and in as an inaccessible place as could be found. A disabled or severely wounded beast would hide up in dense cover until death released it from torment. The remains of groups of elephants in any one particular spot might indicate one of three possibilities—a wholesale slaughter by human agency, a sudden epidemic of disease, or the consumption of some deadly poisonous food. But it would be rather far-fetched to suggest that this was an habitual " elephant cemetery."

In all my years of wandering about Africa, I have only once found the body of an elephant that unquestionably had died from natural causes, though other cases have been suspected as being so. In thirty odd years, one may cover a great deal of country ; and I have traversed practically every part of the game-lands of the continent of Africa.

This solitary exception was found early in 1929 on Toms' Farms, near Wankie in Southern Rhodesia. When in the company of H. G. Robins, the owner of this estate, Lieut.-Colonel A. J. Tomlinson, the secretary of the Automobile Association of Rhodesia, and a Matebele named Jim, we found the body of a young cow elephant that had died in calving down ; and then only two or three days before our discovery of the body. She was an oddity also for the reason that she possessed but the right tusk : the other had never grown. This cow was so very recently dead that the vultures and other scavengers of the veld had not had time to do more than devour the tip of the trunk and a small part of the tail.

The cow had died when kneeling or else when resting on her belly. The trunk was extended along the ground in front of her, and the fore and hind legs were doubled up under the body. The great bulk of her remained just as she had died, and had not fallen over sideways. The cause of death was quite obvious, even to the most inexperienced eye. We found all that remained of the newborn calf about a quarter of a mile from the mother's body, and it had been eaten completely. When we reached the spot, the vultures were picking clean the bones of the small skeleton. We hoped that it had been stillborn, and had not died from attack from wild beasts or hunger.

Of course elephants do die from natural causes; but I have no hesitation in denying that there exist one or more select places, and most carefully hidden, to which all go directly death seems to be imminent. Such a myth, while romantic and picturesque, strains one's credulity to the breaking point.

I have found the skeletons of elephants in various parts of Africa, some of which have been speared or else shot with a rifle; and a few others which may or may not have died from natural causes. It was impossible to say. But there was never a tusk near the bones, and it was plain that they had been hacked out of the skull. If search had been made in the neighbourhood, it is possible that they would have been found stored in some local chief's ivory cache and awaiting a purchaser; or else the killer of the beast had carried away the rich prize. In any case, I was never fortunate enough to stumble upon a free gift of ivory. I had to work hard for it, and take big risks. That was what made it so much worth while when once the tusks were in your hands.

Once, in the Kedong Valley below Kijabe, I found the complete skeleton of an elephant: complete, that is to say, but for those precious bars of ivory which are the rightful equipment of every self-respecting pachyderm. Others had been there before me. The beast must have been dead for some considerable time, for the bones were bleached as white as snow by the fierce tropical sun. I could find no trace of any bullet-hole or spear mark on skull or bones, and can only presume that death had occurred from natural causes; but it might have died from either poisoned arrows or spear-heads shot into the flesh by native hunters. Judging by the size of the skeleton, I am of the opinion that it had been a bull. This discovery further confirmed my disbelief in the existence of any " elephant cemetery."

I have often heard it said that one of these mythical spots existed in the Kedong Valley, but I have tramped over almost every inch of it and have never found anything of that sort. I know of no man who has. At a spot known as " The Kedong Stink Hole," there are always skeletons, bones and bodies of animals scattered about the place; but none of elephants. They may have been responsible for the fable. In actual fact, they had all been asphyxiated by volcanic gases issuing from a deep fissure in the rock-face of a hill. This was one of the pipes letting off poisonous gas from Mount Longonot, an extinct volcano, or from some other point of this widely extending volcanic region of Kenya.

So much for the delightful myth of the " elephant cemetery," which is still so persistently believed throughout Africa and even much further afield. Like the old fable that you may never find a dead donkey, this fantastic belief will probably live for ever.

CHAPTER XXX

FACING A STAMPEDE

ONE very often reads about elephants charging *en masse* in a regular stampede. They do, and it is an awful, nerve-shaking experience for the hunter. When a shot among a herd causes such a stampede, the forests resound to the first crash of their mad panic. It resembles an avalanche down a mountain-side, and is very terrifying. Once, when motoring across Sumatra, the whole side of a mountain suddenly came crashing down upon the road ahead of me, just missing my car and completely blocking the road. The noise of the immense mass of earth, huge boulders and giant rocks, and big trees cascading down the slopes was paralysing. After the tumult had subsided, a thick fog of dust blotted out the landscape and filled my nostrils, eyes and mouth ; and, when it finally lifted, I gazed upon a quarter-mile wide path of desolation.

The stampede of a wild elephant herd is rather worse.

But once their initial panic has died down, however, they can disappear from sight without making more than a faint whisper of sound. Trees have been uprooted, bushes and grass laid flat, and there remains over all a thick haze of dust.

When hunting in Uganda, I once encountered a large herd travelling beyond Nimule beside the Nile. The grass stood from six to fifteen feet in height, and the whole countryside was studded with thick bush and the thorny Acacia trees, yet the only sound they made was that of a faint breeze stirring the grass. It was no more than the echo of a sigh, such as one may often hear in a wheat-field in England. It was remarkable that such huge bodies could collectively move across such a type of country so noiselessly. Had they been feeding as they travelled, the constant snapping of tree-branches and the rumbling of their digestive organs in operation would have been heard.

Often I have been tracking a herd on the move and been

fairly close up to the tail of the procession, and then lost them unaccountably. Their spoor would have been simple enough to follow, had there not been so many other quite recent tracks. I could not hear their movements. Only when I found their droppings was it possible to locate the path they had taken. If sound alone had been my guide, then I should not have found them again.

On another morning, I picked up the very fresh spoor of a small herd of elephants, also not far from Nimule; and one pad-mark in the dust of the road indicated that a really big bull was with them. The measurement of the circumference of the pad-mark gives a fairly accurate idea as to the size of the brute and also the weight of ivory carried. It is not an infallible guide, perhaps, but is seldom far out.

It was the beginning of the breeding season, and I knew it was probable that this bull would be well in advance of the cows; and the hunting, therefore, would be fraught with grave perils. I considered the problem for some time, and then decided to make the attempt. Hamisi advised strongly against my doing so, but another careful measurement of that giant footmark clinched the argument. He was obviously worth getting, risks or no risks.

Followed by Hamisi and one of my Muganda hunters, I set off on the track of the herd. It was easy enough to follow them through that twelve-foot high elephant-grass, for they had left a path as wide as Regent Street. Unknown to us, we got within the cows. I could hear absolutely nothing, see less. Suddenly, Hamisi signalled me to drop flat on the ground; and, though knowing no reason for it, I obeyed instantly. He crawled slowly and silently to my side, and whispered: " *Tembo, Bwana !* "

Still I could see nothing, though he pointed to a spot just in front of me. I strained eyes and ears, every sense keenly on the alert. All at once I heard a curious sibilant sound, closely resembling the gentle kiss of a light wind on the tree-tops. Swish—swish—swish; no other sound, and nothing to be seen. Then, suddenly, my eyes caught a slight movement near a tree to my immediate front.

I almost shouted aloud in fright and surprise. There, so close that I could have touched her with my hand, was a huge cow elephant. I crawled away hastily, only to meet still another. Then I realized that we had ventured inadvertently into the cows and were surrounded by them. The game laws prohibit the killing of a female, even in self-defence, as a result of much abuse and also because this excuse has so often been employed to explain a breach of the regulations.

We dared not move, yet wanted to get away from our unhealthy predicament immediately. We set ourselves to wait patiently until the animals moved off. They displayed not the least inclination to do so, and appeared to have settled themselves in the spot for a noontime siesta. It was most provoking—and dangerous ! The hours dragged by interminably, while we waited quite motionless, legs and arms cramped, and scarcely even daring to breathe. At last I could stand the strain no longer, and decided to break the tension for good or ill. I was desperate, and ready to take big chances to free myself one way or the other from the chains that bound us to this dangerous spot.

Silently, I took the Baganda's spear from his hand, gradually raised myself to my feet, and got ready to assault that cow vigorously on the rump. It was the only target she offered, and was so well proportioned that a blind man could not have missed it. I swung the spear and struck with all the strength in my body. The spear-head hit the cow's colossal posterior with a resounding thud, and the shaft broke into three pieces. I dropped the stump like a red-hot coal, and seized my rifle from Hamisi's outstretched hand. I heard him laugh as I took the weapon—a rare event for my gun-bearer !

The cow sprang into life, uttered a shrill and piercing scream, tucked her tail between her legs and galloped off into the bush. When last seen, she was going some ! All around us now were sounds of great activity. We could hear the rest of the herd crashing off through the jungle-growth after their outraged sister, smashing down trees and tearing off branches as they went, and trumpeting loudly. They had gone away from us, luckily, but several passed too close to be at all pleasant.

I never saw that cow again ; and didn't want to, either !

Realizing that they had cleared off, we hurried on after the bull as fast as we could trot, chuckling heartily over the gross indignity inflicted on that most surprised she-elephant. Making a wide detour, we tried many times to get in between the cows and the bull. We failed. Every time we seemed to bump into the females, who were now feeding as they travelled forward. It was getting near sundown when I called a halt, admitted defeat, and abandoned the futile quest.

When an elephant wishes to create a noise, however, he can

make more row than any known animal in the world. A herd of several hundred, such as one often finds in Uganda, will trample down the entire acreage of a native village and destroy every particle of the growing crops, and, in doing so, can make as much noise as a severe earthquake or tornado. The brute is inordinately fond of raiding the crops of the long-suffering African villagers, and the night-raids on the agricultural lands cause terrific devastation and bring the wretched people to the brink of starvation. If a cyclone was at work, it could not do more damage than a herd of elephants on the rampage in the mealie-fields of an African village.

Many of the instances of herds charging *en masse* are merely due to the animals having been severely frightened, and their consequent anxiety to escape instantly from threatening danger. Scent being the strongest sense in most animals, when one or more are disturbed it is only natural that they should wish to get up-wind without delay. This is their only chance to smell the danger from their front. In doing so, they often appear to come deliberately for the disturber of their privacy, and may rush over the hunter or photographer in their acute anxiety to come round toward the wind. Their sole object, at that precise moment, is not to kill or injure the intruder, but to gain a strong strategic position either for attack or defence as the occasion demands. Nothing could be more understandable. Everyone likes to face any danger threatening, not to be soundly kicked from behind.

Should a herd of elephant or buffalo do this on being startled by the unexpected appearance of a human being in their immediate vicinity, almost invariably they split up and pass to either side of the invader of their haunts. I have had this experience with both animals, and am never likely to forget the mental torture and paralysing fear that I suffered in those brief but tense moments.

When a herd of elephants suddenly charges down upon you, trumpeting loudly to express anger or intimidation, it is quite possible sometimes to stop or turn them without even killing a single beast. A shot from your rifle at the top of the skull may achieve this, but cannot be reckoned on as a certainty. A charging elephant is very rapid in motion, and probably travels at the rate of twenty miles an hour. When you are facing up to one coming at the gallop, its speed seems double that. Russell Bowker was once charged by an infuriated bull on the Mau

Plateau, when riding a fleet South African mare, and he told me that it was just about as much as his mount could manage to keep ahead of the brute.

When a hunter is on foot and is charged, it is best to stand absolutely still if facing a massed stampede. This takes a lot of doing, for the most natural instinct is to seek safety in flight. That is suicidal. The slightest movement discloses your whereabouts, and the result is almost certain to prove fatal. Whenever I have acted wisely in this manner, the charging herd passed on either side and left me unharmed.

Such experiences, however, are not those after which one hankers. It requires a strong command over your nerves to act sensibly when facing up to a herd of wild elephants at full gallop in a charge.

Generally speaking, when an elephant is charging, the trunk is hanging down in front of him ; but I have known them rush at me and scream loudly, while the trunk was extended in the air or straight out in front of the beast. This occurs usually at the start of the attack. When they settle down to really gallop, the proboscis is dropped down in front of their chests and the tip turned in toward the forelegs.

Once, when hunting elephants in the Congo, a herd stampeded in my direction. I knew the wisdom of standing perfectly still and managed, by a great effort of will, to do so ; but my soul ached for wings to make myself scarce. To be perfectly frank, I was simply paralysed with terror, and it was due more to this than any sense of wisdom that I remained motionless throughout that terrific ordeal. If I had been a block of stone, there could not have been greater immobility. I hugged my rifle and stared straight ahead at that advancing avalanche of mountains of flesh, waving trunks, wide extended ears, thundering feet and flashing ivory, and my ears were deafened by the terrific roar of their loud trumpeting and passage through the jungle. The sweat poured out of my body and ran in streams down my face and body, drenching me through and through. When it was all over, there was not a dry stitch of clothing on my trembling body, and I felt that I must vomit any second.

As they crashed through the bush and trees, leaving a wide wake of utter ruin and desolation behind, trumpeting shrilly as they galloped, I was conscious of only one sensation—a sickening, deadly fear. I felt powerless to utter a single sound, think or even act until the storm had passed me by, uninjured,

MARMADUKE, THE CHAMELEON, GETS THE FLY

The noise rang in my ears and brain for a long time afterwards, and I was able to hear only with difficulty. The whole picture before my eyes seemed filled with mammoth slate-grey bodies, growing ever nearer and larger, of swinging trunks, and of cruel and gleaming bars of ivory. The whole earth shook and quivered to that thundering roar of giant feet beating on the ground.

"Fear" is defined by the Oxford Concise Dictionary as "a painful emotion caused by impending danger or evil; a state of alarm; anxiety for the safety of oneself, or others." It is all of that; and a very great deal more besides, if judged by the standard of emotions created by facing a herd of over a hundred madly charging elephants. I know. Those cold words do not begin to express adequately the state of my mind on such an occasion.

Even when the ordeal was safely passed, and I found myself untouched, I still stood rooted to the spot and unable to fully grasp the reality of my escape. How long I stood thus I do not know. I was recalled to my senses, and the immediate necessity for getting away to a point of safety, by the gentle touch of Hamisi on my arm. He had stood loyally and gallantly beside me throughout that mad minute or more, even as he had bravely come to my aid, and suffered, on the Aberdare Range.

I turned to stare incredulously into his face, and he merely grinned at me. Silently he pointed a forefinger in the direction we ought to take, turned and led the way. I followed, unquestioning and speaking no word.

Had he seen the hallmarks of the ghastly fear I had suffered? If so, he gave no sign, never even hinted that he knew. Hamisi was far too loyal and good a sportsman to attempt to make capital out of his master's momentary weakness. We had hunted too long in each other's company for other than perfect friendship and complete understanding to exist between us. To some, the idea of the possibility of any friendship between a white man and the black man of Africa may sound not only absurd but impossible, yet there can be a bond between a master and servant that is deeper than all ordinary ideals of such a relation. When they have faced death side by side, year in and year out, there can exist a friendship that transcends all others. Colour is no bar to that deep sense of mutual loyalty, consideration, understanding and perfect companionship. Speech is unnecessary; acts and service alone count. And it was thus between Hamisi and myself.

Because of all this, neither of us ever referred to that dreadful, terrifying test of our manhood. Such things are best locked up in one's own private skeleton cupboard. The momentary lapse into weakness can be forgiven ; a perpetual habit, not so. Yet I never wholly conquered my instinctive dread in the first moment of facing up to elephant. Once the issue was beyond recall, the whole outlook changed immediately and I was a normal man again. At school, I remember, I never really minded the actual lickings often received, but I loathed the period of waiting before the first stroke fell. Is that fear ? Or is it merely sensitive anticipation ? I do not know.

Towards the end of 1904, I went out with Captain Noel Monckton at Muhoroni after the famous herd of elephant in that area. They enjoyed a particularly evil reputation for savagery and for charging at the least hint of any danger. We had been warned by many that this Muhoroni herd was far best left in peace. I would not have tackled them alone, to be frank ; but with Monckton at my side, it was quite a different story. I would have faced any real danger with him, and in preference to any other man with whom I have ever hunted, except only Hugh Stigand or Jim Sutherland.

A native had reported that a couple of really big tuskers had recently been seen with this herd. We had both just taken out new game licences, and wanted to get a good pair of tusks, or two good pairs, to christen them. We agreed to combine forces with this end in view. I am glad to-day that we did.

Before dawn we started out with our native trackers and gun-bearers to the point where the herd had been seen on the previous evening. Soon we had picked up their spoor, and, shortly afterwards, had located them in thick bush and thorn-trees. There must have been fully two hundred, but our glasses told us that they were mostly cows or small bulls. There seemed to be very few calves. We manœuvred for position, testing the wind direction anxiously every few moments, eyes keenly searching for the alleged big tuskers. But there seemed to be nothing much over thirty pounds in weight, and they were far too small fry to even interest us. Our licence only permitted two bulls, and we wanted two pairs of heavy stuff in the way of ivory.

We halted at a spot about five hundred yards from the outskirts of the herd, and held a whispered consultation. It was soon agreed to write down our native informant as the usual type of liar. We decided to abandon the hunt and return to the Dak Bungalow at Muhoroni for breakfast.

I turned to have another look at the herd and, at that very moment, saw four immature bulls suddenly detach themselves and advance in line towards us. I called out a warning to Monckton, who had started to move off, and got my rifle ready. Hamisi shouldered up, with my heavy weapon held ready to exchange swiftly with me. I was in two minds about using this latter weapon first, but thought better of it.

Now I could hear the rest of the herd crashing away noisily from us. They had soon gone from sight and hearing. All my attention was concentrated on the attackers. They were coming at a fast walk in extended order, with the immense ears widespread. They presented a glorious spectacle as they came sailing along, all canvas set. There is no other way to adequately describe the motion of an elephant when seen advancing at a walk through long grass. They might have been four of Nelson's battleships under full sail, and with their ivory now and again gleaming white above the yellow grass.

At four hundred yards they broke into a trot, and charged straight for us. Their heads were well up, tails erect, and trunks waving about in front of them, arched and menacing. They meant business, and I had no doubts on that score. The situation looked distinctly unhealthy, especially as neither of us wanted to kill such small tuskers. I found myself ardently wishing that I was having breakfast, at that particular moment, in the Dak Bungalow in Muhoroni. Instead, there was to be a fight to the death on our hands. The bulls or ourselves must kill, or be killed. There could be no burking that issue now.

Monckton, cool as if on parade, shouted to me to take the pair on the right while he attended to those on the left. After my shouted " Right O ! " not another word was spoken. I knew Monckton to be a really first-class shot, far beyond even the average, and always wise, fearless and deliberate. I reposed the utmost confidence in his marksmanship, but had doubts about my own ability to shoot straight and kill.

On came the four bulls, still in perfect alignment. Three hundred yards—two hundred yards—one hundred yards ; my range was continually being lowered. Now they dropped their trunks on to their chests and turned in the tips, and broke into a thundering gallop. My rifle was to my shoulder, sights

on the right-hand animal of my pair, and finger gently caress-
ing the trigger. I was obsessed with an insane desire to shoot and
chance it ; but I knew this would be madness, rank suicide. The
others depended on me, even as I depended upon them. I *must*
keep cool and take no chances, for death galloped hard at us.
I must wait, and then shoot straight.

Monckton's rifle spoke when the bulls were about sixty
yards from us.   Then his second shot rang out ; and I gently
squeezed my trigger. I saw my target crumble up and go down
with a loud, earth-shaking thud. Instantly I had swung round
to face the other, sighted and fired. again.   The second bull
went down on his knees, slid forward a few yards, picked himself
up quickly, and came on again at top speed. Out of the tail of
my eye I saw my first target had not moved. Hamisi quietly
slipped the other rifle into my outstretched hand, and withdrew
the empty one.

Thirty yards—twenty yards, and the wounded bull was still
going strong. I sighted for his chest and was about to press the
trigger, and then Monckton's rifle spoke twice in rapid succession
from my left. I saw the young bull come down and slide forward
for a few yards, and then he toppled over almost at my feet.
He was dead.

Another second or two at most—for at the gallop an elephant
easily covers a dozen yards in under two seconds—he would
have been on top of me, and I must have been killed or badly
injured.   I stared blankly around me, scarcely believing the
evidence of my eyes. The four gallant young bulls were all
stretched out in their tracks, quite close to us and each other.
All were dead.

I walked over to Monckton, held out my hand and gripped his
like a vice.

" Thanks awfully, old chap ! " I stuttered.

That was all said. What is the use of speech on such tense
occasions ? There is no word in the stolid English vocabulary
capable of expressing the genuine gratitude I felt.

I was brought back to mundane things by Monckton's crisp
words : " That busts our licences for this year. Two bulls
each, and not a damned tusk over the thirty pounds ! Tough
luck, what ? "

Honestly, I did not care. All I wanted was a stiff neat
brandy at that moment : damn the ivory and licences,

And I had it !

CHAPTER XXXI

THE ELEPHANT'S INTELLIGENCE

MOST people believe that they are quite familiar with elephants, and their general appearance and characteristics. If the truth be known, the majority delude themselves. Of all the wild animals on this earth, the elephant is the best known and, at the same time, actually the least known. Paradoxical as this may sound, nevertheless it is perfectly true.

The majority base their ideas on a knowledge of elephants on those animals seen in some circus or zoological garden. If you were to ask any man in the street what an African elephant looked like, he would consider it a most simple question to answer; and probably write you down as an ignorant fool to have asked him. This widespread and popular impression, however, is erroneous except in its broadest sense. So also are many of the beliefs entertained in regard to the actual habits and general characteristic features of the African species.

In the first place, the elephants mostly seen in captivity in Europe or America, or elsewhere for that matter, are of the Asiatic species of its kind. All are undersized, even the very largest of them, in comparison with the African species. The two varieties differ as much from each other as they do from the mammoth and similar extinct forms that were common enough in the " Stone Age."

A full-grown African elephant stands at least a foot higher at the shoulder than any Asiatic specimen ever brought out of the Orient, while the tusks are both larger and heavier. The ears of an African bull, when fully extended in charging, sometimes measure as much as fifteen feet across the forehead from tip to tip. They are enormous, and considerably larger than those of the Asiatic species.

There are other clearly-defined distinctions between the two varieties, notably in the forehead, back, position of the brain, and the absence of the soft depression so fatal to the Indian elephant. A large African bull may often stand from eleven to twelve feet in height, measured at the shoulder, and weigh anything up to six tons. Their age is uncertain, but, in captivity, they have been known to live for 120 years.

To anyone who is familiar with both species in their natural habitat, these distinctive differences in form become apparent immediately. I have just seen a news-reel in a cinema, purporting to depict AFRICAN elephants in training as timber-workers. They were of the Asiatic species, and not African at all. Their small ears, apart from other distinctive characteristics, clearly proved this fact. Apart from size, weight and other special qualities, the African elephant is more savage than his cousin in Asia. In the matter of intelligence they are identical.

The ancient civilization of India boasts as one of its really great achievements the taming of the Asiatic species of the elephant family. In the ancient lore of that early form of civilization, this fact plays a very distinguished rôle. But I know of only one place in the world where any degree of success has crowned repeated efforts to tame the African variety. That is at Abi, on the Bas-Uele River in the Congo.

A training camp for African elephants has been established there for a number of years, and a considerable measure of success has been gained. I very much doubt, however, if the experiment will produce a really permanent supply of trained elephants or in a large enough number to be of any widespread utility in the development of the hinterland of Africa. Certainly never to the same extent as in India, Burma or Ceylon.

It may be stated with emphasis that no experiments in animal training ever have failed so signally as those tried on elephants in Africa. This failure is in no way due to a lack of intelligence on the part of the elephant family. They are not one whit less brainy than their cousins in Asia. It simply goes to prove that the African species positively declines to be tamed and trained for service to mankind. They have decided never to become the ready slaves of human beings. It is a very thoroughly British spirit. They are residents in a British possession and consider themselves British. Their national anthem is : " Elephants never, never shall be slaves ! "

The Government of Uganda once tried a carefully-thought-out plan to capture and train African elephants in the same manner as is done in the Orient with the Asiatic variety. Sir Hesketh Bell, who was then Governor, imported an elephant from India with this laudable object in view. The experiment proved a dismal failure, for it never advanced much beyond the actual importation of the Asiatic beast from Bombay. That elephant caused a lot of trouble and proved a costly immigrant !

The first indication that trouble loomed lifted its head on the railway journey from Mombasa to Kisumu. The elephant travelled with his mahout in an open goods truck, admired by all beholders at every station en route ; even the game beside the track ceased grazing to stare at the strange spectacle of the lord of the forests travelling first-class or saloon on the railway. All went well until Lumbwa was passed, and then the real fun began. Like all self-respecting railways, that of Kenya was endowed with one small tunnel. It had been built more for show than necessity, was short in length and situated on a curve in the line between Lumbwa and Fort Ternan. A railway without a tunnel is akin to a cat without a tail, so the wise engineers made themselves a very nice tunnel. It was always much admired, for the job had been neatly and expertly done.

When the train conveying the lordly elephant and his mahout arrived at Lumbwa, the Irish guard bethought himself of the tunnel. He had his doubts if it was high enough for the passage of the beast, when standing on his truck-platform. He consulted the babu station-master and ascertained the height of the tunnel ; then he wanted to measure the elephant. The latter would not play. So they started off, the Irish guard having warned the driver to go slow at the tunnel. The locomotive and half of the train had entered the tunnel, when the guard found the elephant was much too big to pass under the arch. The train was stopped, and the crew went into conference.

The guard finally insisted that the elephant must be detrained and walked over the top of the hill, and then entrained on the far side of the tunnel. The idea was excellent, and gave the elephant some exercise ; but the problem was how to get him off the truck and back into it again. Once more the guard came to the rescue, and pulled off the door of his compartment to make a bridge for the elephant to cross from the truck to the embankment. The beast was in no hurry, and the mahout felt the same about it. They took a long time to cross the hill over the tunnel, the grass being green and the scenery very beautiful. At last, they appeared ; and, after a further delay, entrained.

In the meantime the single line was blocked, and thoroughly disorganized the railway traffic on this section of the railway. But the elephant arrived at Kisumu, embarked on the steamer and crossed the lake to Entebbe.

Shortly after the arrival at Entebbe, it was discovered that the Agent of the Uganda Government in Bombay had shipped a shikar elephant instead of a labour-machine. On receiving the order for an elephant, he had instructed one of his babus to procure one in the bazaar. As Sahibs generally wanted shikar beasts, one such was duly purchased and shipped. They had asked for an elephant, and one had been sent. The Bombay Agency took their commission on the transaction, and forgot the incident.

But they could not lightly shelve the matter in Entebbe. After various efforts to extract useful work from the shikar elephant, it was decided to abandon the scheme. About the only job of work that elephant ever did, and that under strong protest, was to drag a lorry with a grand piano from the pier to Government House. The road was uphill all the way. Then the beast went on permanent strike.

The Government tried to sell this incubus, but nobody wanted such an expensive pet. Besides, the mahout would not be separated from his chum, and the elephant would not part with the mahout. You took both together or neither. So nobody bought it. Then a travelling circus arrived in Entebbe, and the Italian proprietor was offered the animal at cost price. He had heard, however, the true facts of the *impasse* and expressed himself as disinclined to buy the elephant. In despair, the Government *gave* him the beast, and the mahout with it.

This was more economical than to maintain animal and keeper in idle luxury for the rest of their lives. That elephant had a royal send-off from Entebbe. We never heard how the tunnel was negotiated on the return journey.

To attempt to make a general habit of taming African wild elephants is entirely another matter to seeing them grow quite accustomed to the presence of human beings. Wild animals may become indifferent to the presence of man if they know themselves immune from molestation, or even after they have grown accustomed to the close proximity of mankind. The experience gained from the various game reserves in Africa prove this to be the case. But they become very shy and nervous when their inherent instincts of fear teach them that human beings are a

JILL, A LIONESS CUB

GOLLYWOG, THE SIAMANG

PETER, THE BINTURUNG

A GENET CAT

menace to their further existence. Elephants do not differ from other animals in these two respects.

Next to the highest types of apes, perhaps, the elephant is the wisest and most intelligent of all wild animals. In many ways they surpass even the great intelligence of the higher apes, who may be said to most nearly attain the degree of brain-power enjoyed by the human race.

Those who have seen the domesticated Asian species at work in the timber depots of Burma, India, Ceylon and Siam, or even working as trained beasts in Malaya, will readily grant that they are amazingly wise and intelligent. Their sagacity is almost incredible : often positively uncanny. Their team work and individual cunning in removing and stacking huge baulks of timber astonish all onlookers. Nor do they often require human guidance in their labours, for many solve their problems by using their own brains.

I have often seen elephants at work in the teak forests of Burma, drawing immense tree-trunks to the sawmills, shifting and stacking huge logs in the timber-yards of Rangoon, and employing their clever brains to overcome seemingly impossible tasks.

Once, when resident in Rangoon, I saw an elephant act on his own initiative and move a very heavy log of teak from one side of the yard to another. It was of such a size and weight that two or more beasts combined might have found it a severe strain on their united strength. This young beast, however, propelled it along with one foot, while using the others for motive power. The task was performed with comparative ease. I was told that this cute method was self-taught ; and, in this manner, he had solved a puzzling problem by the use of his intelligent brain.

Often two elephants will carry a big baulk of timber between them ; and I have also seen four animals combine to shift a really heavy log of teak and carry it over other stacks of timber.

When camped at Koba on the Nile, on my way through Uganda in 1910, I spent a night with a band of fearless elephant poachers of the Congo. The conversation turned on the subject of an elephant's intelligence. It was all very interesting. A small, quiet man suddenly spoke up with great earnestness on this matter, and offered to give an example. No one objecting, he told us the following story :

" I was hunting the tuskers in the Lado Enclave," he began solemnly, " and one day saw an elephant acting very queerly.

He was a solitary bull, with only fair tusks. I stood and looked at him for some time, and noticed that he seemed to have a sore front foot. He kept on putting it to the ground gingerly, and then picking it up sharply as if the pressure hurt him real bad. After a time, I went up closer. He made no attempt to move, and so I gradually drew nearer. Taking a big chance, I went right to his head, lifted the sore foot and examined it. He did not seem to mind a bit. I found a nasty wound caused by a spike from one of the Muganda foot-traps. The spike was still in the foot ; but, after a lot of trouble, I managed to extract it. " Thinking it unwise to hang about him, I withdrew to a safe distance. For a short time the old beast stood still, and every now and again tested his foot on the ground. Then he turned round and stared at me for a long time. I thought he was making up his mind to attack, but such was not so. A few minutes later, he wheeled and limped off slowly into the bush. I let him go. I noticed that one of his ears had been badly torn, and would have known him again anywhere. But I did not see him any more.

" Some years later I was in London on a short holiday, and pretty broke. One night I went to see the circus at Olympia and sat in the shilling seats, not being able to afford anything better. One of the items was a performance by trained elephants. When this part of the programme was reached, a big beast was led into the arena and climbed up on a tub. It struck me at once that there was something damned familiar about the beast, and then I recognized him for the old chap I had helped in the Lado.

" Unaccountably, that old elephant refused to perform. His trainer beat him and jabbed him with his toasting-fork, but the beast would not do a single trick. All the time he was sniffing round the arena with his trunk. Suddenly, he climbed down and walked slowly round the arena, sniffing at the people. When he came to where I was seated, he halted, sniffed hard toward me, thrust out his trunk and gently clasped me round the waist.

" Then, very tenderly and deliberately, he carried me across the arena and dumped me into an empty five-guinea box. This done, he returned to his tub and gave a polished performance.

" Now, that's what I call real intelligence—and real gratitude —in an elephant ! " He rose to his feet, smiled round at us all, and made for the tent door. " Well—good night all. I'm for bed."

There was a long and strained silence as the little man took his departure. He was a stranger to me, and I asked one of the ivory poachers what was his name.

" Ananias ! " he retorted bluntly.

He reached out a large hand for the bottle of whisky, poured himself a generous measure, and swallowed it at a gulp.

" The blarsted liar ! " he growled. " Why he's never shot an elephant in his life. He's the engineer on a little sieve of a launch on the Albert Edward Lake."

He spat vigorously into the night.

CHAPTER XXXII

SOME HUNTERS AND THEIR TUSKERS

ARTHUR H. NEUMANN, undoubtedly, was one of the most interesting and famous of the old-time elephant hunters in Africa. He spent most of his life in pursuit of ivory on the Anglo-Abyssinian border, and very rarely was seen in Nairobi. He hunted alone and led a life of solitude in the wild regions. He insisted that he preferred it, and I can understand his viewpoint.

Neumann always was credited with having amassed a large fortune out of ivory, but this popular rumour had no real foundation in fact. I met him on a number of occasions, and once spent two very enjoyable days with him in his isolated headquarters on the Abyssinian border.

I remember vividly one of the many thrilling stories of his adventures with elephants. We were sitting round his camp-fire after dinner, smoking our pipes and gossiping about hunting big game, when he narrated the following ghastly experience he had with a cow elephant.

He said that he was following up a large herd, when a cow, with very small tusks and accompanied by a young calf, charged full at him and his party of native hunters. The attack was most unprovoked and wholly unexpected. They all managed to elude her, and escaped from the neighbourhood. Neumann had no wish to kill or even wound a cow with a small calf at heel.

Once rid of her unwelcome attentions, Neumann trailed on after the herd. He followed a narrow path in dense bush, keeping as close as possible to the tail of the fast-retreating elephants. As he walked round a sharp bend in the path, suddenly he came face to face with three elephants. Among them he recognized the same vicious cow and wee calf. She came for Neumann at once, full gallop. He stood to face and meet her charge this time, for there was no other alternative.

He threw up his rifle to the shoulder, preparatory to shooting into her chest as she came in a mad rush at him, without raising her trunk or uttering a sound. He told me that it was the most deadly and determined charge he had ever seen, and fully realized that he had to kill or be killed. Somehow he must stop or turn that charge, and the range was very close. He pressed the trigger, and the sharp click of the striker alone sounded. His cartridge had failed to explode, unaccountably.

Rapidly he worked the bolt, but no cartridge was ejected from the breech. He had worked the bolt after killing a bull earlier in the morning, and then the empty case had flown clear on being ejected. He was quite unaware that the mechanism of his rifle had failed, and no cartridge had been inserted in the barrel. In this very desperate situation, he knew that his case was practically hopeless. The enraged cow, by this time, was within a few strides of him, and the narrow path, on which he stood, was stoutly walled on each side by thick bushes. In an instinctive effort to escape, he turned about and ran as hard as he could, being closely followed by the cow and her calf. She overhauled him at every stride.

As Neumann ran those few yards, he made spasmodic efforts to work the faulty mechanism of his treacherous magazine-rifle. He pointed the muzzle behind him, without pausing to look round, and tried to fire again, but still the rifle failed to work. The mechanism was still jammed, and refused to function.

The cow now was all but upon his back, and every instant he expected either to be seized in her trunk, knocked down flat or impaled by her sharp-pointed tusks. Dropping his rifle, he sprang out of the path to the right. Then he threw himself back-wards into the brushwood, in the hope that the elephant might pass him and keep straight ahead down the path. But she was too close, and had seen this manœuvre to dodge her charge.

Turning upon him like a terrier after a rat, she was on top of him almost as soon as he was down on his back in the brush-wood. In falling, Neumann's feet pointed toward the path ; and he was stretched out on his back, face upwards, and head propped up by the thick bush. The sky and bush-country were completely blocked out by the huge frame of the cow standing over his prostrate body.

Kneeling over him, she made three distinct lunges at his body. Her left tusk penetrated the biceps of his right arm, and also pierced through his right ribs. Luckily, she was not touching his body with her feet, which must have been, he thinks, on either side of him. At the same time, she pounded his chest with the thick part of her trunk and crushed in his ribs on the left side. At the first vicious butt, some part of her huge head came in contact with his face. It barked his nose, and skinned his face in several places. Neumann thought that his skull would be crushed to a pulp, but managed to slip it backwards out of reach of that cruel battering head.

He told me that he was wondering all the time how she would kill him, for he had, of course, abandoned all hope of escaping from this terrible ordeal with his life. He was convinced that his death was inevitable, but hoped it would come soon. What hurt him most, he assured me, was the severe grinding his chest underwent from the cow's head.

Whether she believed that she had killed him, or disliked the smell of his body or blood, or else bethought herself of her small calf, Neumann did not know, but she left him abruptly. He saw her running off into the forest, trumpeting shrilly for her calf. That was the last ever seen of the savage cow.

His native followers had bolted immediately Neumann had been charged. When the infuriated cow abandoned her victim, however, they came running back to his help. Where these Wandorobo cavemen had run, Hamisi would have stood beside his master.

They found Neumann more dead than alive. His clothes were badly torn, he was covered with blood, and, in addition, was sorely bruised and lacerated all over the body. He had been gored by the cruel tusks through arm and ribs, and the bones of his chest had been crushed in and broken. Some of his minor injuries were not found until a week or more later.

His native followers carried him gently to a shady tree, under which Neumann sat, supported from behind by one of his own men who sat back to back with him. He was unable to sit erect without this help. They stripped him to the waist, tore up his shirt for bandages, and did the best they could for his multiple wounds and injuries. All the time, though suffering intense agony, Neumann directed their crude surgical attentions.

For three months Neumann was nursed back to health by the devotion of his native servants. He was far from all medical aid, and mostly had to allow Nature to do her own work for him. For two weeks or so, Neumann told me, he did not think that it

A FALLEN MONARCH *Photo by Dr. L. R. Magoon*

THE COW ELEPHANT WHICH DIED IN CALVING

was possible for him to live ; and did not mind much whether he did. He said that he suffered untold tortures throughout those dreadful weeks of unending pain. He turned the corner, how-ever, and slowly began to get well; and, in course of time, regained his full health and strength.

Undeterred by this dreadful experience, he continued hunting elephants for another decade or so. He died in London, when on a brief holiday, as the result of a gun accident. He was cleaning a revolver, when it suddenly went off and killed him instantly.

Jim Sutherland was, perhaps, the greatest of all modern professional elephant hunters. His only peers were " Karamoja " Bell and Arthur Neumann. His recent death in the heart of the wilds of Central Africa was a great grief to the many who knew and loved this great-hearted sportsman, myself included. Sutherland had been hunting elephants for something like forty years at the time of his death from dysentery, and was still in pursuit of them. He had a record in four figures, all shot with his own hand.

When hunting with him on one occasion, he told me an amazing experience with a wounded beast in the forest-belt of the Congo. The animal came full at him, and Sutherland's rifle jammed at the critical moment. He was seized round the waist by the trunk, and thrown into the air. He came down sitting astride the elephant's back, with the beast at full gallop. He told me that it was the most uncomfortable ride he had ever had, and never desired to repeat it. It was most difficult to retain his precarious seat on that gigantic back, and so grabbed hold of the great flapping ears. Every moment he expected to be scraped off or brained by the branches of the trees. He managed, finally, to catch hold of a bough as his mount passed beneath it, and swung himself clear of the beast's back.

Once the elephant had passed onwards, Sutherland dropped to the ground, ran back hastily for his rifle, saw to its efficient working, and then gave chase to the wounded animal.

" I got that swine," he assured me, vehemently. " I've never been so mad with an elephant in my life. I was sore for weeks after that rough ride, and could only sit down with acute dis-comfort."

Jim Sutherland died, as he would have wished, still in harness and hunting elephants. I have before me a letter received from him only a few months before his death. It is so very typical

of the man, that I quote a few extracts. It clearly indicates
his character, ambitions and viewpoint on life.

" Only taken nine solid months for your altogether welcome
letter of December 3rd to reach me," he wrote. " Been following
me around the Belgian and French Congo. However, I'm
damned glad to hear of you, old man. I swear it seems like a
thousand moons since I saw you last. East Africa takes a lot
of beating to live in, or rather vegetate in, as you know full
well. . . . As for my own piffling self, I'm still after the tuskers,
and always will be. Financially, 'tis a wash-out now. Still,
all in all, roaming about the ' Blue ' is not such a bad life. And
I, for one, will roam into the depths of the wilds until the very
end of the chapter. Am just off again, starting from Mengo,
Fort Portal, for the Belgian and French Congo ; and, barring
accidents, will make a bee-line for the Sudan and the Old
Country about the autumn of this year. If you are in London
then, do let's meet and discuss the glorious past and the uncertain future. . . . Let's meet soon, old lad, and fix up another
hunting trip together. I'm yours to a cinder at that joyous
game."

Poor Jim ! He did not get to the Old Country, nor did we
meet again. The uncertain future enmeshed him.

My old friend, the Hon. Charles Craven, told me of a most
extraordinary adventure he had with elephants near Mahagi on
the shores of the Albert Edward Lake. He was hunting them in
a gorge with tall grass on every side, and found himself within
twenty yards of an elephant feeding. The bush and grass were so
thick that it was difficult to see more than a few yards ahead.
He could only tell of its presence by the waving of the leaves
of trees above where the beast stood. By making a detour, he
managed to strike his way up-wind and within twenty feet of it.
Now he could distinctly hear it breathing and the internal
rumblings as it digested its food, but still was unable to get a
glimpse of the brute. At last, the elephant moved and showed
its head, apparently having an idea that something was amiss.
It received a mate to that idea in the shape of a heavy bullet.
Down the steep bank rushed the huge animal, taking the bark
off one side of a tree in its passage, while Craven stepped round
the other to avoid the beast.

Again he got home with a bullet as the elephant rushed by
him, and head over heels went the animal like a shot rabbit.
Trees, bush, chunks of earth and rocks vanished like chaff, till

a stout tree pulled up the huge body about fifty yards down the bank of the gorge. There the elephant lay, legs waving in the air, screaming loudly, and vainly struggling to regain its feet. There was a path, like the marine parade at Brighton, leading down to it. Another well-placed bullet finished its career.

A few days afterwards, Craven was crossing a marsh below his camp by a path that, in its tortuous windings, led into a pit of water some twenty feet deep. One of his native hunters ran up to him and reported that some elephants were close at hand. Eventually, he located them. One was standing under a small tree, about four hundred yards away, while another was up to its belly in mud, about two hundred yards from him. The latter's stern was just visible behind a tuft of reeds.

After watching them for some time, the elephant under the tree moved off. In a leisurely fashion, it strolled up to its companion in the mud-wallow. As it emerged from the long grass round the mud-hole, Craven took the only chance offering. He fired a half-side head shot. The elephant drew itself up into a bunch of indignant protest, as much as to say : " Who in the name of thunder, did that ? " But a second bullet failed to elucidate the matter, and the beast swung round and crashed across the gully. At the same moment, the second beast bolted off straight ahead.

Craven ran along the side of the slope from which he had fired, stumbling, tripping, rolling and diving over grass which he could not force his way through, until a sudden drop of ten feet landed him on his stomach in a stream of running water. He had not seen this from above, but it was painfully evident now. By great good fortune, his rifle was undamaged by the fall. He scrambled out of the water and reached a small ridge from which he could see the wounded animal. It was standing quite still, less than three hundred yards away.

After a somewhat hot pursuit, Craven killed him. To his astonishment, he found that his victim possessed but one large tusk. He was quite positive, he told me later, that he had seen two tusks plainly when he had first fired. He came to the conclusion that the animal now killed must have been the one of which he had seen the rump in the mud-wallow, and not the one under the tree.

Back over the trail ran Craven, intent upon bagging the elephant with the pair of tusks. He was startled to find the other beast dead, lying on its side a few hundred yards from where he had first hit it. This animal also had but one tusk. Craven was never able to explain what had really occurred, but imagined that there must have been two elephants standing beside the tree, though he had only seen one, and each had a single tusk ; and that the one in the mud-bath had made good its escape. It certainly sounds a logical solution to the problem.

One of the tusks measured five feet in length ; and the other was seven feet three inches. The combined weight of the two tipped the scales at one hundred and forty-five pounds—a good morning's bag, with ivory selling at just over thirteen shillings a pound.

Charles Craven died at Koba a few months later, and is buried there.

When I was stationed at Kisumu from 1907 to 1908, there used to be a fair-sized herd of elephants on the German East African border, between Kisii and Shirati. There were a few quite good bulls, but the cows were much in evidence. I had one successful hunt after them and got two quite useful pairs of tusks ; but the herd was very dangerous to tackle and their habitat most difficult.

At the conclusion of the Kisii Expeditionary Force in 1908, my troops were relieved at Kisii by a company of the King's African Rifles. I told the Company Commander about this herd, but strongly urged him to leave them alone as he had never hunted elephants. I emphasized that the beasts were very savage, and the grass so high that it would be difficult to run if occasion demanded.

On my return to Kisumu, I received a letter from him, sent in by a native runner, to inform me that he had been out after the tuskers but had failed to get one as they had charged so viciously. There was a postcript, which read : " I thought you said I couldn't run ! "

Later, I heard that he had equalled, if not beaten, the world's record for the mile ; and this, in spite of the tall grass, rough going and stunted tree-growth.

CHAPTER XXXIII

THE CLASSIC OF BIG GAME HUNTING

I T has been my experience that elephants, where generally unmolested, rest and wander about at all times of the day and night ; and feed without much regard for fixed hours. Morning or evening, noon or midnight, the herds may be met on the move or else seen resting in the shade of trees. During the very hottest hours of the day, however, I have rarely seen an elephant feeding ; as a general rule, they may be observed standing still and resting in the shade.

I have noted that, when so resting, they usually sleep in an upright position. They then oscillate gently backwards and forwards, rather like the monotonous movement of a rocking-chair. It has always made me sleepy to watch them doing this, especially when tired out after a hot day's work tracking them. There was something hypnotic in their dreamy motions.

Sometimes, however, they do lie down to sleep ; but this is rare. When they do so, the sloping bank of a convenient ant-hill is a favoured spot against which to rest their massive heads.

Often I have observed that the sharp crack of a stick or dry reed, when trodden upon, instantly awakens a sleeping beast ; especially if you have the misfortune to make the noise when near at hand. It rather goes to prove that the animal is pretty wide awake, even if seemingly asleep. I have never actually seen an elephant stretched out on the ground when resting or sleeping ; but other hunters have assured me that they have done so, but only when the beast was sick or very infirm from old age.

When hunting elephants, it is well to remember that the herds generally move on to new feeding grounds in the very early hours of the dawn, and even before then. It is the early man who kills the good bull elephant !

I have stated that cows are not allowed to be killed, even under the plea of self-defence. The reason for this law is the laudable desire to save the elephant family from complete extinction. That risk is an ever present one.

In so far as I am aware, there still remains considerable doubt as to the actual period of gestation in the African female elephant, though I have always understood it to be about twenty-two months. If this is correct, the species cannot increase very rapidly, even with the cows protected from being killed off. One calf at a time is about all a cow can undertake to produce. The slowness of reproduction is a forceful argument in favour of rigid protection. The ivory is so valuable that it proves an irresistible incentive to any white or native hunter to slaughter elephants for profit. And the tusks of the female obtain a far better price on the market than those of the male.

It is absolutely imperative that restrictions should be imposed, and rigorously enforced, with a view to the preservation of this species. The vast improvement in sporting rifles and the rapid development of easy means of access to the habitat of the herds would soon bring elephants to the point of complete extermination. A check on wholesale slaughter is essential.

It would be a dreadful calamity if the lordly king of the African forests was to be wiped off the face of the continent; and that danger is never entirely absent. Civilization, in its determined advance into the wild regions, has been driving back these great animals from their former haunts; and, consequently, they are becoming more and more difficult to find. One may well ask when they will be allowed to find some really safe sanctuary from this constant attack and aggression? The big tuskers have nearly all been killed; and their smaller brothers go in constant fear of sharing a similar fate. All lovers of the fauna of the British Empire must feel regret that such is the case, and should whole-heartedly support any sane and sound measures for the effective control of elephant hunting.

Within recent years, wise protective laws have done much to stem the holocaust. Since poaching has been checked in Uganda and the Sudan (that part of it which was formerly the Lado Enclave territory of the Belgian Congo), the elephants have found a safe asylum therein. In his annual report for some years past, the Game Warden of Uganda has commented upon the enormous herds to be found in that Colony, and noted that they have increased very considerably in numbers within the past decade. The elephant population in the Toro district, for example, in addition to natural increase has been largely augmented by immigrants from the Belgian Congo. In that territory they are subjected to much heavier molestation, and have naturally sought out a safe refuge from attack. They have found it in Toro.

In Uganda, however, elephant control has been effectively in operation for a number of years ; and the herds are kept down to reasonable proportions by professional hunters employed by the Government. The beasts are forced to respect inhabited areas. This system of control has now been found inadequate in Toro, where there are huge areas of forest land and mountain ranges, both of which afford security to the animals and enable them to make periodical raids into the settled areas. It was recently decided, therefore, to kill off some six hundred elephants in order to thin out these herds and teach them to keep back in the remote regions.

It would seem that the African elephant is its own worst enemy. Civilization's needs must be respected by them, and any serious encroachments suitably punished. Happily, the king of the forests soon learns a lesson.

The sight of the elephant being so bad, while its powers of smell and hearing are so strongly developed, it is imperative that the sportsman should use the utmost caution in attacking them. Stigand always insisted that an elephant could smell a human being from a distance of over six hundred yards, provided that the wind favoured the beast. The hunter, therefore, must always keep a close watch on the wind and any sudden variations in its direction. It is equally essential to make as little noise as possible in stalking up to the beasts. To keep close tab on the wind and be noiseless are the elephant hunter's chief safeguards. Neglect these, and the penalty may well be a really terrible death.

I know of nothing more exciting and dangerous than hunting the African elephant on foot in tall grass or in forest-clad country. During the past thirty years or more, I have shot most kinds of dangerous animals with rifle or camera, but still would place the elephant at the head of the list.

You have to approach so close to them, and yet so seldom can get a clear view of the vital spots at which to aim, that danger is never absent. The only thing to do then is either to wait in the hope that some slight movement may bring your target into full view, or else go in still closer to your quarry. Both plans are equally dangerous, but are risks which all elephant hunters must take cheerfully.

These animals make such extraordinary noises while you are waiting and watching for a clean shot, that your nerves are keyed up to fraying point. At every crash of a branch torn down from a tree, you think they are stampeding in your direction. Again the wind is so fickle. It is constantly changing its course in thick cover, and one light puff of wind from you to the elephants will set them off, and most probably in the least desired direction. In every instance where I was forced to wait and watch for a chance of a safe shot, I experienced the sensation of sitting on top of a heap of dynamite and expecting it to explode every single second. It was a damnably unpleasant feeling !

A long range shot is supreme folly. When wounded, they have a nasty knack of looking to see who threw the brick. A whole regiment of lions cannot produce the same demoralizing effect as a single infuriated elephant when he spreads those immense ears, draws himself up to his full height and looks toward you, and at the same time utters a most blood-curdling scream of fury and intimidation. In all probability, invisible companions of the beast are stampeding on all sides with the din of a mammoth earthquake. Such moments in a hunter's life are very far from pleasant. But the experience seems worth while later on, the more so when you admire your ivory trophies and remember the sport they gave you to make them your own.

An African elephant seen in his native environment is a colossal beast. You seem to shrivel, and the very rifle in your hands to dwindle into a mere pea-shooter. Try as you will, it is not easy to face up to one ; and you always feel an insane desire to turn about and run for your life. At the crucial moment, I have never quite been able to overcome a sinking feeling at the pit of my stomach as I stared full at an elephant about to charge at me.

There are two recognized shots for quick effect—the brain and the heart. Few hunters, unless forced by circumstances over which they have no control, attempt the heart shot if the brain is available as a target ; for it is rarely fatal immediately. If you take a line from the top tip of the ear to the shoulder and then dissect it in half, you can generally place a bullet in the centre of the heart. But this is always an uncertain and unsatisfactory kind of shot to make, for the beast is still capable of travelling some distance and committing a great deal of damage before the blood has all pumped out and he collapses.

The much more fatal shot is that for the brain. This is most generally used by experienced hunters when opportunity is quite favourable for so doing. If you look at an elephant's head, you will observe that there is a kind of small cavity in the temple, between the eye and ear. This cup-like depression is not so marked as in the Asiatic species, nor is it exactly in the same place; but it roughly covers the brain. As there is little or no bone protection at this part of the huge skull, you may be reasonably sure that a heavy bullet placed therein will stun even if not kill instantly.

The surest sign, within my knowledge, that a bull elephant has been brained by this type of wound is that, a very short time after the fatal bullet has hit this mark and the beast is down, an organ which is usually hidden from sight is extruded and a general evacuation ensues.

The brain target, of course, is a small one; and, for this reason, you must creep up close so that it is easy to see and hit it. Thus only can you hope to kill instantly. A fraction of an inch off the centre of your bull's-eye may make a whole heap of difference to what happens once you have gently squeezed the trigger. In my opinion, it is by far the safest shot for an elephant; and many others agree in this. But it is not always possible to get near enough, or on the flank of a beast, to obtain an accurate aim at this vital spot. If such be not feasible, then the sportsman must use his own judgment. Unless actually forced to do so, never have I attempted any other shot. The professional hunter generally reckons one bullet, one elephant; and seldom is far out in his calculations.

I have heard it stated a number of times that " Karamoja " Bell, the famous elephant hunter of my time in Kenya, went into the Congo during one trip with only 350 rounds of ammunition. He returned with 349 pairs of tusks. Only once did he have to shoot twice at an elephant, and then got it with the second bullet. But he was a noted marksman!

I often discussed shooting with Bell, and he always held that elephant hunting was no child's play but the real classic of all big game hunting. He ought to know. Few men have killed anything like as many elephants, unless it was Jim Sutherland or Arthur Neumann. Bell has assured me, more than once, that he considered it both the most dangerous and

most profitable sport in the world. It was the excitement and
not the financial rewards which provided him with the lure to
take grave risks, year after year, in the pursuit of big tuskers in
Africa.

Some twenty or more years ago, there was a rather famous
herd of over two hundred elephants roaming the Nile country
between Nimule and Gondokoro. They were always known as
the Gondokoro herd, and most hunters had ample cause to
anathematize them. I am told that they are still there, and
more savage than ever. In those days, the herd consisted chiefly
of cows with small calves and immature bulls; but the cows
had a very large majority. I know of many famous hunters
who have pitted their brains and skill against this particular
herd, only to admit failure. I never heard of one single man
who ever got close enough to be positive that there was even
a worth-while bull among them.

When I was hunting in this district, native reports persistently
confirmed the rumour that there was one bull with tusks of fully
two hundred pounds each. I made three or four desperate
attempts to get near the herd and verify this statement; but
was never allowed within distance for a sporting shot, let alone
to inspect them thoroughly. I have been unable to find anyone
who could state truthfully that he had ever actually seen this
alleged giant. It may have been true; but, most probably, was
not. I do not really know.

The herd was so notoriously dangerous that nobody really
attacked them in grim earnest. The cows always put a damper
on their courage at once; and not even the native hunters
would willingly molest them. They must have been real savage
for such born fatalists to give them a wide berth. I can only
say that, each time I went near them, the cows immediately
charged as soon as they got my wind, heard or saw me. They
were really most ungracious in their reception of a stranger in
their midst.

When hunting in the Lado Enclave of the Belgian Congo, I
had a very nasty experience while trying to cut out a really
magnificent bull from the centre of a herd of about five hundred
cows and young bulls. There was also a fair sprinkling of calves
of varying ages. I was in company with W. Bennett, an ivory
poacher in the Congo; and Hamisi and Bennett's gun-bearer
were with us.

The local natives had told Bennett that there were a few

COLONEL THEODORE ROOSEVELT'S ELEPHANT

ELEPHANT LABOUR-MACHINES IN BURMA

real big tuskers in the herd, but we had our doubts. It is quite generally accepted as a fact that really large tusked bulls are not to be found in big herds; but this is not always correct. To my own knowledge, sometimes they are so found: though rarely. The old bull elephants you may meet roaming about in solitary state, such as the one I killed on the Aberdare Range and the other at the foot of Mount Kenya, are almost invariably senile old gentlemen who have been sent to " Coventry " by the rest of the herd. Or they may be those who have developed such a vile tropical liver as to make their company positively intolerable.

The bulls found with the herds are mostly in the prime of life, and usually only have small tusks. I grant that point readily, and without any reservations; but I have also seen and killed a real big bull with large tusks in a numerically strong herd. This particular splendid specimen was an exception to the rule.

We saw him on this day, but had to abandon the hunt. The old chap was surrounded by young bulls and irate cows. They would not let us get near enough to the old patriarch for a safe head shot; and neither of us was taking any undue risks. Time and time again, we tried to get close up to him; but never succeeded in approaching nearer than the fringe of vicious cows guarding him. Immediately they got our wind or heard us, they stampeded in every direction.

After abandoning the hunt, Bennett returned to camp; but I kept close to the herd, for I was interested in watching their actions. It was a most instructive day for me, and I learned a great deal.

In a large herd such as this, there are generally cow-leaders —or queen-elephants—who are cursed with extremely vile dispositions and ugly tempers. These are mostly very old cows. The very instant they scent danger, the chief body of cows crowd round the bulls and protect them. This makes it utterly impossible to get close enough to the big tuskers for a safe shot. In this instance, the cows had only to see, hear or smell Hamisi and myself, and they charged down deliberately at us. But I noticed that enough of their number were left to guard the bulls. Their sense of hearing and smell was so acute that our presence was detected from a distance of over five hundred yards. They could not have seen or heard us, for we stood perfectly still; and an elephant cannot see even a hundred yards distinctly. It could only have been that they had got our wind.

That day was full of thrills—enough to completely satisfy even the most adventurous of spirits !

Two days later Bennett and I tried again to cut out that old bull from the same herd. This time we managed to get within close range, and saw there were three other males worthy of our shots. One by one, with great risk and infinite patience, we killed all four big tuskers. The cows were charging right and left all the time, but this day we had agreed to take every risk to attain our object. We rather spoke out of our turn. If we had known all it entailed, we might have reconsidered that decision ; and, probably, would have done so.

When the last bull dropped to my bullet, we deemed it wise to get away temporarily from the scene of our activities. The battle-ground was most unhealthy. We wanted to give the maddened herd time to calm down, and then move off from the dead bulls. I saw some cows trying to lift up the bodies, while the rest galloped hither and thither in search of the enemy. It was a critical moment for us, for we were within the infuriated mob of elephants. Time and time again, I tested the wind. There was not even a suspicion of a faint breeze. We were lucky.

Down on our knees we got, and began to crawl away to safety. Our hearts were in our mouths ; at least, I know mine was. Those tense and anxious moments dragged by slowly, seeming like centuries to me. In crawling away, we were often so close to the cows, who were now stationary and seeking our wind, that we could have patted them on the legs. I had taken my own line of retreat, for it was every man for himself. I did not know where the others were, and did not even look round for Hamisi. I was interested only in escape.

All at once, I found my way barred by a dense ring of gigantic cows, a forest of huge legs and waving trunks, and a sea of burnished ivory. For a short time, I hesitated : at a loss what to do for the best.

Taking my courage in my hands, I crawled onwards and passed beneath the belly of the first unsuspecting cow. She lifted a hind foot and only just missed planting it down again on the small of my back. I almost screamed aloud in my fright. Now my heart was pumping like a dynamo, and the sweat pouring down my face and almost blinding me. The stench was simply nauseating, for few animals have a stronger scent than an elephant. In their habitual haunts, the air is permeated with their aroma and stagnant with it permanently. There is no mistaking it. A clinging vine has nothing on the smell of elephants, and the scent is not of violets. The ground, trees, vegetation and even atmosphere were saturated with the vile stench of them. A farmyard is attar of roses in comparison.

Ahead were still more forests of legs and swinging trunks, and bars of glistening ivory ; the same to my right, left and rear. I crawled slowly onwards, being careful to make not the faintest sound, testing the direction of the wind every few seconds, and missing been trampled upon a dozen times or more.

No words can possibly describe that ghastly crawl under the bellies of those giant cow elephants to a point outside the ring. I was conscious of nothing except the acuteness of my desire to rise and run ; and a terrible, sickening fear. At times, I had to pause and fight for control of myself, for I felt that I must be violently sick. The physical effort to restrain from retching was almost beyond my powers. The only sensations which I can remember vividly were a combination of intense fear, severe nausea, and an overpowering wish to end that mental torture.

It is quite impossible to say how many times I crawled through elephants' legs, but I seemed to be doing so continually for hours. It was a ghastly experience, without any compensating features : except only that I finally won through to safety.

At last that maze of legs, trunks, bodies and ivory tusks ceased to block out my horizon, and I crawled out clear of the outer fringe of the herd. I did not stay there. As soon as I could control my nerves, I rose and walked steadily away, all my faculties keenly alive to make no sound and keep strict watch on the variations of the wind. I found myself walking with the wind, which was now blowing from the herd. I began to breathe more freely, my nerves steadied and my heart stopped racing. When I had reached a point about half a mile from the herd, my legs gave way under me. I collapsed under the shade of a tree, only half-conscious. I had even forgotten my companions in their dire peril, which was unpardonable. But I was incapable of the physical effort of going to their aid, no matter how great their need.

After a time my strength returned to me, and I sat up and

took a long drink from my water-bottle. The liquid was tepid from the burning sun, and tasted very nasty ; but it was wet, and my mouth and throat were parched. If it had been neat spirits, I should have been much happier. In all my life, I never remember a greater or more urgent need for neat brandy.

It was some time before the four of us were reunited. The others related similar dreadful experiences to mine ; and all were badly shaken and unnerved, Hamisi more so than I had ever seen him. The two gun-bearers were very yellow about the gills, and still shaking as with an acute attack of ague. Bennett was in about the same state of mental and physical exhaustion as myself ; and that is saying a great deal. He was ghastly white of face. I strongly suspected that my own cheeks were the colour of a bed-sheet just returned from the steam-laundry.

We were poaching in Belgian territory ; and, if caught, about the least penalty we might expect was ten years' hard labour in a chain-gang. I would rather endure this than repeat that morning's awful experience.

The four of us rested in the shade of a large tree for a couple of hours, in order to regain a grip on ourselves, both mind and body, and also to allow the herd time to move well away from the neighbourhood. When once we deemed the coast to be clear, we returned very cautiously to our four dead elephants. There was no sign of the herd, only that rank, musty, strong body odour heavily tainting the air. All around us were their recent droppings and a sea of devastation caused by their stampeding. We hurriedly cut out our prizes, and retreated to camp.

They were all good tusks. The big fellow's pair weighed one hundred and seventy-seven pounds, and the others were all over seventy pounds each. A good day for us !

As I had helped to carry the trophies back to camp, I kept asking myself if the game was really worth all that we had endured. Was it ?

Now it is all past and done with, I have to admit that it certainly was. It is probable that others will not agree with this view ; but elephant hunting is a most fascinating adventure.

I know none better.

CHAPTER XXXIV

HAMISI'S LAST SAFARI

I KILLED my last elephant in the Akuma Forest, between Wadelai and Gondokoro, on the Uganda bank of the Nile. That encounter ended in a terrible tragedy. Never again have I hunted an elephant with a rifle, though in later years I did resume hunting them with nothing more deadly than a camera.

The meeting between that last elephant and myself was staged unexpectedly. In Africa, it is always the unexpected that happens. We were never formally introduced, and his near presence was unsuspected by my faithful Hamisi and myself. Had it been otherwise, that chance meeting might have concluded very differently and far less disastrously.

We were tracking down a splendid bull buffalo, and walking silently up a narrow rhino-path through the dense Akuma Forest. Hamisi was immediately behind me, carrying my heavy rifle. No sound broke the stillness of that grim forest, except our soft-footed tread and the warbling notes of birds in distant tree-tops. Once I heard the noisy blasphemy of two grey parrots, who were engaged in a shrill word-warfare like a couple of fishwives. Then again there was peace, and a deep hush descended. Gorgeously winged butterflies flitted hither and thither; a bird flew light and swift across our path; and a couple of monkeys swore at us angrily, as they climbed higher into the boughs of their trees.

Once again there was a deep silence. We trod virgin jungle, seldom touched by foot or hand of man. Go fifty yards off that well-defined rhino-path and you would probably be lost; and possibly only would recover it again by happy chance. The jungle is an eerie place, always in twilight, full of strange sounds and smells, and harbouring unfamiliar reptiles and insects, flitting ghostly little birds, raucous-tongued creatures and sudden death.

Life moves upon the face of the jungle surface and upon the tree-tops warmed by the sun and lashed by the rain, but you see it not. Its creatures are here free from man's idle curiosity, from his wanton interference, even from his reverent appreciation of their wonders.

Over all broods a mystic, menacing silence. There is no sound save a rare bird's whistle from the depths, or a rarer crash as some beast, you know not what, hears your quiet movement through those dim aisles of giant trees. Deserted it may seem to you, but nothing is more certain than that, through every yard of your course, some jungle-dweller's eyes are fixed upon you. However silently and cautiously you move forward, you are sure to be heard. They have not waited for you to come to them. They have watched you come, alert and ready for flight or attack. Then they have given you a wide berth, and you have not heard them go. The scenery is wild and savage ; and so are the beasts dwelling therein. You walk along those animal-paths at your peril.

Neither of us had a thought that we faced death at that very moment. We were quite unprepared for the Reaper's sudden summons.

I lifted my eyes from the path, having been occupied in a search for the buffalo's spoor, and looked straight up at a huge elephant with very big tusks. I halted immediately, and up went my rifle to the shoulder. He had come abruptly and silently round a bend in the path, just ahead of us. Instantly he saw the intruders, the charge started. There could be no mistaking the deadly nature of that mad rush. He came at a swift trot, trunk hanging down in front, and the tip curled inwards.

A second or two later he was in top gear, screaming with fury ; and now the trunk was held straight out in front of him. He started to gallop at a point less than fifty yards from us. I stood my ground and fired full into his chest. It was futile trying any other target for there was no time, and no bullet could turn him in that narrow, forest-walled path. I was up against the law of the wilds, with a vengeance : either I killed him, or he killed me or both of us.

The big beast crumbled on to his knees as my bullet went home in that big chest ; and, before he could rise again, I let him have the other between the eyes. I should have preferred to have broken one of his knees ; but he was on them. Before

HAMISI BIN BARAKA

I could exchange rifles with Hamisi, the wounded bull had regained his feet and was upon us. He was now not more than ten yards away from me. There was no chance to do anything, for my rifle was empty; but I expected to hear Hamisi fire from my right. No shot rang out. I could see the huge bulk of the beast overshadowing me, the great mouth wide open as he screamed with anger and the lust to kill, and the trunk was stretched out menacingly into my very face. The next instant I felt myself seized in the trunk and swung off the ground by my waist. Then I was hurled through the air, and landed with a nasty jar in a nest of long and sharp thorns in the topmost boughs of a squat Acacia tree.

I had dropped my rifle as I was hurled skywards, and yelled with pain as the sharp tooth-pick thorns imbedded themselves in my back and posterior, as well as other portions of my anatomy. Fortunately, no worse injury befell me. No bones were broken; but my shirt had been ripped half off my chest by one of the tusks, and the skin was grazed and bruised. I had been converted, moreover, into a pin-cushion for a particularly evil brand of long thorns.

As soon as I regained control of my senses, I struggled to get clear of the tree and drop to the ground. At that moment, I heard an agonized shriek from Hamisi. The elephant had seen the red tarboosh he was wearing that day, a most unusual thing for him to don when hunting, and this had acted like a red rag waved in the face of a mad bull. The gun-bearer must have turned to run for it, as I saw he was some short distance from where he had been when I was thrown skywards. The elephant had made straight for this offending splash of bright red colour in the dim cathedral aisles of that forest, and now had got Hamisi down. That tarboosh probably accounted for my own miraculous escape from being selected as the chief victim. I had been merely thrown out of his path, like a truss of hay, in his eagerness to get at that spot of challenging colour.

When I dropped to the ground from the tree, I could see poor Hamisi stretched out flat on the ground with the elephant's great body standing over him. The big beast was stabbing at him viciously with the cruel tusks, and trampling him savagely under immense feet.

I recovered my rifle rapidly, tested and found it quite undamaged, inserted two cartridges, and ran to Hamisi's aid. I had no clear idea of what I proposed to do, except that somehow

I must save my gallant gun-bearer and drive off the wounded brute from him.

At close range, I fired at the elephant's colossal stern. I sent the contents of both barrels full into those massive hind-quarters, and hit him just beneath the root of the tail. The two bullets shook him badly. He raced off into the forest, with tail well tucked in and screaming shrilly.

That was the last I saw of that elephant. But my native trackers found his dead body two days later, and retrieved the splendid tusks. Hamisi was revenged. But I took less than no pride in those two bars of solid, gleaming ivory. I would have given them, and a very great deal besides, to have had my loyal Hamisi restored to me, uninjured and in good health.

Once the elephant had made himself scarce, I ran to the poor fellow's side. One swift glance at his terribly mangled body told me that his case was utterly beyond all human aid. The elephant had gored and crushed him almost out of any resemblance to a human being. The wicked tusks had ripped Hamisi from the waist to the neck, partially disembowelling him. His legs and arms had been broken in many places by those great feet ; and the spot where he lay, scarcely breathing, was a shambles and swimming with his blood. Even the heavy cartridges of my second rifle, worn in pockets on his shirt-front, had been twisted almost double. My rifle, I found afterwards. It had fallen clear or Hamisi had thrown it away, and was quite unharmed. How I wished that the elephant had picked on the weapon instead of on my gun-bearer.

That savage brute had left behind him not a human body, but a pulped mass of flesh and bone.

I did all that was possible to ease his passing ; but he died as I moistened his twitching lips with water. His eyes opened and looked into mine, and I seemed to read in them a message of sorrow at the forced parting. Then, just a faint sigh, a light but convulsive shudder, and he had ended his last safari.

Poor, brave Hamisi ! He had served me well and faithfully over a period of many years. We had been through some very tight corners, side by side, and never once had I known him fail me. I was heartbroken at his death. I knew no human being could have averted his inexorable fate, but wished the end had been more kind and less painful. I knew I was blameless for what had occurred, but found no particle of consolation in the knowledge.

He had been with me on my first thrilling adventure with a wild elephant, years before, and then had suffered five broken ribs in his effort to save me from injury or worse; and now he had met a ghastly death at the feet of this one.

As I stood over his mangled body, I vowed that it should be the last elephant I would ever hunt to kill. I have kept that oath ever since.

We buried my faithful African servant and friend, my stout-hearted co-adventurer and comrade, in the depths of the lonely Akuma Forest. The night was closing down as we laid him to rest within the grim shadows of the jungle-belt, not far from the life-giving waters of the mighty Nile. No prayers were uttered; no funeral service read; but the mournful sadness of master and fellow-servants, as they covered his body with earth for the last long sleep, surely was enough.

For a long time after the others had returned to camp, I stood beside his grave, staring down blankly at it, my heart as heavy as lead within me; and thinking, thinking, thinking. No more should I have this splendid African at my elbow; no more listen to and follow his sage advice; no longer enjoy his sturdy companionship and silent understanding. God! it was a loss. I turned on my heel, and walked slowly back to camp. Dinner went untasted; sleep refused to comfort me; and I could not even speak of the matter to Sefu or those others. They were silent, too. My porters' talk was hushed, and they did not lift up their voices in their customary song about the camp fire.

Hour after hour, I sat before my own fire, brooding and sad. I have always liked the natives of Africa, generally speaking, and got on well with them. I have understood them; treated them firmly and justly; known them for the great big children they were. Yet never had I thought that the loss of one of them, a man like my Hamisi, could have affected me so deeply.

Next morning, I searched for and found a flat stone which would serve as a headstone for his grave. With infinite labour, I cut and chipped my last message on its face. It was a simple epitaph, but in large and bold lettering:

HAMISI BIN BARAKA,
KILLED BY AN ELEPHANT TO SAVE
HIS MASTER'S LIFE.
TRUE AND LOYAL FRIEND, AND FAITHFUL
SERVANT.
R. I. P.

That dreadful experience occurred just on a quarter of a century ago, but I still retain a vivid memory of it. Sometimes, even now, I can see that wild elephant's great body crashing toward me, overshadowing my puny form as I was seized and thrown skywards.   I can still hear that agonized shriek of terror from Hamisi bin Baraka.   It is a real nightmare that must haunt me to the day of my death.

Just as strongly, I sincerely mourn the man, with a black skin but the soul of a white man, who lies buried in the deep recesses of the Akuma Forest in Uganda.

In my memories of those years of hunting big game, the only real regret I have is the death of my gallant African comrade.

Sleep on, and well, Hamisi !   And good hunting in the Great Unknown !

INDEX